CAPE MAY
COURT
HOUSE

Investigative journalist Lawrence Schiller, the bestselling author of *American Tragedy* and *Perfect Murder, Perfect Town*, goes behind the scenes of this unusual case to explore the question: was a young wife and mother's death an accident . . . or murder? *Cape May Court House* gives you more than enough evidence to be your own judge and jury.

"A compelling picture of love, betrayal, admitted adultery and greed . . . A real-life story waiting for an end."

Daily News

"Fascinating . . . South Jersey is an unlikely place to set a Greek tragedy, but the sad and awful story of Eric Thomas fits the bill."

Philadelphia Inquirer

"Compelling."

Publishers Weekly

"Page-turning suspense."

Port St. Lucie News

"Gets to the heart of the case without dragging the reader through a sea of legalese."

Camden Courier-Post

American Tragedy

"Valuable, gripping and illuminating . . . great narrative power."

New York Times

"A stunner . . . there's an eye-opening revelation every few pages . . . A fascinating page-turner."

Entertainment Weekly

"The juiciest book yet! . . . The most fascinating aspect is its insight into Simpson's frame of mind throughout the ordeal: He emerges as a calculating, tortured character who gives this book the force of a great crime novel."

People

Also by Lawrence Schiller

AMERICAN TRAGEDY
PERFECT MURDER, PERFECT TOWN
INTO THE MIRROR

In Collaboration

LSD
by Richard Alpert, Ph.D., Sidney Cohen, M.D.,
and Lawrence Schiller

LADIES AND GENTLEMEN, LENNY BRUCE
by Albert Goldman from the journalism of Lawrence Schiller

CAPE MAY
COURT
HOUSE

A DEATH IN THE NIGHT

LAWRENCE SCHILLER

HarperTorch
An Imprint of Harper**Collins***Publishers*

HARPERTORCH
An Imprint of HarperCollins*Publishers*
10 East 53rd Street
New York, New York 10022-5299

Copyright © 2002 by Lawrence Schiller and KLS Communications, Inc.
Quotations from interviews by Lawrence Schiller are copyrighted © 2001 and 2002 by KLS Communications, Inc.
A continuation of this copyright page appears on page 369.
ISBN: 0-06-000668-4

First HarperTorch paperback printing: November 2003
First HarperCollins hardcover printing: September 2002

HarperCollins®, HarperTorch™, and ♥™ are trademarks of HarperCollins Publishers Inc.

Printed in the United States of America

Visit HarperTorch on the World Wide Web at www.harpercollins.com

10 9 8 7 6 5 4 3 2 1

To my mother, JEAN

Contents

CAPE MAY
COURT
HOUSE

ONE

Hand Avenue

Earlier in the evening a light snow had fallen in the small town of Cape May Court House, New Jersey. Some nights, even in the coldest winters, the sea air from the Atlantic Ocean and Delaware Bay warms the barrier islands and the entire cape, so that slush seldom freezes. Tonight, Saturday, February 8, 1997, slush had not frozen.

Dr. Robert Fitzpatrick, a local veterinarian, was just returning home from a party in Wildwood. At forty-five, Fitzpatrick was a strong man with rough hands capable of subduing a rottweiler. On that night, alone in his Chevy Astro, he stopped at the local Wawa convenience store, where he bought a bottle of Gatorade. The time was 1:45 A.M. As he drove away, he noticed that all the other local businesses were closed. Even the volunteer ambulance service building was dark and deserted.

Dr. Fitzpatrick then turned west from North Main Street onto Hand Avenue, the route he usually took to his house. A few seconds later he stopped at a traffic light on the corner of Dias Creek Road and Hand. The night was unusually dark. He noticed that he had the road to himself.

After passing a few houses set in the woods, Fitzpatrick saw some white and red lights up ahead. He thought an SUV had pulled over onto the berm on the other side of the road. As he came closer, however, the odd angle of the vehicle made him take a second look. That was when he noticed some sagging electric wires. Just then a battered white pickup truck approached from the opposite direction and stopped. While Fitzpatrick pulled his own car to a stop, a man got out of the pickup, walked to the SUV, and tried unsuccessfully to open the driver's door. As Fitzpatrick rolled down his window, the man yelled back to him, "There's people in there."

Instantly, Fitzpatrick reached for his cell phone, punched in 911, and got out of his car. As he reported his location he saw that part of a utility pole was hanging from its wires. That's when he realized the SUV, a Ford Explorer, was in a ditch.

"An officer will be there in minutes," the 911 dispatcher told him as he ran across the road toward the accident. When he reached the rear of the car, the driver of the pickup asked if he had called the police.

Fitzpatrick nodded.

Before he could say another word, the driver said, "Then I'm getting out of here." And within seconds was gone.

The Explorer's left headlight was broken, but the fog lights were still on. Fitzpatrick tried the driver's door. It wouldn't budge, but the rear passenger door on that side opened easily, and the dome light came on. There, staring at him from the backseat, were the wide eyes of a baby, still strapped in its padded car seat. Almost immediately, the baby started to cry. Fitzpatrick then saw a driver and a passenger in the front seats. Neither was moving. The driver's head slumped toward the window, and the passenger's head hung down to the side. Fitzpatrick saw no blood.

Brushing his hand against the baby's face, Fitzpatrick took hold of one of the child's hands. The baby's cheek and fingers were cold. Then he noticed that the air inside the truck was not as cold as the outside air. As he leaned forward between the front seats, he saw that the driver and passenger were, like the baby, African American.

"Hello? Hello?" Fitzpatrick said. He repeated it a third time, and even louder. Neither person moved.

He could tell that the air bags were now deflated and the seat belts were still drawn tightly around the passengers. The man in the passenger seat appeared to be unconscious. His skin was cool when Fitzpatrick reached for his neck to find a pulse and determined that the man had a sluggish, rhythmic heartbeat. Next, Fitzpatrick turned to the woman in the driver's seat. Her leather jacket was open, her neck was exposed, and her skin was cold to the touch. Fitzpatrick probed for a pulse. Nothing. Again, he pushed hard on the carotid artery. Zero.

He stepped out of the car and redialed 911. "I think she's dead," Fitzpatrick said to the dispatcher. "The police had better hurry." Then he went back to the Explorer and reached between the front bucket seats to the dashboard. Though the

engine was no longer running, he turned off the ignition, fear-
ing the car might catch fire. He took the child's hands again,
and managed to quiet it almost immediately. He continued to
murmur to the baby as he stepped back outside the car. As he
waited for the police, Fitzgerald fought the urge to remove the
baby, who he now realized was a girl. He knew better than to
try to remove either of the adults in the front. As he stood there,
no cars passed on the deserted road.

At 2:01 A.M., just nine minutes after Fitzpatrick's first 911
call, Medic 9 arrived. As the first paramedics, Lisa Schulthies
and James Cline, climbed out of their vehicle, a white police
cruiser pulled up, its lights flashing. An officer got out and
quickly surveyed the inside of the Explorer through its closed
windows and called for another ambulance. Then he removed
the baby from the backseat.

Fitzpatrick wanted to help, but the officer told him not to
touch anything. Just then a second police car arrived.

Schulthies had difficulty getting to the passenger side of the
SUV through the bushes and a gully, which was full of water.
The ground was swampy. The male passenger, who was leaning
against the window, appeared to be unconscious, and Schulthies
decided to enter the vehicle through the same rear door from
which the baby had been removed. The baby was checked for
injuries by a second set of medics, who had just arrived, and
then placed in the ambulance. As Schulthies waited to reach the
passenger, her partner, Cline, managed to get the driver's door
open and immediately saw that the female driver was pregnant.
Her pupils were dilated, fixed, and did not respond to the
medic's flashlight. Her mouth was clamped tightly against her

protruding tongue. There were several open and moist abrasions on the right side of her face. Cline hooked up a Life Pack/EKG portable unit. The driver had no vital signs. Her color was ashen. The medic estimated she'd been dead for at least fifteen minutes.

From the backseat of the SUV, medic Schulthies began treating the male passenger. His glasses were askew on his face, but not bent or broken. The baseball cap he was wearing didn't seem to have budged, and he had no obvious physical injuries. However, he failed to respond to verbal or tactile stimuli. As the medic attempted to place a C collar on him, the man came to. He lifted his head and opened his eyes. He looked around and easily responded to Schulthies's questions. What is your name? What is your wife's name? Is this your baby? What is the name and age of the baby? Where are you from? Do you have any pain or discomfort? Eric Thomas was his name, he said, and he was a dentist. His wife's name was Tracy and the baby was eighteen months old. Her name was Alix. He said they lived nearby.

When Thomas had answered the questions, he asked about his wife. The medic didn't tell him that she was dead. Then Thomas told Schulthies that his daughter had a fever and that he and his wife were on their way to the hospital.

The accident was unremarkable as accidents go. There was little interior damage to the car—no broken windshield and no visible damage to the dashboard. Both air bags had deployed and were now deflated, hanging like punctured balloons. There was no obvious open trauma to any of the car's occupants and there were no visible injuries. And yet the pregnant driver had died.

Cline released the driver's seat belt, which was very tight, riding high on her left shoulder and into the neck area. Since the seat was positioned forward, very close to the steering wheel, and also adjusted to the highest position, it took a few minutes to remove the driver from the seat without moving the seat itself. She was put on a body board and placed on the ground on the opposite side of the ambulance so that her husband couldn't see her. Thomas, too, was then removed and placed on a board for transport in the same ambulance the baby was in. Now he seemed unaware of what had happened and where he was. He asked about his wife several times. Though the medics answered his questions, he repeated them. He, along with the baby, was then taken to Burdette Tomlin Memorial Hospital in Cape May Court House, a few minutes away.

At 2:38 A.M., Lawrence Pratt, the medical investigator on the scene, pronounced Tracy Thomas, thirty-seven, of Cape May Court House, dead.

The headlights of all the cars on the scene illuminated the path the Explorer had taken. As Robert Fitzpatrick stood there answering Officer McHale's questions, he could see tire tracks on the road. It looked as though the car had traveled straight down the road; there was no indication of yawing or swerving. It seemed simply to have turned off to the side, hit a utility pole, and landed beyond the shoulder in the ditch.

At 2:35 A.M., after the paramedics had left for the hospital with Thomas and the baby, Detective Sergeant William Webster arrived to take over the investigation. The covered body of Tracy Thomas was still lying on a body board on the road, adjacent to the ambulance. Inspecting the scene with Officer Robert McHale and Captain William Shea, who had just arrived, Webster noticed that while the Explorer's one good headlight and fog lights and taillights were still on, the windshield wipers were off, but in an upright position. The three officers moved to the front of the car, where they noted that the pole had damaged the left headlight and the hood and had dented the roof on the driver's side. The rearview mirror inside was turned upward and the glass had broken. Having finished the initial review, Webster spoke to the medical investigator, Pratt, who represented the medical examiner, Dr. Elliot Gross.[*] They discussed when the autopsy would be completed.

Next, Webster and Officer Steve Ginyard walked along the tire tracks, as far as they could follow them, looking for what might have caused the accident. Webster noted that no other vehicle was involved. He then checked for deer prints, but found none.

At about 3:00 A.M., Webster photographed the accident scene. One of the first shots was of Tracy Thomas still lying on the board. After he had taken the pictures and road measurements, Webster instructed Officer Ginyard to have the vehicle impounded and secured at the township's public works garage. After looking at the tire tracks again and noting that the car had hit nothing but the pole, Ginyard, with his many years of experience reviewing accidents, concluded that the car had not

---

[*] In New Jersey a coroner is referred to as a medical examiner.

skidded but had simply driven off the road and hit a pole. The driver had probably fallen asleep at the wheel.

At Burdette Tomlin Memorial Hospital, Donna Hess was the documenting nurse who saw the passenger, Eric Thomas, in the E.R. Hess took notes as Marilee Olsen, the primary nurse, made her assessment. Thomas was slow to respond to questions and lethargic at times. He couldn't lift his arms on verbal command. His grip was weak. He had no visible injuries, but he complained of some upper back and head pain. When Dr. Teresa Bridge-Jackson, the physician on call, asked him what had happened, Thomas said that a deer had crossed in front of the car.

A few minutes later, Eric's uncle Rudy and aunt Minnie Callender arrived. They had been called at Eric's request. He had said they were the family's nearest relatives. Meanwhile, the baby had been examined and found to have no injuries or fever. Since there was nothing wrong with his daughter, Eric asked that she be released to his uncle and aunt.

At about 3:30 A.M., Detective Webster and Officers McHale and Ginyard left the scene of the accident and drove to the hospital to interview Thomas. According to Dr. Bridge-Jackson, Thomas had told her that the family had been at home when their daughter became sick with hives and a fever. She had seen the pediatrician for the same problem just last week. Now all three officers stood beside Thomas's bed in the emergency room as Detective Webster took his statement.

Thomas was upset, still unaware that his wife was dead. He told them that he, his wife, Tracy, and daughter, Alix, had left their home between 12:15 A.M. and 12:30 A.M., after he had seen the first part of *Saturday Night Live*. His wife was driving, and she spotted a deer in the road. The snow made it hard to see, he said. Thomas told the officers that his wife had screamed and then he remembered a loud thump. The next thing he remembered was a flashlight shining in his eyes. Then he told Webster that during the past week, his wife had experienced blackouts because of her pregnancy. Almost as an afterthought, he said that Tracy had lost her balance and fallen as they left their house to go to the hospital that night. But he was sure that she did not black out then and was not injured from the fall. Webster considered Thomas groggy but responsive and cooperative.

After Thomas's X-rays were reviewed by the hospital staff, he was diagnosed with cerebral concussions and herniated nucleus pulposus, better known as herniated discs. The staff thought his condition could be better treated at Atlantic City Medical Center's Trauma Unit, and he was transported there at around 5:30 A.M.

Tracy's parents, Doris and Donald Rose, were asleep in their home in Hyannis on Cape Cod when the phone rang. It was a little after 3:00 A.M.

Doris wasn't sure who was calling, but it sounded like her son-in-law's aunt, Minnie Callender. All she could make out was that Tracy and Eric had been in a bad accident and a doctor would be calling them back. Just let one of them be alive, Doris said to herself as she woke her husband and told him the news. Donald started crying.

When the phone rang a second time, Donald couldn't bring himself to pick it up. A woman doctor informed Doris that her daughter Tracy had died. Please God, let Eric and Alix be alive, she cried to herself. Then the doctor told her that her granddaughter and son-in-law were okay.

Donald could not control his emotions when he heard that Tracy was dead. Doris knew that her husband couldn't drive all the way to Cape May Court House in that condition.

Doris called her other daughter, Wendy, who lived in North Jersey, and told her there had been an accident and that Alix was okay but she didn't remember what was said about Eric.

"And Tracy?" Wendy asked.

"Just go down there," Doris pleaded.

"What's wrong with Tracy?" Wendy repeated. All she could make out from her mother was that Alix and maybe Eric were all right.

"Please, just go down and see Eric and Alix," Doris repeated. "You're much closer."

When she hung up, Wendy called the hospital and reached Eric's uncle, Rudy. "Is my sister all right?" Wendy asked.

"No," he replied.

Wendy was stunned. "I'll be there in a few hours" was all she could say. By the time she left Plainfield with her twenty-five-year-old daughter, Bre, at about 9:00 A.M., she had learned that Eric had been moved to Atlantic City Medical Center. She and Bre set out down the snowy Garden State Parkway.

Rudy Callender met them when they arrived at the Center. He led Wendy and Bre to the intensive care unit, where a nurse said they could visit Eric, but only one at a time. Rudy left to make a phone call.

Seeing him in a neck brace, with medical equipment hooked up to his body, and not knowing what condition he was in, Wendy was afraid to embrace Eric. She sat beside him and rubbed his arm. Bre stood off to the side, leaning against a wall.

"Wendy, you know with all my medical training, I couldn't do anything, I couldn't save her," Eric said. Wendy couldn't understand what he meant. She'd just been told that Eric was found unconscious, so how could he be feeling guilty that he hadn't been able to save Tracy?

"Wendy, you have to help me," Eric said. "You have to help me with Alix," he continued. "She needs to be brought up on the Cape." Wendy looked over at Bre. She found herself remembering how important it had been to her sister that everyone spend summers on the Cape with their parents.

Eric said he didn't want to have Tracy cremated but that it had been her wish. Tracy wanted her ashes brought back to Hyannis, she had told Eric. She wanted them spread over Dennis Pond, where her dad used to take her when she was a child. Wendy had to leave the room. She couldn't handle what Eric was telling her. In the corridor, she found a pay phone and called her mother.

When Wendy told Doris what Eric had said about Tracy being cremated, Doris yelled to Donald, "She wants to be cremated." Wendy had never discussed it with her sister, and now her mother was telling her that Tracy had once, not too long ago, mentioned it to her. Apparently, she'd told the same thing to Eric's sister, Lisa Jenkins. Wendy didn't know what to think. All she wanted to do was go and see her sister, wherever she was.

Wendy and Bre arrived at Burdette Tomlin Memorial Hospital only to discover that Tracy's body was at the medical examiner's facility at Shore Memorial Hospital in Somers Point, some twenty miles away. Wendy had no idea where Shore Memorial was, and in any case she was told that Tracy couldn't be shown to them there. Instead, she and Bre went to see Alix.

At the Callenders' house, they found Alix playing quietly. Minnie Callender and one of her friends were taking care of her. Minnie was a deeply religious woman and she and her husband, Rudy, had worked in the Middle Township House school system for years.

After hugging the baby and talking to Minnie for a few moments, Wendy noticed a pile of clothes on the sofa—a brown leather jacket, a blue denim shirt, and a pair of black sweatpants, all ripped. Then she noticed they were all cut open in the front. They must have been the clothes Tracy had been wearing last night, when she and Eric had had the accident. Distractedly, Minnie was fiddling with a purse. Wendy recognized it. It was Tracy's. "We were supposed to go shopping for drapes," Minnie said over and over.

While Wendy and Bre were at the Callenders', Dr. Elliot Gross, the intercounty medical examiner of Cape May and Cumberland, was performing an autopsy on Tracy Thomas. Gross had been told the circumstances of the accident by the medical investigator. The car ran off the road and struck a pole. The weather had been bad, with poor visibility. Gross was also told that the victim had been properly restrained in her seat at the time of the accident and that her air bag had deployed. The time of death was between 12:15 A.M. and 2:00 A.M., when the paramedics had arrived at the scene.

Tracy Thomas was five feet four inches tall and weighed about 145 pounds. Immediately, Gross made the following pathologic diagnoses: contusions of the face and neck; petechial hemorrhages of conjunctivae and epiglottis; focal hemorrhages surrounding the hyoid bone and cricoid cartilage, right; extradural hemorrhage, cervical spine.

In layman's terms, Tracy had suffered injuries to her larynx and the surrounding neck tissue, including hemorrhages in the eyes, hemorrhages in the muscle of the back of the neck, and hemorrhages surrounding the spinal cord in the neck. She also had some cuts and bruises on her face—one on the left earlobe, another on the left lower lip, and several on the right side of the face, as well as a contusion over her right eyelid. Gross noted no other damage, and no injury to the spinal cord itself.

Gross dictated the report during and after the autopsy on February 9th, but it would not be transcribed until March 4th. His findings were inconclusive, pending further study and investigation.

He still had to complete the toxicology and review the emergency personnel records and police reports. His first opinion was that Tracy Thomas's death was due to blunt force, also known as physical force, but he didn't know exactly how the force had been applied. Hemorrhaging in the eyes was usually caused by compression of the neck, and in Gross's opinion, Tracy had suffered some neck injury. But he knew that hemorrhaging could also be caused by suffocation. Gross wanted to look at the vehicle and wanted to know more about air-bag-related deaths before he made a final determination about the cause of death.

Wendy didn't know what else to do. After she visited Alix, she called her parents and told them that the baby was okay. Unable to see her sister, Wendy decided to take Bre and go home to Plainfield for the night, a three-hour drive.

Early the next morning, Monday, February 10th, Doris and Donald left Hyannis and drove to Wendy's house, where they picked up Bre, who would drive them the rest of the way south. Their first stop would be to see Eric in Atlantic City. They did not know exactly what shape he was in. Wendy had said very little—only that Alix was okay and that she'd not been able to see Tracy. The Roses didn't know who had been driving the car or where the accident took place.

When they arrived at the hospital, Eric's sister, Lisa, his cousin, Iris, and uncle, Rudy, were in the hallway. Doris couldn't bring herself to go in and see her son-in-law. Her daughter was dead. She didn't know what to say to Eric.

Donald was puzzled that Eric's family didn't try to comfort him and Doris. He went in to see Eric alone. As he leaned over to hug his son-in-law, all he could think was *Thank God Alix and her father are alive.*

"I'm glad nothing happened to you," Donald said.

"I thought I was going to be able to take care of her," Eric replied.

Donald had seen a lot of accident victims during his thirty years in the construction business, but despite Eric's neck brace, Donald didn't think he talked or looked like someone who had been in an accident. Doris, who had just joined Donald at Eric's bedside, was also struck by the feeling that something didn't fit. There had been a terrible accident that had killed her daughter, yet nothing seemed wrong with Eric.

Just then some of Eric's relatives came into the room and the conversation turned lighter. There was even some joking. Doris knew it was time for her and Donald to leave.

That afternoon Eric would be released from Atlantic City Medical Center. Diagnosed with a bloated cervical disc and a herniated cervical disc in his neck, he was asked to return in a week for a follow-up visit.

On the drive down to Cape May Court House, Donald decided that he didn't want to see Tracy's body. He didn't want to remember his daughter in that condition. All he thought of now was Alix. He and Doris drove to Tracy's house, where Eric's mother, Louise, and his stepfather, Willie, were staying after arriving the night before from South Carolina. Minnie Callender was there, too, with Alix. On the way over, the Roses had driven past the site of the accident without even knowing it. At Tracy and Eric's home, the phone rang. Minnie, who answered it, was told that Tracy's body had been released. She asked Doris to talk to Eric and "get something planned," meaning a memorial service. Whatever Eric decided, Doris knew she also wanted a service in Hyannis, where Tracy had been so happy.

Earlier that morning, Detective Webster had paid a visit to Eric and Tracy's house. He found nothing out of order, briefed Eric's parents, and asked them for a family history. He also asked them about Tracy and Eric's relationship, and was assured that nothing was out of the ordinary between them.

Webster told them that the accident was under investigation. Willie asked to see the car. Webster agreed, and they drove to the public works garage to look at the Explorer. They stayed for about half an hour. Neither man said much. After dropping Eric's stepfather off at the Thomases' house, Webster returned to the garage to meet the medical examiner.

Dr. Gross and Detective Webster met at 1:30 P.M. to examine the Ford Explorer. Both of them photographed the purple SUV and then took additional measurements of the seat positions in relation to the steering wheel and other interior areas. They found no sign that the car had hit a deer.

The two men then sat down and tried to piece together what had happened. Could the air bag have killed Tracy Thomas somehow? Gross said they would have to wait for the full toxicology report before assessing that possibility. Then the medical examiner asked Webster to get him some additional information on air-bags—how they deploy and the type of injuries they were known to cause. Gross asked Webster to have someone call the Ford Motor Company, the maker of the Explorer, to get as much information as possible on the air bags they used. Since there were no major visible injuries to Tracy's liver, chest, or head, Gross also wanted to know what other documented deaths could be related to a motor vehicle accident. The two men discussed Tracy's proximity to the steering wheel, the tightness of her seat belt, and how her pregnancy may have played a role. Webster could see that Gross was unsure of the cause of death.

The situation was puzzling. There was no severe trauma and

no severe damage to the car, yet Tracy Thomas had died. Since the damage to the car was not consistent with a fatal accident, Gross suggested that the cause of death was a police matter.

When Eric returned home from the hospital Monday afternoon, the family looked for an appropriate picture of Tracy that could be used at the funeral home and the memorial service. Late at night, Eric sat alone in the family room and returned some calls. Donald, Doris, and Bre stayed the night.

FATAL CRASH VICTIM IDENTIFIED
AS WIFE OF MIDDLE TWP DENTIST

Police identified Tracy E. Rose Thomas as the pregnant woman killed early Sunday when the vehicle she was driving went off the road and struck a utility pole on the side of eastbound Hand Avenue in Cape May Court House.

A memorial service will be held Wednesday at 10:00 A.M. at the Radzieta Funeral Home at 9 Hand Ave. in Cape May Court House.

Both wife and husband were wearing seat belts and air bags deployed.

Police said snow and slushy road conditions likely contributed to the accident.

THE PRESS OF ATLANTIC CITY
Tuesday, February 11, 1997
By Jeanne Dewey, Staff Writer

Detective Webster had left word with Eric's parents that he wanted to see Eric when he was discharged from the hospital. First thing Tuesday morning, Eric called Webster and made an appointment to give the police his formal statement. Thomas then called his receptionist to say that she should reschedule his patients.

At around ten A.M., on their way to the police station, the Roses, Bre, and Eric, who was still wearing his neck brace, decided to stop at the funeral home, where Tracy's body had been taken. There, the director gave Tracy's rings to Eric. For a moment, he fidgeted with them. Then he stared at them. When the director asked if he wanted to see his wife, Eric replied with a simple "No." Doris was surprised. The Roses liked to see their people before they went, but out of respect for Eric, they simply stood there and wept silently. After arranging for the service, to be held the next day, they left for Eric's eleven A.M. appointment with the police. Driving there, Eric didn't say a word about the accident. When they arrived at the station, Doris stayed in the car. She liked being alone; it was her time to cry. Donald walked into the building with his son-in-law.

Webster met them in a tiny office, where he sat in a metal chair on one side of the room, while Eric and Donald sat on the other side in identical chairs. Webster said that the tire tracks made it seem as if the wheel had been turned deliberately to the right before it hit the pole. The wheel had not been yanked as if the driver might be trying to avoid something, like a deer, he said. Donald thought the detective was waiting for Eric to respond. His son-in-law said nothing.

"Do you mean to tell me that it was foul play?" Donald interjected.

"No, no, no. Not at all," Webster replied. "I'm not suggesting anything."

Donald explained that he didn't mean to imply that his son-in-law might be involved. He just meant to ask if someone had done something intentionally.

Eric remained silent.

Webster used the word *asphyxiation* when he described how Tracy had died, how the strap had been tight, how she in fact may have choked to death.

Again, Eric said nothing.

Donald interjected, "Asphyxiation—what do you mean?"

"Like I said, she may have choked to death," the detective replied.

Webster then suggested that he and Eric move to another room so that the doctor could give his formal statement.

Donald left the room and the building and joined his wife in the car. Neither of them said a word.

In the interview room, where Webster had set up a tape recorder, Thomas was told that he was not compelled to say anything if he chose not to. He then signed a waiver of his Fifth Amendment rights.

Thomas said that three days before the accident Alix had had a slight fever, around 102 degrees, but that he and Tracy weren't worried about it. On Thursday night, they checked in with the hospital and were told that they were doing the right things, but they may not have been giving Alix enough Tylenol or Motrin.

"Uh . . . * Friday . . . Thursday . . . Friday, Tracy called to make the appointment because that night [Alix's] fever had

---

* In this transcript of Detective Webster's taped interview, three ellipsis points after a word like *Uh* indicates a long pause in the conversation or a stutter.

really scared us, she was at 104 . . . 104.5 . . . so we were able to get an appointment at the Harbor View, I think at five o'clock or something on Friday. Found out that she had a virus, she had an ear infection, she was teething; so a lot of things were happening; so everything was kinda working out together.

"So Saturday, we kept her in the house all day and I had to go to work Saturday morning to see a patient or two. . . . Uh . . . so we just kinda loafed around all day, and you know, we did things in the house and everything . . . cleaned up, and uh . . . she wasn't feeling . . . uh . . . Tracy was a little tired and the baby was sick, so my aunt had a little drop-in for some friends . . . so I went and picked up some food to bring back to them.

". . . Alix was being very cranky and irritable, so we put her down early, probably about seven P.M., 'cause she normally goes between seven-thirty and eight o'clock to sleep . . . and uh . . . but we were worried about her because she went to sleep very fast and she didn't resist us or anything, like babies do.

"Tracy came down and told me that the baby's temperature is going up instead of going down . . . and it seemed like it was climbing for some reason and I don't know why.

". . . Tracy decided that we needed to take her on in, just so there wouldn't be any problems when she gets older from a fever we possibly could've controlled.

"So I went out and, you know, cranked the car up and got everything ready, the truck . . . the Explorer thing . . . and uh . . . got everything ready and Tracy was getting the bag ready for her, the bottles and stuff. Um . . . uh . . . put on her . . . uh . . . winter jumpsuit thing, because it was snowing outside and then . . . uh . . . because Tracy was feeling a little . . . uh . . . she'd get . . . I told you before that she was getting a little clumsier with the baby's weight and everything, she was losing her balance, so she felt more comfortable with me carrying the baby because the doctor, the obstetrician, told us stay away from heavy lifting. . . . So uh . . . she's clumsy anyway, kinda dropsy, so sure enough she fell outside . . . just slipped on the snow and I think she was reaching for the car . . . the other car parked next to it. And um . . . you know, helped her up and things were moving so fast by this time because it was snowing and sleeting and whatever it was doing.

"Um . . . so we get in the car and uh . . . I remember, I think she . . . I think her gloves were wet, she had some gloves, but I think when she fell in the snow, the leather gloves got wet or something. So I think she took them off somewhere down the line, because she was slipping on the wheel or something. Um . . . we drove down Hand Avenue towards the hospital. Uh . . . um . . . and . . . as we, I guess, got closer and closer, I remember we were trying to look through the window because the snow and stuff was starting to freeze on the windshield wipers and it was kinda scrappy, or you know, I don't know how to describe that . . . and um . . . she started to get a little . . . uh . . . uh . . . not irate, but just kinda excited, and started to scream because she can see better than I can . . . I wear glasses, and she said, 'I see a deer down the street.' And I said, 'I don't see a deer.' So I'm trying to look through the mirror—through the window—and I do see it . . . so what do I do? What do I do? So she, you know, tries to snatch the car or get around the deer . . . from what I remember . . . and then right after that, I remember a couple booms or knocks to the car . . . and . . . then I saw a little flash of light or something and then that's all I remember from there."

Thomas went on to describe coming to, telling the paramedics about why they were going to the hospital and having watched *Saturday Night Live* and the cheerleaders skit.

Webster asked what the family had done in the days before the accident. Thomas said they had gone to see a pediatrician at the "Harbor View in Cape May Court House" on Friday. In response to the detective's next question, about Tracy's "blackouts," a word used in a statement Thomas had made at the hospital just after the accident, he said the following: "Uh . . . she can't . . . she wouldn't be able to sit up . . . uh . . . because of the weight on her stomach. If she lays on the couch, I'd have to help pull her up. Um . . . uh . . . she would stand up and complain that she would be dizzy and I'd try to explain to her on the medical side that the weight was pressing against the major vessels in her back, and that's causing it . . . to try to reposition herself all the time. And uh . . . she's been having, she was having problems with a lot of congestion. She had that checked out a while ago, and the doctor, you know, just told her to try and prop her head or do different things . . . antihistamines or whatever to try and help with that. But stay away from that as much as possible, but because she would . . . she would snore a lot, and sometimes I actually thought that she would be stopping breathing in the middle of the night, which concerned me."

Since Eric had not answered Webster's question, he asked it again, "Did she black out at all?"

"No, not that I remember," Thomas answered.

"She just lost her balance?" Webster asked.

"She just lost her balance in the snow and in the commotion of us trying to get out, you know, at night kinda thing," Thomas replied.

"Was there any outward sign of injuries that you could see?" Webster asked.

"Uh . . . I know I brushed her off, she brushed her face off, and you know there was snow," Thomas answered.

"Did she hit her face on the ground?"

"I think she did . . . looking back, I probably should've looked at her a little closer, but I didn't," Thomas said.

"Why did she drive that evening?"

". . . I guess, because one: she wanted to."

"She wanted to drive?" Webster asked.

"And I know not to argue with her to a certain extent. I was . . . I was cranking up the car, I was . . . putting the baby in on the other side, so I was doing all that stuff . . . so you know, she was like, you know, let's go. You know, let's just kinda go, and she was just, like, I'm driving . . . and uh . . . and just took it from there. I wish I was driving at this time now because I feel maybe I . . . maybe it would have been me instead of her and the baby, right now. I run this in my mind all the time."

All of a sudden, the town's fire siren, which sounds loudly at noon every day for a test, interrupted the interview.

After it stopped, Webster asked Thomas about the car's defroster. "The defroster was on, but I guess it wasn't thawing it

as fast," Thomas replied, "as fast, yeah, I didn't see the deer at
first because I . . . she sees farther than I do, but I guess as we got
closer, I started to . . . I saw the deer, I saw the deer."

"And that was on the passenger side of the truck?"

"The side that I was on, yes."

The interview had taken twenty-four minutes.

When Eric returned to the car, Donald didn't say a word.

That afternoon, Detective Webster called the National Highway
Traffic Safety Administration and asked for whatever literature
they had on air bags and air-bag fatalities.

On Wednesday morning, the first of two memorial services was
held in Cape May Court House at the Radzieta Funeral Home
on Hand Avenue, just a few miles from the scene of the accident.
Eric's relatives from South Carolina were there, along with
Wendy, her husband, Faquir, her son, Farrad, and daughter, Bre,
from Plainfield, and Donald and Doris from Hyannis. Eric's staff
and some of his dental patients also came, as well as the many
townspeople Tracy and Eric had come to know: Dr. Callaway,
who had sold his dental practice to the Thomases the year
before, and his wife, members of the school board and the township government, including the mayor also attended. The
Thomases had made a lot of friends in the year they had lived in
Cape May Court House.

Wendy asked to see her sister, but the understanding was
that Eric didn't want anybody to see Tracy. Like her parents, she
accepted his wishes.

There was no casket and no urn, only a gold-framed photograph of Tracy, in a denim shirt, lips covered in shiny red gloss, and her hair slicked back to perfection.

Eric read a poem, "If I Had Known," and one of his friends became so emotional while singing "Amazing Grace" that he forgot the words. Eric's sister, Lisa, had to hold her brother up most of the time, yet when Doris looked over at him, she felt that there was no real sadness in his eyes. Donald noticed the same thing. Perhaps people are different. Some hide their feelings in public, but in private they cry and cry.

That afternoon, Tracy was cremated.

After the service, everyone went for lunch at a local restaurant. To Bre it felt like a reunion for Eric's family: Eric seemed more interested in his family than in sharing his feelings with Tracy's family.

When the brunch was over, Eric suggested that they all go over to his aunt Minnie's house and leave him and the Roses alone at his and Tracy's home. Wendy and her husband and son left for Plainfield. Bre stayed behind.

Donald and Doris noticed that when they reached Tracy and Eric's two-story wood-sided home on Woodlawn Avenue and took seats around the kitchen table, Eric stood at the back door, facing some woods, and stared out.

"I thought I would feel guilty, but I don't," Eric said quietly, as if to himself. But Donald was sitting just a few feet away and wondered whether Eric knew he could be overheard. Donald decided that Eric was troubled about letting Tracy drive that night and thought no more of it.

Doris was in the kitchen, sitting in a chair crying, when Eric walked in and said, "Well, I've only had one other girlfriend, and Tracy had—what's his name, the last one." Doris looked up, puzzled.

Then it struck her that Alix no longer had a mother.

The next morning, Eric's family returned to South Carolina, and the Roses drove back to Hyannis to prepare for Tracy's memorial service there. Bre stayed behind to help Eric with Alix.

Eric told Doris he would bring Tracy's ashes with him so they could spread them over the pond.

On February 21st, Eric arrived in Hyannis in time for the services the next day. Tracy's ashes were in the same plain metal can in which he'd received them from the funeral home.

TWO

Family

Tracy, Doris's youngest daughter, was born on July 26, 1959, in Hyannis. She looked like her father, with big bright eyes. He said that she made him feel that life was worth living. She was his favorite.

Four years earlier, in November 1955, Donald, just out of the army, had found a job and was saving money. Soon after, he and Doris were building their house in Hyannis when Doris's mother began losing her sight; then her father died suddenly. With her husband and four-year-old daughter, Wendy, Doris moved into 215 Old Yarmouth Road, the house her parents had built, to care for her mother. She never left, and she and Donald rented out the three-bedroom house they had built for themselves.

Donald, a third-generation Cape Verdean from the resort town of Harwich, on Cape Cod, was always trim and fit. He had married

Doris in 1952, when he was sixteen. She was sixteen too, half–Narragansett Native American and half–African American.

One day when Tracy was in the first grade, she passed out at Sunday school and was taken to the hospital. She was found to have a defective heart valve. But in time, her heart problem just went away.

Tracy had a zest for life. She loved floating on rafts in nearby Dennis Pond and playing street ball or croquet in their large front yard. But education came first with the Roses.

In grammar school, most of Tracy's friends were African American, Cape Verdean, or Native American. That was also where Tracy found dance to her liking. In junior high her mother would drive her for two hours each way to and from Boston twice a week for lessons with the Boston Ballet.

Wendy was extroverted; Tracy was the shy one. When Tracy was upset by something, she'd say, "Don't tell Dad; he'll get angry." She kept her emotions to herself.

Tracy was an excellent student in high school, well organized and disciplined. She always had at least one job, and saved to buy a car: a Ford convertible that her parents helped her buy in 1978 for $400. A good wash was all it needed.

Tracy went away to Skidmore College, a small school in upstate New York, and paid the $1,200-a-year tuition with her parents' help and student loans. Tracy often told her parents how much she appreciated what they were doing for her. One year she worked in the kitchen and another in the dean's office. By her second year her major was business and dance was her minor. She traded in her convertible for a station wagon and on holidays drove home to the Cape.

Tracy's most serious relationship was with a fellow student, Gregory Shepherd, from Princeton, New Jersey, who was planning to go into finance.

After Tracy graduated in 1982, she got a job at the Cape Cod Bank and Trust. A year later, she told her parents that she was moving to Boston to get a master's degree at Northeastern. Tracy put herself through business school, got her M.B.A. in 1985, and took a job as a computer graphics specialist.

It was then that she met Eric Thomas, who was five years younger than she. He was five feet eleven inches tall, she was five four. They met at a formal party for African American professionals at Boston College. They each arrived alone. A few days later Tracy called her parents and told them about Eric, describing him as smart, nice, handsome, a good cook, and still a little immature, but ambitious—like herself. She said he was studying to be a dentist at Tufts.

Eric had gone to South Carolina State University on an ROTC scholarship, and after he graduated he went to Fort McClellan in Alabama and then on to dental school. After dental school, he would have to serve another four years as repayment for his education.

Tracy was attracted by Eric's pursuit of her. He doted on her and she loved it. When he wore his glasses, she thought he looked like an intellectual. Most of Eric's friends were African Americans; Tracy's were mixed. In Boston he had been living with a girl named Stephanie Arrington, who had recently moved out. As they got more serious, Tracy and Eric went on vacation to Disneyland, and then to the Caribbean. It wasn't long before Tracy moved in with Eric, in a little apartment in Quincy. In 1989, Eric took a job at Boston City Hospital, where Tracy was working as assistant director of the nursing department.

Donald and Doris had assumed that someday they would marry. From time to time Tracy would ask her mother, "Do you think I'm too old for him?" Doris would answer, "No, you seem a lot younger than Eric."

One summer morning Eric showed up at the Roses' home in Hyannis wearing a tailored shirt and shorts. It was a two-hour drive from Boston, so when he walked in the back door, Doris thought something was wrong. "Where's Tracy?" she asked. Doris had never seen Eric without Tracy. Eric said, "I've come to ask for her hand in marriage." He was charming. How Southern, Doris thought. She admired him for this gesture. A few moments later he told Tracy's father. There were big hugs all around. Not long afterward, Eric started calling Doris "Mamma D." and Donald "Daddy Rose."

Eric told Tracy that he'd been raised mostly by his aunt Minnie, who had moved to Cape May Court House, New Jersey. She was an active member of the local Christian Women's Club and taught weekly Bible classes.

On a Sunday in May, the entire Rose family attended Eric's graduation at Tufts. But Eric's family hardly celebrated the event and this made Tracy sad.

It took Eric a couple of tries to pass the dental boards. He liked to play golf and go drinking with the boys, which he preferred to studying. Right out of school he wanted an expensive car. Tracy said no and the couple settled on a VW.

The wedding was planned for September 21, 1991, at the

First Federated Church of Hyannis. Tracy and her mother made little gift baskets for the families. Tracy found a very old quilt, which she gave to her mother as a present.

Donald Rose beamed as he walked down the aisle with his daughter. Tracy was radiant. Eric looked pleased.

During the ceremony, Tracy would look at Eric and stroke his arm. When Eric's eyes teared, she dried them with her handkerchief.

At the New Seabury Resort, overlooking the golf course and ocean, where the reception took place, Eric's stepfather, Willie, who was a minister, gave an enthusiastic opening toast. When the first song, "All of My Life," was played, it was clear that Eric couldn't dance. An African American who couldn't dance? That was bad, Doris thought. But it didn't bother Tracy. She was in love with Eric.

Tracy's sister, Wendy, however, remembered that Eric's mother had told her that she would have preferred her son to marry someone else. She didn't say who, just some other girl. Wendy never forgot this.

A year later, in October 1992, Eric was transferred to Germany and assigned to an advanced cardiac life support and trauma unit. In late 1994, Tracy became pregnant while still in Germany.

On August 9, 1995, Eric called Donald and Doris and said that Tracy had given birth to a little girl. She was going to be named after Tracy's imaginary childhood friend, Alexandra. They would call her Alix.

Eric's four years in the service were up shortly after Alix was born. Tracy and Eric decided to leave the army and buy a dental practice in southern New Jersey, a move that Eric's aunt Minnie had suggested.

Cape May Court House, a town of four thousand people, is some thirty miles south of Atlantic City, a flat expanse of marshland and pine forests on a peninsula that separates the Atlantic from Delaware Bay. From the town's center, a network of roads fans out to surrounding communities.

To most tourists who stroll the boardwalks, sail, fish, and vacation at Victorian inns along the Jersey coast, Court House, a few miles inland, is off the beaten track. Unless poor weather draws some of the sixty thousand or so tourists from the beaches at Avalon and Stone Harbor to the local zoo, there is no reason to drive to town. It has no movie theater, no shopping mall, no amusement park, no sports arena, and few attractions other than its many churches and freshly painted single-story wood houses occupied by small businesses.

Its charm lies in its old homes and the stately courthouse, built in 1765. It is the administrative crossroads of the county, home to its commissioners; a superior court; the county jail; the prosecutor's office; the medical examiner's office; and the health, planning, and public-works departments.

When Tracy called her mother in October 1995, from South Jersey, she said that she and Eric needed some financial help to buy the dental practice. Doris didn't hesitate at all. "What do you need?" she asked.

"Ten thousand dollars," Tracy replied, 10 percent of the purchase price.

"Are you sure that's enough?" her mother asked.

Tracy hesitated.

"Well, why don't we send you twelve thousand?" Doris said without even asking her husband.

Then Eric picked up the phone and became emotional. He was close to tears.

"Don't worry about it, you got it," Doris said to her son-in-law. From the way he talked, Doris wondered whether he had tried many other people before calling her.

A week later, when Tracy called, Doris asked, "Are Eric's parents helping out?"

"No, Mommy."

It bothered Doris that Eric's mother and stepfather, who drove a Jaguar and had a house ten times the size of hers and Donald's, weren't there for Eric the way she and Donald were.

The price of the practice included the little house that served as the dental office, the land, and the client list of its owner, Dr. James Callaway.

Callaway, now seventy, was, like Thomas, African American, successful, and well respected in the community. He was a pay-as-you-go dentist, and he prospered in a place where people needed help. He was one of only a few African Americans in the local government, the first to sit on the school board and the city's planning board.

In April 1996, after sending Tracy and Eric the money, Donald and Doris drove to New Jersey in their old Volkswagen bus, with tools and supplies, to help fix up the dental office. By then Tracy and Eric and their daughter, Alix, were renting a recently renovated old house on North Main Street, Route 9, right on the highway.

The practice stood on West Atlantic Street, a stone's throw from the Court House water tower and the Cape May Seashore excursion rail line, which runs from Court House to Cape May.

The single-story wood-sided building sat in a large lot some twenty-five feet from the street. If you drove past, you wouldn't notice it. There were no other businesses and only a few wood-framed and renovated aluminum-sided two-story homes set back among trees.

Fixing up the dental offices took a week. To celebrate, Tracy, Eric, and Alix; Donald and Doris; Wendy and Bre; Minnie and Rudy Callender; and Eric's cousin Iris Dracket all posed for group photographs in front of the building. Facing the house, Doris decided she didn't like the sign, with its black calligraphy, that Eric had had made for the front lawn. Cape Cod had nice-looking signs. This one, she thought, looked as if it belonged to a funeral home. But Doris did like the off-white paint and blue shutters that Tracy had chosen.

Eric now started to establish himself in the community. His aunt Minnie was the best friend of Dr. Callaway's wife. Minnie and Rudy, who was membership chairman for the Cape May County Democratic Party and involved in several senior-citizens' organizations, introduced Eric to the locals.

Eric set his sights on emulating his well-respected predecessor. First, he made an appointment to meet the mayor and the superintendent of the school that was just a few blocks away.

He wanted to join the township's planning board and country club. He attended meetings of the Middle Township Democrat Club and the American Legion and also some AARP functions.

Dr. Thomas, as he soon became known around town, enjoyed his new life. He was soft-spoken, young, good-looking, and immaculately well-dressed—he made a good impression. People liked him. At the high school's Career Day classes, he soon became one of the most popular and inspiring speakers.

Eric had always paid attention to his clothes and the kind of car he drove. Now he bought a new Volvo for Tracy, and leased a new 1996 Ford Explorer for himself and the family. He was beginning to live a little above his means.

Soon Eric was golfing at the Wildwood Golf and Country Club with Vincent Orlando, the township's engineer, and Dr Callaway. Not long afterward, he was invited to become a member. It was the same club where Arnold Palmer had played when he served at the U.S. Coast Guard base in nearby Cape May.

Doris considered herself fortunate. She had three grandchildren and things were going well for both her girls.

When they started out, Eric and Tracy were the only people working in his office. Tracy would drop Alix off at day care, then go to the office, answer the phone, do the bills, file the insurance claims, mop, clean up, and help her husband mow the lawn.

Then Eric told Tracy he wanted to have another child. Tracy was surprised, since they had discussed waiting until she went to law school. Alix would be four then and the practice would be showing a profit.

I'm working full-time, she told Eric. Sometimes I fall asleep at the desk in the office. I'm expected to do this and that? I haven't even lost weight from having Alix, and where is the time for us to enjoy her?

It was during one of her trips to Court House that Doris saw something was wrong.

"Eric won't touch me," Tracy said.

"Oh my God," Doris replied. And when she took her daughter into her arms, Tracy wept.

"Don't tell Daddy, don't tell Daddy," she sobbed.

Doris tried to console her daughter without prying. "Things like that happen," she told Tracy. "You're starting a business. There's pressure on both of you. It's just something he's going through."

Alix spent her first birthday, August 9th, in Hyannis. The entire family drove up to Provincetown and lunched at Michael Shay's. That same week, Tracy told her mother that Eric wanted another baby and she didn't. "I'm so tired from running the business and taking care of Alix," she said.

"Well, maybe you should just wait, hold off," Doris replied. "Tell Eric that Alix is so young."

Then Tracy wept again, as if she were trying to tell her mother that Eric didn't want sex unless he could have a baby.

Doris could see that her child was hurting, but she understood it was a private matter. Tracy was so much in love with Eric that she would do anything for him.

Tracy was still unhappy in early October 1996. It was during one of the Roses' regular visits to Plainfield to see Wendy's and Tracy's families together that Eric told the family Tracy was going to have another child. This was the first the Roses had heard if it; Tracy hadn't told her parents that she was pregnant.

Tracy's pregnancy was easy, but she wondered about Eric's new habit of stepping outdoors to take calls on his cell phone. The phone would ring, and he'd walk out the door. Back inside, he'd tell her it was patient business.

In late October 1996, the Thomases' one-year lease on their home expired. Now they needed a larger house, where they could raise their children. Eric started looking at subdivisions of custom homes in the area. He wanted to live near his office. It would be good for business.

By mid-November Tracy and Eric had settled on a four-bedroom house, nestled in a forest, on an acre and a half on Woodland Drive, out near Hand Avenue. The two-story gray-sided house was set back from the road, among towering trees, just outside the Cape May National Wildlife Refuge, less than three miles from Eric's office. When Donald saw the $175,000 price tag, he thought they were overreaching a bit. Doris waited for Eric to ask for money, but he didn't.

At the same time, through the American Dental Association, Eric and Tracy applied to Great West Life and Annuity Insurance Company for term life insurance, to protect the new mortgage and the business debt they were accumulating. This was their first home, and they hadn't had any insurance since leaving the military. Eric thought that $400,000 on his life and $150,000 on Tracy's would cover the debt and provide sufficient funds for the family if he died.* Eric wanted Tracy to be taken care of.

Though they would close on their house on December 20th, Eric thought it was still important to attend a dental conference near Secaucus, New Jersey, scheduled for mid-December. He said he wanted to keep up on the latest technology. The gathering lasted four days. While he was away, Doris came down to help her daughter pack and to watch Alix, since Tracy had to work at the office.

By New Year's Day the Thomases had moved into their new home.

Doris, who was back in Hyannis, was eager to return to Court House to take care of Alix while Tracy worked on the new house. The week she was there, Mayor Mike Voll appointed Eric to the planning board as an alternate. It was just afterward that Eric left for Boston, to attend another dental conference and speak to a group of students. Before Eric returned, Donald joined Doris in New Jersey to help Tracy, who was now six months pregnant.

On Saturday, February 1st, Eric and Tracy dropped Alix off at Wendy's house in Plainfield on their way to Newark International Airport. They were going to visit some army friends in Texas. The day before, Doris and Donald had taken a train to Wendy's, where they would help with Alix for the week. Tracy and Eric arrived in a rush. When Tracy took Alix's

---

* A month before Tracy's death, Eric and Tracy increased this amount to $200,000. In addition, the policy had a provision that in the case of accidental death, the death benefit would be doubled.

things upstairs to the room where she was going to sleep, Eric called out to her to hurry up or they would miss the plane. Tracy rushed downstairs and ran outside to catch up with him. But while Wendy was still at the front door bidding them good-bye, Tracy suddenly returned to say something to Doris. "Mommy, if anything happens to me, take Alix to Cape Cod," she said. Doris and Wendy were stunned. They had never heard Tracy talk that way before. They said nothing.

Perhaps, Doris thought later, she was nervous about flying without her baby and meant only that if she and Eric died, she wanted her parents to raise Alix. Still, Doris worried.

It was a quick trip. Tracy and Eric were back three days later, on February 4th. They hadn't called while they were away, and the Roses didn't know where they had been staying.

Alix was sniffling with a mild cold, and Tracy wanted to get home from Wendy's to care for her daughter. The next day, before dark, they made the three-hour drive back to Cape May Court House. Tracy, who was still tired from the trip, sat in the back with Alix.

On Friday, Tracy called her parents to thank them for watching Alix. The baby still had a fever, she said, and they were thinking about taking her to the pediatrician later in the day.

Tracy was giving her Tylenol, on the advice of the local hospital. By Friday afternoon, Alix's temperature was on the rise again and Tracy was worried. When they took Alix to the pediatrician at Kids First in town, they were told that Alix's chronic ear infections and teething were making her feverish. By Friday night she was better, with only a slight temperature.

On Saturday, February 8th, Tracy decided to stay home with

Alix, and Eric saw a few patients. Six and a half months pregnant, Tracy had difficulty moving. Sometimes Eric would have to help her up from a chair.

After dinner, while Eric watched TV, Tracy went upstairs, put Alix to bed, and settled in herself.

Hours later, he was watching *Saturday Night Live* when Tracy came downstairs and said Alix's temperature was rising, even with the Tylenol she'd given her. Tracy wanted Alix taken to the hospital so that her fever wouldn't do permanent damage.

Eric put on his jacket and baseball cap and went out to start up the Explorer. After brushing off the windshield, he returned to the house. Tracy had dressed the baby in a winter jumpsuit and was getting the bottles and the diaper bag as Eric walked in. Shortly afterward, Tracy left the house with Eric, who was holding Alix.

By now the snow had stopped falling.

THREE

The Investigation

The temperature was still a crisp thirty-one degrees on Thursday, February 13th, four days after Tracy Thomas died. On that day Detective Webster met with a representative of the USAA Insurance Company, Eric's carrier. Together they visited the scene of the accident on Hand Avenue, and then examined the Ford Explorer at the impound garage. At the scene, Webster showed the adjuster how the vehicle had been traveling east just before it turned right and hit the utility pole. Only the utility pole stump remained as evidence of an accident. The two men wondered if an air bag might have caused Tracy Thomas's death.

Between seeing patients and dealing with dental emergencies, Eric Thomas normally worked a forty-hour week. Three weeks after his wife's death he returned to work on a reduced schedule, but found it hard to concentrate. Since the accident he had worn a hard collar and now he switched to a softer one. From time to time he felt pain and could not move easily. Thomas went to an orthopedic surgeon and a neurologist to track down the source of the pain and of the numbness and the occasional tingling in his fingers. Gardening, swimming, and heavy lifting were painful. For months Eric would feel encumbered by stress and pain.

Toward the end of February Eric contacted the medical examiner to ask about the cause of his wife's death. Dr. Gross told him that he was still waiting for the toxicology reports and hadn't made a final determination. In late March, Thomas would call again. This time he would get the impression from the medical examiner and Detective Webster, whom he also spoke to, that the air bag had probably killed her.

Also at the end of February, Eric called the Great West Insurance Company to tell them of Tracy's death.

In early March, Eric's sister, Lisa, called Doris in Hyannis to find out how she and Donald were doing. As they chatted, Lisa mentioned that Eric had been ill. Eric had told Doris he had Lyme disease, but Lisa said she wasn't referring to that. She wouldn't elaborate, but in fact, Eric was depressed and had seen a psychologist, named Chareny, about a half dozen times since Tracy's death.

He wasn't yet back to work full-time. He thought about playing golf, but his neck and back still hurt, and he had difficulty turning his head. He thought it would be good to get away for a while, and he made a short business trip to Secaucus, where he had attended the dental conference the previous December.

By the end of March Detective Webster had finally heard from the National Highway Traffic Safety Administration about child car seats, but nothing about air bags. When he called to complain the agency suggested that he call Ford for the information. In fact, Webster had called them two or three times. The people at Ford seemed concerned that an air bag may have caused Tracy's death, but no one from the company, as far as Webster knew, followed up, nor did Ford send Webster the information he'd asked for.

Periodically, the detective talked to the medical examiner and gave him status reports. Webster told Gross he had exhausted all means of finding out about air bags. Gross told Webster that he had also come up empty-handed.

At first, the medical examiner gave Webster the impression that the tightening of the seat belt, the position of Tracy's body in relation to the steering wheel, the pressure of her uterus pushing against her diaphragm, causing asphyxia, could have killed her.

Dr. Gross asked Webster to document what he knew to date so that he could complete the record. In typing up the report of his conversation with Gross, Webster noted that from the medical examiner's point of view, there was no need to go any further with the investigation.* The cause of Tracy Thomas's death would be made without reference to air bags.

---

* In an oral deposition, taken on October 21, 1999, Gross would deny that he made such a request. "I would not tell a police officer not to go any further with an investigation. That's not me."

Also in March, Webster met with Jim Rybicki of the Cape May County Prosecutor's Office to discuss the circumstances surrounding the death. They were both struck by how unusual it was that Tracy Thomas had died in this otherwise unremarkable accident. Could Dr. Eric Thomas have done something to cause the accident or his wife's death? Was he hiding something?

But they could find no evidence of family problems. All they had was the accident, the pregnancy, the location of the fetus, the tight seat belt, and the air bag. And who could say that a deer *hadn't* appeared in the roadway? There were no eyewitnesses.

With foul play ruled out, the investigation into the death of Tracy Thomas was coming to a close.

That year Easter fell on March 30th. On that day Eric took Alix down to Orangeburg, South Carolina, to visit his parents. This was the first time in a long while that he had attended Easter services without Tracy. At church, he ran across an old friend, Stephanie Arrington, who was also visiting her parents. He had dated her in high school and lived with her for a while during his first year at dental school. Since then she'd married Sean Haley, a graduate student, in Austin, Texas, where she worked for IBM. The marriage was not going well, she told Eric.

At home and in day care, Alix had been having crying jags. She suffered from repeated earaches and seemed confused and sad. The doctor had discovered a painful blockage of her ears, which contributed to her continuing colds and fevers. Now that Alix and Eric had returned from their Easter visit to his parents, Alix had minor surgery on her ears. When she came to, with Eric sitting beside her, she cried, "Mommy, Mommy." The Roses were now in Court House to help with their granddaughter.

Soon after Alix returned from the hospital, Thomas left again, this time to attend the Masters tournament in Augusta, Georgia, where Tiger Woods was playing. The Roses thought it was a good idea for their son-in-law to get away, and Doris didn't mind staying longer with Alix. On this trip, however, she realized that Eric hadn't left her a number where he could be reached in case of an emergency, and this worried her. It wasn't right. Eric returned a week later after seeing Woods defeat defending champion Nick Faldo.

On April 8, 1997, two months after the accident, Dr. Gross issued his autopsy findings on Tracy's death. Gross reported that the cause of death was blunt force trauma with asphyxia.

AIR BAG PLAYED ROLE IN MIDDLE TOWNSHIP WOMAN'S DEATH

. . . air bag was among several elements mentioned in the report Gross completed this week.

"The positioning of Tracy Thomas in the vehicle at the time of impact, as well as the pregnancy and the effects of restraints and the sudden deployment of the air bag" were contributing factors, Gross said.

In response to deaths caused by air bags, a consumer outcry, federal safety regulators last month gave United States automakers approval to install less powerful air bags in new cars and trucks.

The National Highway Traffic Safety Administration issued a rule that allows car companies to reduce the force of a deploying air bag by between 20 percent and 35 percent.

Twenty-three small adults—most of them short women—and 38 children have been killed by air bags, mostly from severe head and chest injuries, said Kara Donohue, spokeswoman for the Insurance Information Institute in Washington, D.C.

Air bags are very effective when used properly. They have saved 1,700 lives in 1 million deployments and have reduced injuries and fatalities by 30 percent, said Donohue.

THE PRESS OF ATLANTIC CITY
Saturday, April 12, 1997
By Jeanne Dewey, Staff Writer

On April 28th, Eric made an application under oath to Cape May County's Surrogate Court. His declaration would determine how much, if any, inheritance taxes Tracy's survivors and beneficiaries would have to pay.

On May 5th, three months after the accident, Doris picked Alix up at Wendy's home in Plainfield, where Eric had dropped her off. He had to fly somewhere, he said, and would return in five days.

The following week Eric called Doris to ask if she could take care of Alix again. This time he said he needed to attend the taping of an HBO Television special in Aruba. On his way back he stopped in Tampa, Florida, to see some friends.

Almost a month later, on June 4, 1997, the Great West Insurance Company notified Eric that payment for Tracy's life insurance policy and accidental death benefits had been deposited in a ready fund account that he could now draw on.

The amount was $400,000 plus $4,763.84 in interest. Although the face amount of the policy was $200,000, accidental death paid double the amount.

Meanwhile, Eric leased an Expedition from the local Ford dealer that had leased him the Explorer, which was still under investigation.

Soon after receiving the proceeds of Tracy's life insurance policy, Eric withdrew between fifty and seventy-five thousand dollars to pay off his dental school debts and his and Tracy's student loans, and spent another twenty to thirty thousand dollars to decorate his office. He then repaid a loan of $5,000 from his parents. Next, he paid off credit card debts amounting to about nine thousand dollars. Altogether, he spent about $115,000. He did not repay Tracy's parents' loan or pay down the mortgage on the home he and Tracy had bought the previous December. He invested the rest of the money.

On June 11th, Detective Webster was contacted by CalSpan, an independent agency that represented the National Highway Traffic Safety Board. David Lee, Eric's friend and an attorney, had suggested that the NHTSA reconstruct the accident. A week later, on June 19th, Webster took Thomas, David Lee, and the CalSpan investigators out to the accident site. Then they looked at the Explorer. Almost immediately, Thomas left and returned to work. The investigators spent two hours photographing the car and taking measurements.

Around the middle of July, Eric called the Roses and asked if he could bring Alix up to Hyannis for a few weeks. He'd decided it was time to remove Tracy's belongings from the house, he said. Doris and Donald understood that Eric had to get on with his life, and they were happy to spend so much time with their granddaughter. Their niggling doubts about the trips Eric took so soon after Tracy's death were all but erased after they saw how much he loved Alix when they were together.

After that visit, Donald and Doris traveled to Court House on August 9th for Alix's second birthday. The entire Rose family—from Hyannis, Plainfield, and Philadelphia— and Eric's relatives from South Carolina met for the occasion. This year there was no Tracy, no radiant smile, no mother to dress Alix in her Sunday best, no mother dressed in her usual shorts.

It was on that visit that Doris first heard the name Stephanie. After Alix's party, Eric told Doris he was going to pick up a friend named Stephanie at the airport the next morning. The Roses had planned to stay another day, but they felt that Alix's birthday was an inappropriate time for them to meet Eric's new girlfriend, especially since it was only six months since Tracy's death. The next morning, before coffee, Donald and Doris left for Hyannis.

Later in August, Eric called the Roses and said he was taking another vacation, this time in Antigua. Would they take care of Alix up in Hyannis? Of course, they replied. Doris and Donald assumed he wasn't going to Antigua alone.

In October Doris drove down to Cape May Court House to help Eric around the house and spend time with her granddaughter. Though Alix was in day care, everyone agreed that the more time she spent with family, the better it would be. One morning while Doris was putting some things away in Eric's bedroom drawers, she found women's clothing that didn't belong to Tracy. Then she noticed a color photograph of a woman on the refrigerator. Doris assumed it was Stephanie. It made her pause for a moment; she was so used to seeing pictures of Tracy, smiling, hair cut short, proudly holding Alix. Later, Alix took her grandmother into the kitchen and pointed to the photograph. "Is my mommy?"

"No," Doris told her. "I don't know who it is." No sooner had she spoken than she regretted that she had inadvertently added to her granddaughter's confusion.

That night Eric told the Roses he had removed photographs of Tracy from the house on the advice of a child psychologist. He told the Roses not to talk about her in Alix's presence. This puzzled Doris. Then Eric said he also wanted Tracy's pictures removed from the Roses' home when Alix visited. The conversation flared into an argument.

Later, Donald reminded Doris that when Eric's father died, his mother had taken down all his pictures, changed the rugs and the furniture, and started a new life. That was how she dealt with her grief.

When the Roses returned to Hyannis, Doris consulted her own doctor and a child psychologist. They advised the opposite approach. "If Alix asks about her mother," Doris was told, "talk to her, but don't push her into anything."

Doris knew she couldn't tell Eric what to do in his own home, but she wouldn't let him tell her what to do in hers.

Later that month, on October 27th, the Roses returned to

New Jersey to pick up Alix for their traditional Halloween visit with Wendy's family in Plainfield. Eric agreed that Alix shouldn't miss the occasion, and invited them to come to Court House beforehand.

On Monday evening Donald was upstairs in bed and Eric and Doris were watching TV in Eric's den when the news broadcast said something about the stock market. Eric stood up, said he was going to call his broker, and left the room. Doris was surprised. With Tracy's life insurance and the dental practice doing so well—well enough that he could invest in the market—why hadn't he repaid the $12,000 she and Donald had loaned him to purchase the dental practice? She said nothing to Eric, and went upstairs to tell Donald. He was not as upset as she was. A few days later Eric would repay half the money he owed them and would promise to pay the rest the following year.

The next morning Doris asked Eric what day during the coming Christmas holidays he wanted Alix picked up for her scheduled vacation with them.

Eric told her that Alix wouldn't be going to Hyannis for the holidays this year. Instead she would spend Christmas with his parents. Doris didn't understand. The plan had been for Eric's family to have Alix for Thanksgiving and for the Roses to have her at Christmas.

"She's not going to Hyannis unless you take down all of Tracy's pictures," Eric said. "I told you—I don't want Alix seeing her mother's pictures. And I don't want you talking about Tracy when Alix is around."

This was blackmail. Doris was furious, and she and Eric argued.

Then she told Donald what Eric had said. Eric's insistence on this point confused the Roses. After all, Alix was old enough to remember her mother. Moreover, the Roses didn't have that many pictures of Tracy in the house. On one wall was Tracy and Eric's wedding picture, and there was a group photo on the opposite wall that included Tracy, wearing her favorite gold-hoop earrings and black-rimmed sunglasses. But Eric had already left for work when Donald went downstairs to discuss the problem with him.

That afternoon when Eric got home and before Donald could mention Christmas, he told his father-in-law that he might sue Ford over Tracy's death. He was sure the air bag had killed her. He wanted to know if his in-laws would join him in the action. "It isn't for the money," Eric said. "I'm doing well. It is for all the other people that have been or might be killed by air bags."

Donald was still troubled by the issue of Tracy's photos and tried to control his anger. "No. I don't want to make a cent off the death of my daughter," he said. Eric dropped the subject. But later, in passing, he mentioned it again. "If things get out of hand and they [Ford] ask too many questions, I will drop it," he told his father-in-law. Eric's statement puzzled Donald. He would never forget it.

When Donald told Doris that Eric was thinking of suing Ford, she got upset. She had never seen this side of Eric. There was now so much tension between the Roses and Eric that the Roses drove back to Hyannis without taking Alix to Wendy's house for Halloween.

At home that same week, Doris and Donald consulted a

lawyer named Diane Boudreau about Eric's demands that Tracy's pictures be removed and that they not speak about Tracy in their granddaughter's presence. They said that they didn't want more time with Alix; they simply wanted their visitation rights protected. The lawyer advised them to retain an attorney in New Jersey and petition the court to set specific times for phone calls and visits. She recommended someone named Lisa Radell, whose office was in Wildwood.

The Roses were depressed not to be with Alix for the holidays. For a time, Doris was so upset that she didn't even want a tree. This was the first Christmas since Tracy's death and Doris had planned to let Alix help put up the decorations Tracy had bought in Germany. Instead, the Roses spent the holiday at Wendy's, where they bought presents for Alix and Eric and mailed them. But by New Year's, the Roses hadn't had a phone call or even a card from Eric.

Then, in January, Eric called Doris to say that she and Donald could see Alix at Wendy's if they wanted to, but not at their own home—unless they took Tracy's pictures down. Since Donald had already taken his vacation, he would have to take the week off from work without pay, but he was eager to see Alix and agreed. Doris said that she and Donald would visit Wendy's next week.

On January 10, 1998, Eric dropped Alix off at Wendy's. Soon after, everyone in Wendy's household came down with a cold. Doris wanted Alix to see a doctor and thought Eric should be told, but when Doris repeatedly tried phoning his office and his home, he didn't return her calls. She discovered he had gone away without leaving a number where he could be reached. By the time Eric came to pick Alix up, her cold was gone.

During February and March the Roses talked to Alix two or three times a week.

Eric let them call as often as they liked.

At Easter, Donald and Doris drove to Wendy's, and Eric delivered Alix to visit with them for the week. Thereafter, Wendy's house in Plainfield became the meeting place for the family to see Alix. They went there about once a month. Between visits, they phoned Alix at Eric's house. Often, a woman answered the phone. They assumed it was Eric's girl-friend, Stephanie, but didn't give her much thought. All they cared about was Alix.

In the early summer of 1998, the Roses visited Lisa Radell, the family-law attorney who had been recommended to them by Diane Boudreau. Radell said that Donald and Doris should estab-lish a visitation schedule, which they were entitled to under the law. Perhaps it was this validation of their feelings that led them to decide during the return trip to Hyannis that they should talk to the medical examiner or the police about Tracy's death. They were now emotionally ready to read the police report.

A few months previously, the National Highway Traffic Safety Administration had published a list of thirty-six accidents since 1991 in which drivers had been killed or seriously injured by air-bag deployment. Ford's thirteen-year-old Taurus appeared on the list eight times. Ford's F150, Escort, Windstar, Probe, Aspire, Crown Victoria, and Contour were each listed once.

So was the Explorer: Tracy Thomas's NHTSA case number CA9723.

The report stated that her safety belt was worn properly and that the Explorer's speed at the time of impact was estimated at fifteen miles per hour. The cause of death noted was similar to what medical examiner Gross had written in April 1997: blunt trauma to the neck, with asphyxia. The lengthy report did not mention chest compression or injury to the spinal cord.

Eric was now ready to sue Ford and had to retain a product-liability lawyer. He went first to a local attorney, James Pickering Jr., of South Seaville, New Jersey, who suggested the law firm Mellon, Webster & Mellon, in Doylestown, Pennsylvania, which had recently won some claims against the tobacco industry.

Tom Mellon, a former federal prosecutor who now specialized in personal injury, medical malpractice, and product liability, took the case: it would be his first automotive air-bag case.

Recent government reports differed widely in their estimates of deaths from air bags in cars at low speeds. NHTSA estimated that as of November 1996, air bags had deployed more than 800,000 times in crashes and had saved approximately 1,664 lives (164 passengers and 1,500 drivers). The agency also claimed that air bags had fatally injured at least thirty-two children, one adult passenger, and nineteen drivers in low-speed crashes. Most of those children who died were unbelted. NHTSA also said that while the number of people saved by air bags was growing annually, so too was the (much smaller) number of those killed.

Mellon, tall and thin, with pale blue eyes, would handle the strategy and public relations. His colleague Elliott Kolodny, a large man with lots of energy, the firm's top litigator, would handle the injury claims. He would try to prove to a jury that the air bag in the Thomases' Explorer had killed Tracy.

The financial arrangements were standard. Mellon's firm would advance all the costs of the litigation. Mellon's expenses would first be deducted from whatever Eric received. Then the State of New Jersey would award Mellon's firm a fee somewhere between twenty-five and thirty five percent. The rest would go to Thomas.

On July 26, 1998, Tracy would have been thirty-nine years old. Now, eighteen months after her death, the Roses would fulfill their daughter's wish. When Donald came home from work, he and Doris walked down the road to Willow Street to spread Tracy's ashes over Dennis Pond. They talked about how she had preferred the pond to the ocean, and recalled how Donald had taught her to float on a wooden raft he had made for her, and how early one winter he'd scolded her for skating on thin ice. Walking back through the woods they talked about their own childhoods and how happy they too had been on the Cape.

By that summer, Doris had been growing increasingly obsessed with what Tracy had said to her the week before her death, when she and Eric left for Texas to visit their friends. "If anything happens to me, take Alix to the Cape." Doris didn't trust Eric enough to ask him if he knew what Tracy had meant. She and Donald now felt that Eric couldn't be relied on at all to tell them the truth. They were also afraid he'd lose his temper and jeopardize their visits with Alix.

* * *

Eric agreed to bring Alix to Wendy's house for her third birthday so that the Roses could have a party for their granddaughter. On August 10th, when Doris opened Wendy's kitchen door, she found Eric, Alix, and a young woman she recognized from the picture on Eric's refrigerator as Stephanie. She was pregnant.

"I want you to know that I've remarried," Eric said.

In fact, he had married Stephanie a month earlier, on July 11, 1998, soon after she divorced her husband, Sean Haley. This came as a complete surprise to the Roses. Months later they learned that part of Tracy's life insurance—ten thousand dollars—was used to pay for the wedding.

Donald took Eric's hand and congratulated him. He understood that it would be good for Alix to have someone taking care of her. Doris was less enthusiastic. She invited the couple to come in. Alix ran quickly to her grandfather.

Doris thought Stephanie looked like a black Barbie doll, in a brown suit jacket, a white blouse, and brown pants. But Stephanie turned out to be polite and friendly and Doris decided that she might be easier to deal with, when it came to Alix, than her ex-son-in-law.

Wendy, however, didn't like what she saw. Eric and Stephanie stayed too long. Wendy thought they didn't want to leave Alix with the Roses. Then, when Donald told Eric that they would like Alix to visit the Cape that summer, Eric said, in almost a whisper, he'd think about it.

Two days later, on August 12th, Eric called the Roses to ask whether they were going to take Tracy's pictures down. Again,

Doris said no. *Nobody* was going to tell her what to do in her own house.

Donald took the portable phone from her hands and sat out on the porch. "I've always been friendly with you," he told his former son-in-law. "I even walked your dog when you asked."

Eric was silent.

"I can't lose two people," Donald continued. "I can't lose my daughter and lose my granddaughter, too."

Eric said nothing.

"I'll do it," Donald said after a long silence.

Eric then told Donald that he and Doris could have Alix from August 15th to the 22nd. They could pick her up at his house.

That night, after finishing the laundry, Doris took Eric and Tracy's wedding picture down. Then she remembered that in their recent conversation, Eric had said nothing about not talking to Alix about her mother. Maybe some progress was being made after all.

The next night, just before the Roses were to leave for Cape May Court House, Eric called again. He wanted to know if the photographs had been put away. Donald said yes. Then Eric called Doris's niece, who lived down the block, for confirmation. He got it.

The fifteenth was a Saturday and Eric wanted Alix picked up by two P.M. It was a six-hour drive from Hyannis to South Jersey on a summer Saturday. The Roses stayed just a few minutes but felt Stephanie had been genuinely affectionate toward their granddaughter.

Alix's visit was a joy. Donald showed her Dennis Pond, where he had taken Tracy at the same age. Tracy's girlfriends who still lived within driving distance visited, and even Doris's relatives from Philadelphia showed up.

In the excitement over Alix's visit, the Roses had put aside their worries. Then, in October, just as the leaves were changing their color, Wendy told her mother that she was going to get the records of Tracy's accident from the Middle Township Police Department. She had talked to someone there who seemed cooperative. On October 29th, Wendy and Doris collected the entire file.

That same morning, Doris called Eric, apologized for the short notice, and asked if she could see Alix. Eric said it was no problem. Alix would be ready at around noon and they could visit with her until about three-thirty P.M. When they rang the doorbell, Stephanie answered. Alix was ready and excited to see them. Their granddaughter and her stepmother seemed to be getting along well. Wendy and Doris took Alix to the shore.

When Doris returned to Hyannis, she wondered whether to hang Tracy's photographs on the wall again. She knew that if Alix saw the pictures and told Eric about them, he might not let her come back to Hyannis. Doris decided she couldn't live like that. She and Donald would have to legally pursue their visitation rights. They were determined to see Alix. They were also determined to know everything about how their daughter had died.

Wendy made a copy of the police reports for her mother and then sat down to read them. The more closely she read, the more she saw that something was wrong. Tracy had never told Wendy about the "blackouts" Eric mentioned to Detective Webster, and it was certainly odd that Tracy had chosen to drive that night, leaving Alix, with a high fever, alone in the backseat. Wendy was sure that her sister would have sat next to Alix and held her hand while Eric drove. Wendy had often watched Tracy put Alix to bed and never saw the baby resist, fuss, or cry, as Eric said she had done that night. And what was this about hives? Wendy was sure that Tracy would have told her if Alix had hives, but she had never mentioned it. Wendy wondered if Eric had lied to the police.

When Wendy called her parents to tell them of her doubts, Donald couldn't bring himself to read the documents, but Doris did. The part about Tracy falling in the snow and Eric letting her drive the car didn't make sense to Doris either. For one thing, her daughter was six and a half months pregnant, wasn't feeling well after her recent trip to Texas, and was unlikely to be driving. Then there was the word *clumsy,* but Tracy was graceful, a ballet dancer! She never fell, even on ice skates. In Germany, pregnant with Alix, Tracy never blacked out, and if she had such problems in her second pregnancy, Tracy would have told her mother.

Doris too began to question the circumstances surrounding her daughter's death. Maybe it *wasn't* the air bag that had killed Tracy.

Doris and Wendy decided to visit the police.

On December 9, 1998, the Roses went to see Lisa Radell in Wildwood about visitation rights. That same day, Wendy and

Bre joined Donald and Doris in South Jersey, where they visited Detective Webster at police headquarters.

Webster, a quiet man who never said much, met them in the same office where he'd sat with Donald and Eric a few days after Tracy's accident. The detective was pleasant, drinking his coffee, and not upset at all that the Roses had come to see him. To Wendy he seemed almost too genial, not a go-getter like the policemen you see on TV. Wendy told Webster that the family had now read Eric's statements and had some questions, but more important, they had some information the police should know.

The Roses told Webster how Eric wanted Tracy's pictures taken off the wall and how he'd said that they shouldn't talk about Tracy in Alix's presence. They said they were upset about Eric's dating, getting remarried, and having a baby with his new wife so soon after Tracy's death. Moreover, they didn't understand how, with such a small dental practice, he could now be driving a Mercedes and how his new wife had a Cadillac SUV, to say nothing about a new swimming pool! They hoped that some of Tracy's insurance money had been put away for Alix.

Doris told Webster that Tracy had said to her, "If anything happens to me, take Alix to Cape Cod," just a week before her death. She also mentioned Eric's cryptic remark, just after the accident, that he didn't feel guilty. Bre then mentioned his comment in the hospital: "With all my medical training, I couldn't save her." Since he was supposedly found unconscious, Bre found this strange.

Webster listened in silence.

Wendy then told him that she'd driven with Tracy in the same kind of bad weather as that night, and her sister was an excellent driver. She always anticipated things. She would have had plenty of time to stop the car, especially at that low speed, before hitting a pole.

Then Wendy raised questions about Eric's tape-recorded statements.

"When there's an 'uh' and three dots in the transcript, what does that mean?" she asked.

"You know, stuttering," Webster replied.

"Was Eric on some medication [at the time of the tape-recorded interview]?" Wendy asked.

"I asked him that, and his answer is recorded," Webster replied. "He said, 'No.'"

"And 'snatching,'" Wendy said, referring to a word in the transcript. "I've looked at the drawing of the tire tracks in the report, and where's the snatching, where's the veering?" Webster agreed that the car had simply turned toward the side of the two-lane road and hit the pole.

Just then Doris remembered that Tracy had told her how, in the months before her death, Eric would step out into the back-yard to talk on his cell phone.

"Did you check the telephone calls that were made to and from the house that night?" Wendy asked.

"Well, we can't just do that," Webster replied.

"You can't do that?" Wendy said. "You're the police. Why can't you do that?"

"There was no probable cause at the time," the detective answered.*

---

* Having more evidence to form a reasonable belief in certain alleged facts.

It was then that Webster said there were things he also didn't understand about the accident—for example, how long Eric was unconscious. Also, there was no damage to his side of the car and very little to the driver's side. Still, Tracy was dead.

"Why don't you call Ford," Webster suggested. "They might be able to help you."

Wendy said that she'd already called. At first, she could get only as far as customer service. Now she was waiting for someone from the legal department to return her call.

Wendy asked if the police had ever asked Alix's pediatrician exactly what was wrong with her that night. Webster said he hadn't.

Finally, she asked Webster about the contusions to her sister's face. Could they have been caused by the air bag or the fall Tracy had taken? He didn't know for sure, Webster replied. Was it actually true that Tracy had fallen before getting into the car? All Webster could say was that Eric had told him so on two occasions. "And the blackouts?" Again the detective could say only that Eric had told him that. Had the police talked to Tracy's obstetrician or gynecologist to confirm the blackouts? No, Webster said.

The Roses were not satisfied with the detective's answers.

But after they left, Webster scheduled a meeting with Jim Rybicki, chief of detectives in the Cape May County Prosecutor's Office, and told him about the family's concerns. Over a cup of coffee, the two men talked, and decided there was no new evidence to justify reopening the investigation. Dr. Gross's final report would stand.

At home, Doris called Ford in Dearborn, Michigan, and

asked if anyone knew about the accident in which her daughter had died. Nobody knew anything. Then she asked to talk to someone at Ford who could tell her about air bags. Each time she called, she left her name and phone number. Nobody returned her calls. But now Wendy got on the case and soon found the names of several lawyers who represented Ford on the East Coast.

By December Eric had learned that the Roses were pursuing their visitation rights through the courts rather than continuing with the arrangement that he felt was working. He couldn't understand why.

Then the Roses began having difficulty reaching Alix on the phone. Donald called Eric to find out why. His call was not returned. On December 21st, however, as they were about to call their attorney, the Roses received in the mail some pictures of Alix from Eric. On Christmas Day they finally talked to their granddaughter.

Meanwhile, Tom Mellon and Elliott Kolodny visited medical examiner Gross at his office in South Jersey. The attorneys wanted Gross to explain his findings to them. Referring to his autopsy report, Gross told them that blunt trauma with asphyxia had caused Tracy Thomas's death. He had noted that there were injuries to the larynx and the neck tissue surrounding the larynx, including hemorrhages in the eyes and in the muscle of the back of the neck, as well as hemorrhaging around the spinal cord in the neck. He also took out some autopsy photographs and pointed out the injuries to Tracy's face.

The coroner said there were other factors involved in the death: the driver, who was pregnant, had been restrained and the air bag had deployed with the driver's seat in the most forward position. Gross added that since there was little deformation of the steering column, and the injuries to the neck and to the face were consistent with the impact of an air bag, Tracy Thomas's injuries may also have been related to the restraint system. He could not isolate which injuries were caused by the air bag and which were caused by her simply sitting in the vehicle at the time of impact. Gross said that Tracy had died as a result of the trauma partly associated with the air bag. He did not say that the air bag had killed her.

On January 3, 1999, Stephanie gave birth to a boy, named Zach. A week later Eric called and told Doris that on January 8th, Stephanie had adopted Alix with the court's approval. At first, the Roses were upset that they were hearing all this after the fact and thought the adoption was meant to circumvent their visitation hearing, which was pending. But the reality was that three-year-old Alix lived with Stephanie, and they decided the adoption was more than likely an act of love on Stephanie's part, meant to reassure Alix when the new baby came along.

FOUR

The Plaintiff

FORD TO OFFER A SAFER AIR BAG

Ford Motor Company has found a new way to make air bags inflate more safely with a computer that senses the car's speed, the weight and positions of the people inside, and the severity of the crash.

Some elements of the new system will begin appearing in cars and light trucks at no extra cost beginning with model-year-2000 Taurus sedans that will arrive in showrooms later this year, Ford said.

Although air bags have saved thousands of lives, their explosive inflation also has been blamed in dozens of deaths, mostly of children and small women.

"We are moving beyond mechanical devices for occupant safety and are now adding to the mix a fully integrated, computer-driven system that 'thinks' about and responds to different conditions," said Neil Kessler, Ford's chief technical officer.

The system will use two-stage air bags that will expand at full force in higher speed crashes, or more slowly in lower speed collisions. They are designed not to inflate in minor fender-benders.

If the driver is closer to the air bag, as determined by seat position, the air bag will inflate more slowly. It also will adjust the front passenger's air bag, depending on the passenger's weight: The bag will inflate with full force with an average size person, but with 'less force' with a small passenger.

"Every accident is as unique as the individuals involved," said Helen Petrauskas, vice president of environmental and safety engineering at Ford.

Starting last year, automakers were allowed to install air bags with up to one third less force than older air bags. Ford, General Motors Corp. and Daimler Chrysler AG have installed the so-called de-powered air bags in their models.

ASSOCIATED PRESS
January 19, 1998
By Justin Hyde

It was raining on the evening of February 1st, when Bill Conroy of the Philadelphia law firm of White & Williams turned off of Highway 476 and onto South Ithan Avenue on his way to his Colonial-style home in suburban Rosemont. There, at the front door, he was met by his wife, Sharon, who had just been watching the six o'clock news. She told him that a lawsuit had been filed against Ford, one of his clients.

"You're probably going to have to deal with this one," Sharon said. "It's been filed in New Jersey."

"Yeah, I'll probably hear something about it," Conroy replied as he switched from channel to channel hoping to find more news on the case.

"The woman was pregnant," his wife continued. "And they are claiming an air bag killed her."

Bill Conroy, a six-foot-seven-inch former college basketball star, was a highly regarded product-liability attorney with a reputation for fairness. However, if a plaintiff's claim went to trial, he would never back down. He often acknowledged to the jury that a product was defective, but argued that the injury wasn't as bad as the plaintiffs claimed or that the product did not cause the injury. Now, at age forty-five, he handled mostly catastrophic cases, where the injured person had been paralyzed or brain damaged or had died. He knew that it was usually easier to try a case in which someone dies than one in which the survivor is severely injured.

Conroy had tried some heartbreaking cases. In one, a videotape made by a surviving adult was entered into evidence. It showed two Hispanic families on vacation, first playing and then resting at a hilltop grotto, where they prayed to the Virgin Mary. Five minutes later, their Ford Aerostar plunged 150 feet into a ravine, killing all seven children and three adults.

Jorge Aguiniga, the only survivor, sued, alleging that the cause of the accident was sudden brake failure. He wanted $100 million to settle the suit. Ford wouldn't settle at that figure, even though Conroy knew his client couldn't win. He expected Ford might have to pay as much as $30 million. The all-Hispanic jury spoke little or no English, so Conroy had to argue the case through a translator.

It took the jury only three and a half hours to award Aguiniga $16 million, a big win for Ford, Conroy thought.

In another case, a mother had been driving with her husband and their two sets of twins when their van rolled over, killing the father and one child from each of the sets of twins. Conroy, horrified by the situation, tried to settle the case, but got nowhere. Once in court, he fought hard. His job was to win. In the end, he did. The plaintiffs received nothing. However, he felt awful.

That morning, February 1st, Mellon, Webster & Mellon filed Eric Thomas's suit.* Hours later Mellon issued a press release, which outlined the multimillion-dollar civil action. It was picked up by all the wire services, and by early afternoon, TV and the newspapers were reporting the lawsuit. The release referred the media to a Web site to find photos of the Thomas family and the damaged Ford, as well as the complaint, with

---

* The suit, Civil Docket No. 99-CV-451, was filed against the "Ford Motor Company, Breed Technologies, Inc., and TRW, Inc. on behalf of Eric V. Thomas, D.M.D., Individually, as Administrator, and Administrator *ad prosequendum* of the Estate of Tracy Rose Thomas, and as Parent and Natural Guardian of Alix Thomas, in the United States District Court for the District of New Jersey."

its exhibits, a history of those involved in the accident, the cause of action as it was filed, and an explanation and breakdown of all the causes of action.

In the media, Thomas was presented as a grieving widower whose only child was now without a mother. There was no mention of his marriage to Stephanie the previous July or her adoption of Alix or the birth of the couple's first child a month before.

Mellon had positioned Thomas as David against Goliath and was sure that this Goliath would lose.

The next morning Donald Rose took a seat in a diner and opened a copy of *USA Today*. He saw a picture of Tracy. That was how he learned about Eric's lawsuit.

CAPE MAY COURT HOUSE MAN SUES FORD, SAYS AIR BAG KILLED WIFE, FETUS

A Cape May Court House man on Monday filed a multi-million-dollar federal lawsuit against Ford Motor Co. in the death of his pregnant wife, who was killed when a driver's-side air bag exploded in a low-speed collision two years ago.

"Although preliminary tests made public by the National Highway Traffic Safety Administration estimated the Ford Explorer's speed at the time of impact at 15 mph, we believe Tracy was actually traveling at a much lower speed," said attorney Elliott Kolodny of the law firm Mellon, Webster & Mellon in Doylestown, PA.

"This should have been a minor accident," Kolodny said, adding damage to the car was minimal.

Ford spokesman Jim Cain said he had not seen the lawsuit and did not know the details of the accident in which Tracy Thomas was killed, but noted that Ford's 1998 and later models are equipped with less forceful air bags, a move aimed at reducing the risk to children and shorter adults of being injured or killed by the devices.

All together, 125 people have been killed by air-bag deployments, including 69 children, according to the NHTSA, while an estimated 3,800 people have been saved by the devices.

Cause of death was blunt-force trauma to the head and torso, with asphyxiation caused by chest compression, according to medical examiner Dr. Elliot Gross.*

> THE PRESS OF ATLANTIC CITY
> Tuesday, February 2, 1999
> By Jeanne Dewey, Staff Writer

That same morning, Bill Conroy read about the suit in the *New Jersey Courier Post*. He faxed it to Ford, in Dearborn.

Later that day, Jonas Saunders, Ford's house counsel, called Conroy's partner, Joseph Pinto, since the lawsuit was filed in New Jersey, and formally asked that White & Williams handle the case. Pinto knew their first job was to hire an investigator and get the police reports and records.

Saunders also said that a member of the Rose family, who wanted to speak to someone about Tracy Thomas's accident,

---

* The words *chest compression* do not appear in any of Dr. Gross's reports or documents, including those that listed cause of death. He used these words only in a press release provided to the *Press of Atlantic City* the day his final autopsy findings were released.

had just contacted the company. There was something Ford should know about, the woman had said, and left her telephone number.

Two years after the death of Tracy Thomas a second investigation into her death was about to begin.

FIVE

Karate Chop

The offices of Mellon, Webster & Mellon were in Doylestown, Pennsylvania, a community of fourteen thousand people and an hour's drive from Philadelphia. In the center of town sat the Bucks County courthouse. Surrounding it on all four sides were small two- and three-story historic homes and other buildings that had been converted to law and governmental offices. Tom Mellon's offices occupied one of these elegant, small stone-and-brick buildings. The interior had been gutted and now featured a fifteen-foot-wide grand staircase that rose from the reception area to a second floor beneath a huge skylight. One side of Mellon's office was a glass wall from which he could look out over the firm's other offices. On his walls were framed magazine and newspaper articles attesting to the success of the firm and its clients.

In the case of Eric Thomas, Mellon didn't do what many attorneys do when they want to settle a product-liability action out of court. In those instances, the plaintiff's lawyers advise the potential defendant in advance that they are going to file a lawsuit. The company investigates, sits down with the plaintiffs, and discusses the matter. More often than not, the case is settled.

Instead Tom Mellon filed his lawsuit without notifying Ford. The suit listed as co-defendants Breed Technologies, which manufactured the air-bag sensor, and TRW, which made the air-bag module. Each of the named companies retained its own law firm. White & Williams would be the lead firm. Bill Conroy, Ford's national counsel, would head the legal team.

The complaint stated that the Thomases' Ford Explorer was traveling slowly when it hit a utility pole. The damage to its front end was minimal. The driver's-side air bag deployed, striking Tracy Thomas in her chest, neck, and head, and, if not for its improper deployment, she and her unborn baby, who had also died, would have survived with little or no injury. In addition, the complaint stated that if the passenger-side air bag hadn't rendered Eric Thomas unconscious, he would have been able to resuscitate or revive his wife and their unborn baby.

The suit stated that Ford designed, manufactured, and sold a 1996 Ford Explorer that was not reasonably fit, suitable, or safe for its intended purpose. The plaintiffs claimed they had discovered thirty separate defects in the air bag, the seat-belt system, the steering-wheel design, and the pedal platforms, all of which were cited. In addition, Dr. Thomas on behalf of himself and his daughter, Alix, sued for loss of consortium and companionship.[*]

Bill Conroy saw that the complaint was well drafted and specific in its allegations. Clearly the plaintiffs had relied upon experts for technical assistance. The right buzzwords were all there.

Tom Mellon's success in his tobacco-liability cases didn't impress Conroy. Anybody who does his homework can settle cases, Conroy knew. He had settled many himself. What Conroy wanted to know was whom he'd be dealing with in court if the case went that far. He thought that Tom Mellon and his colleague Elliott Kolodny were not formidable opponents.

The first order of business was for White & Williams to get all the reports, findings, interviews, and documents that pertained to the case. Conroy's staff issued subpoenas for the medical examiner's records and the police department files.

On February 5, 1999, four days after Doris Rose spoke to an attorney in the office of Ford's general counsel, Conroy assigned investigator Tom Fuchs to contact the Rose family. But before Fuchs reached the Roses, Doris called White & Williams herself and was told that the attorney handling the case would call her back. After months of frustration, Doris Rose was relieved. She could now tell Ford her suspicions about Tracy's death.

The day the Thomas case hit the headlines, Bill Conroy was handling more than twenty other cases around the country and

---

[*] The relationship and all of the accompanying benefits enjoyed by a married man and woman.

had direct responsibility for another fifteen, but he knew instinctively that he personally had to return Doris's phone call.

"I really would like to talk to you about some of the inconsistencies of my daughter's accident," Doris told him. "But I'd become too upset to discuss it." She told Conroy to call Wendy.

That afternoon Conroy called Wendy, who described the Rose family's doubts, including their conversation with Detective Webster the previous December. Conroy told Wendy that Ford was already aware of the case and would be looking into all aspects of the accident. He assured her that his investigator would visit her as soon as his staff had reviewed the files. In a subsequent conversation, Conroy told Wendy that he would not share with the family information he had developed but that he would be asking them for help, explaining that he would probably be taking their depositions himself and didn't want their statements to be tainted. The Roses said they understood.

From the beginning, Conroy knew it was important to keep an open and cordial dialogue with the Roses, especially if the information they provided was not tarnished by vindictiveness and was factually correct. If the case went to trial, they could become an important asset.

Sometime later, when Tom Fuchs visited Plainfield to interview Wendy, she told him that she didn't think the air bag had killed Tracy. She believed that Eric Thomas had killed her sister. Fuchs said he didn't want to include that statement in his report because it might be given to the plaintiffs in the normal course of discovery and Thomas could then sue her for slander.

Fuchs then asked Wendy about Thomas's lifestyle and tastes. He wanted to know what kind of golf clubs Eric owned and what type of car he now drove. Did he own an expensive fountain pen, for example. Wendy told him that her brother-in-law had taken a lot of vacations just after her sister's death.

Conroy knew from past cases that the speed of the car at impact could be a factor in air-bag-related deaths.* Air bags are designed to deploy in the blink of an eye, inflate, and protect the occupant before that person moved a couple of inches.

In slow-speed accidents, injuries could be massive if the driver was not wearing a seat belt or was out of position or was leaning forward to pick up something from the floor, with his head pressed against the dashboard, or was sitting very close to the steering wheel. There were documented cases where an air bag had snapped the head back and broken the neck. At thirty miles per hour, catastrophic spinal cord injuries and basal skull fractures are possible. In some accidents, the most common allegation made is that air bags are too powerful and too aggressive. But Conroy couldn't find in the reports what speed the police believed the Thomases' car had been moving at on impact.

In the early 1990s, carmakers had been criticized and even sued for not installing air bags; by the late 1990s, they were being sued for the improper manufacture of air bags. Since

---

* Car speed is determined by different types of measurements: "Delta V" and "miles per hour." Delta V is the stopping velocity—how quickly the car stops on impact. "Miles per hour" is the designation for speed while the car is still traveling. An air bag should not deploy with a Delta V of seven miles an hour or less, and had to deploy with a Delta V in excess of fourteen miles or more.

1994, automakers had been sued twenty-three times on allegations that a faulty air bag had caused catastrophic injuries or death. Juries returned verdicts against the car manufacturers in only six of those cases. In October 1996, four months before Tracy Thomas died, a six-year-old child was killed in a low-speed car accident. The lawsuit, filed by the boy's father, focused on Ford's failure to warn car owners that air bags can kill children and claimed that air bags were not designed for small people and low-speed accidents.[*] David White of Lexington, Kentucky, who was six-foot-six, also sued Ford, claiming that an air bag deployed in a Ford Escort in a minor crash broke his neck and left him a quadriplegic.[†]

Bill Conroy understood that air bags exemplified a pure form of risk versus benefit. In noncatastrophic cases, they could break a nose, injure the eyes, bruise a face, but they might also save a life.

In the weeks following the Thomases' lawsuit, Ford received calls from *Dateline, 20/20, PrimeTime,* and *60 Minutes.* They wanted the carmaker to respond to the suit's allegations. For the networks this could be a coup; for Ford it was a problem. Ford said it couldn't comment on pending litigation.

Conroy recognized the strengths of Eric Thomas's public relations campaign: not only was his pregnant wife dead, but Thomas was well respected in his community and highly credible. He would make a good witness.

---

[*] The case, which did not involve an Explorer, has been settled and neither party to the action will provide any settlement information.

[†] This case is still pending.

But Conroy also thought that the plaintiff's attorneys were unfairly stating some facts. Tom Mellon presented Tracy Thomas as small, fitting the category in which most air-bag deaths occur. But she was five feet four inches tall, large-boned, and weighed about 145 pounds.* Five-four was at the high end of the child/small women category. Her normal weight (when she was not pregnant) would have been at least 125 pounds, well above the category.

Bill Conroy had read the autopsy report several times but couldn't determine the cause of death. After laying out all the photos of the accident site and the autopsy on his desk, he didn't see injuries he was used to seeing in other cases. He didn't understand what "petechial hemorrhaging in the eyes and neck" had to do with an air-bag death, and he'd never seen a medical examiner's report in a product-liability case in which the cause of death was "blunt force trauma with asphyxia." Joseph Wills, the Ford engineer who had been assigned to the case, was also puzzled by the medical examiner's report and the cause of death. He and Conroy agreed that the medical examiner probably didn't know how Tracy died and that this case was different from other air-bag accidents they had handled.

Conroy was also struck by the fact that Thomas was unconscious for at least an hour and a half and yet didn't have a mark on him. He was still wearing his baseball cap and his glasses when the EMTs arrived, and within a couple of minutes he was asking questions and seemed normal.

---

* Tracy Thomas's weight was within the normal limits for the stage of her pregnancy.

Thomas's explanation of why his wife had been driving that night also disturbed Conroy. She had fallen in the driveway, had been experiencing blackouts, and was six months pregnant. Conroy, who had two kids of his own, knew that in a similar situation his own wife would have been with their child in the backseat and that he would drive. It didn't make sense that Eric Thomas would be in the passenger seat that night.

On February 14th, Conroy retained James Benedict, a leading expert on air-bag-related injuries. Benedict, from San Antonio, Texas, was a medical doctor with emergency room experience, but he was also an engineer who had devoted much of his practice to air-bag-related injury cases. He was often called upon by the automotive industry.

But Benedict's schedule was tight. He couldn't drop his other clients and Conroy would have to wait his turn.

Meanwhile, Donald and Doris were pursuing their visitation rights case with their former son-in-law, who still insisted that they not mention Tracy to Alix. If they would agree to his request he would allow the Roses more time with Alix, but Doris wouldn't agree.

David S. DeWeese, also of Wildwood, who was now representing Eric Thomas on the matter of visitation rights, wrote to Lisa Radell that Dr. Thomas has been more than responsible with respect to the Roses' visitation schedule. He pointed out that as Alix grew older, her school schedule and social activities with her friends would limit the Roses' time with their granddaughter. He added: "Finally, I would like to reiterate that my clients are insistent that no discussions occur between the Roses and Alix regarding Tracy Rose Thomas. My clients will advise the Roses when they determine that any discussion is appropriate."

Doris and Donald asked their attorney to tell Mr. DeWeese that they would see Eric Thomas in court. A date for oral arguments was set: July 6, 1999.

By the end of March 1999, Thomas's case against Ford had been assigned to federal judge Stephen M. Orlofsky, in Camden, New Jersey, where the suit had been filed. Camden was once a thriving industrial center, home to Campbell's Soup and RCA. Today, the city, which looks across the Delaware River to the Philadelphia skyline, is depressed, its hulking factories abandoned, its warehouses boarded-up. The white-limestone federal courthouse, built in the 1930s, sits on Market Street, in the heart of Camden, across from the local campus of Rutgers University.

Motions and other pretrial matters would be heard by Judge Joel B. Rosen, a federal magistrate who handled cases ranging from bank robberies to fraud to large drug busts. He liked to get cases settled quickly and managed his docket aggressively.

On April 29th, Rosen called the attorneys from both sides into his office for a conference. When they were all seated, Tom Mellon began by recommending that Ford take his client's deposition as soon as possible, in order to get quickly up to speed.

The judge picked up on the suggestion immediately. Could Conroy's firm take Dr. Thomas's statement within thirty days?

Conroy knew, of course, that in civil suits you only get one chance to depose someone unless the opposing side agrees to further statements. It worried him that he might not get a second crack at Thomas, and his investigation had only begun. Who knows what further information they might turn up on Thomas, but with the medical examiner's and police reports already in hand, it was unreasonable for Conroy to ask for more time.

Conroy was also preparing for another trial in Baltimore and turned Thomas's deposition over to his colleagues Robert Devine and Michael Horner.

Within days, Tom Mellon suggested to Bill Conroy that Ford informally "interview" Thomas rather than take his formal deposition, to learn his version of the accident and evaluate him as a witness. The suggested date for the "interview" was May 26th, the same day the deposition was to take place, and a few days before the next scheduled conference with Judge Rosen. Both sides knew the court would set a mediation date at that time, hoping for a settlement. Rosen liked to see action, and Mellon seemed to be forging ahead. But Conroy preferred to move more slowly. He decided against the "interview." Because the doctor's previous statements to the police had raised more questions than they'd answered, Conroy wanted Thomas's statement on the record and under oath. If Mellon hoped for an early settlement, he would be disappointed. Conroy wasn't thinking of a settlement at all.

Finally, on May 26th, Robert Devine and Michael Horner took Eric Thomas's deposition under oath in a small white-walled conference room at the White & Williams offices in West Mount, New Jersey. Also present were George McDavid for Breed

Technologies and Ann Marie Walsh for TRW. Representing Eric Thomas were Tom Mellon, Elliott Kolodny, and Thomas's personal friend and attorney, David Lee, from Knoxville, Tennessee.

A deposition is not intended to be adversarial, though the atmosphere can become tense. Its purpose is to gain information, preserve the witness's testimony in case the person may not be available at a later date, and preserve his testimony for admissions and impeachment if required.

Besides pinning down Dr. Thomas's story of what had taken place, Devine wanted to explore the basis for his claim of damages to himself and his daughter. Loss of income and short- and long-term injuries were issues that had to be addressed before it could be determined whether Thomas's claims had any merit.

Devine began by asking the standard questions: name, social security number, marital status, and so forth, and then took Eric through his life story. In a quiet voice Thomas told the attorneys about his ROTC scholarship, his undergraduate and professional schooling, his meeting and subsequent marriage to Tracy, his training in the army, and his buying and building up of the dental practice. He described how he and Tracy had worked together to make it a success. By the end of the first year, he said, they had five employees and he had time for a round of golf every week.

Thomas said he'd never been separated from Tracy and that they had never had any marital counseling. "Life was very good," he told Devine. However, he was unable to remember the name of his daughter's pediatrician. He knew only that it was someone in a medical group called Kids First in Cape May

Court House. Now he said that Tracy's pregnancy was normal, and that during her pregnancy she had never blacked out.

In depositions, attorneys often move from subject to subject for no obvious reason and then return to topics covered earlier. Now Thomas was asked whether he and his wife had understood the features of the Ford Explorer they were driving that night, including the air bags. Thomas said he had read the owner's manual and the warning labels posted on the window visors. He said he had reviewed the recommended emergency procedures.

Thomas then responded to questions about the positioning of the Explorer's seats and how he and his wife had adjusted them. Ford and the other co-defendants wanted to know how Tracy wore her seat belt during her pregnancy. Thomas said she placed it just under her belly.

They both used the steering column in the same position and were not in the habit of readjusting it.

Eric said that it took him and Tracy about thirty minutes to get Alix ready for the hospital. Eric left the house first and turned on the engine, the heater, and the defroster. Afterward he scraped the snow off the windshield and returned to the house to get the baby.

"As we were getting ready to go, I was carrying Alix. Tracy was—we were locking up the house, and we were leaving the house. Tracy was ahead of me, so she went out. There's really no—to the best of my recollection, that's how it happened, that she walked out ahead of me.

"From the door to the driveway is not that far. I would estimate maybe ten, twenty feet, something like that. Of course, I wanted to keep Alix indoors as long as possible before we took her outside," Thomas told Devine in a matter-of-fact tone.

"Did Tracy fall in the driveway prior to getting into the Explorer that evening?" the attorney asked.

"Yes," Dr. Thomas replied, before taking a sip from his water glass.

"On the walk from the house to the vehicle?" Devine asked.

"Yes," Dr. Thomas said.

"Where did she fall?" Devine asked.

"She fell where we have some, I believe they're called railroad ties or landscaping ties, that divide the driveway from the actual walkway. And from what I can recall, she was trying to negotiate walking across the railroad tie and slipped."

Then Devine asked about the driving conditions that night, whether either of them was near- or farsighted, how Tracy held the steering wheel while driving, and if the windshield was fogged up or otherwise impeded visibility. He also asked what Thomas was doing while Tracy drove, whether they had been in any way negligent. Thomas said nothing that took place inside the car had contributed to the accident.

"As you and your wife were driving down Hand Avenue prior to the accident . . . did your wife say something to you just before the accident took place?" Devine asked.

"She said that she saw a deer in the road," the doctor replied.

"Were you looking through the windshield or tending to Alix or something else when your wife made the comment?" Devine asked.

"When she made that exact comment, I'm not sure," Thomas said.

"Had you already seen the deer, or a deer, when your wife made that comment?"

"No."

"When your wife made that comment, did you then observe a deer?"

"At that point, that's when I tried to locate one," Thomas answered.

"And did you have difficulty locating a deer?"

"I had difficulty locating a deer because I wasn't sure where to look. I wasn't sure whether it was right, left, in front of us, rearview mirror. I don't know," the doctor said.

"At some point, did you observe a deer?"

"Yes."

"Where was the deer relative to Hand Avenue when you first observed the deer?"

"I would say the deer was in the middle of the road," Thomas replied. "The deer was standing still."

Thomas then said that his wife "tried to veer off to miss the deer. . . . It was a sudden change. She was trying to avoid hitting the deer."

"Do you know of any eyewitnesses to the accident?" Devine asked him.

"From what I understand, there were no eyewitnesses of the accident except the deer," Thomas replied.

Devine then asked about Tracy's debts at the time of her death and how much cash the Thomases had in their checking and savings accounts. As for Tracy's life insurance, Eric said that he had received about $15,000 in accidental death benefits from his car insurance policy and that the benefit from Tracy's death from Great West Life was $200,000.

Then Devine asked Dr. Thomas if he and his wife knew that car passengers had to sit back in their seats in order to avoid risking injury when an air bag deployed. Thomas said that they did.

Thomas stated that he believed he was unconscious for over an hour and a half. He remembered when he had left his home and had since noted the time he was first observed at the accident scene, which was recorded in the police reports. The total elapsed time was one and a half hours. He told the attorneys that he had injured his C5 and 6 vertebrae and that he had one bulging disc and one herniated disc.

"Had you had any neck injury before February 9, 1997?" Devine asked.

"No," Thomas replied, and explained his reduced range of motion following the accident and his difficulties in returning to a normal life because of his discomfort.

"Was there a . . . time that you could not practice dentistry following the accident?" Devine asked.

"Yes."

"How long was that?" the attorney inquired.

"Four to eight weeks after the accident," Thomas answered.

Devine then asked, "If I suggest to you Dr. [Scott] Strenger released you to go back to work March 11 of '97, does that sound right?" Devine asked.

"I'm not sure," Thomas replied.

Devine then asked about lost income. The doctor couldn't put a dollar figure on it because his patients were rescheduled, he said. He confirmed that even though he had disability insurance, he'd made no claim against his carrier. When asked why, he said that he'd had other things on his mind.

Ann Walsh, representing TRW, questioned Thomas next. What was the basis of Thomas's allegations that the air bag had hit his wife and killed her? Thomas took a moment before answering, then said his conclusion was based on what he had ascertained from the medical examiner, Gross, and the police department. Walsh inquired whether Thomas knew that his wife had sustained injuries to her face when she fell in the driveway. Thomas said he couldn't recall anything related to those injuries.

Thomas told George McDavid, who represented Breed, that a month before filing his lawsuit he had returned the Ford Expedition he'd leased after the accident and replaced it with a General Motors Escalade.

Tom Mellon, Elliott Kolodny, and David Lee did not question their client. Eric waived his right to read and correct the transcript of the deposition, and Tom Mellon did not provide an errata sheet with any changes. The deposition had taken four hours.

On May 28th, two days after Thomas's deposition, Bill Conroy received from Tom Mellon a report issued by Dr. Donald Jason, an attorney and a board-certified forensic pathologist, who had served as a medical examiner in New York City for twenty-six years.

The report had been requested by Mellon, who had sent to Dr. Jason the medical examiner's report, microscopic slides from the autopsy, autopsy photographs, and the results of lab tests that were conducted because of the autopsy. In his report dated May 25th, Dr. Jason concluded that the "mechanism" of Tracy Thomas's asphyxia "was injury to the upper spinal cord at the level where bleeding was found, causing paralysis from the neck downward, thereby making her breathing impossible."

Conroy was puzzled. Gross's autopsy report did not mention a spinal cord injury.

Conroy decided to hire a pathologist of his own to look not only at Jason's report but at Gross's findings.

On the following Tuesday, June 1st, Judge Rosen, a burly man with a salt-and-pepper beard and mustache, convened the first joint conference. Rosen wanted to know if the attorneys were moving in the direction of a settlement now that Thomas's deposition had been taken. Mellon, knowing that Conroy had just received Dr. Jason's report, waited for Conroy's answer. Conroy told the judge that he was still working through the discovery process, that Thomas's deposition hadn't been transcribed, and that Tom Mellon had just sent him new information that required further investigation. Rosen asked both sides to move the case along quickly.

From Thomas's deposition, Conroy learned for the first time that Eric had married Stephanie Arrington Haley, who had recently divorced, and that the couple had had a child seven months after they were married and just a month before Thomas filed his lawsuit against Ford.

Conroy was startled. Eric Thomas was not a grieving widower with a small child.

Meanwhile, Conroy thought Thomas had not been pushed hard enough at his deposition. For example, when Thomas said that his home life was "good," Devine accepted this answer without attempting to probe further. He had also failed to pursue the matter of Alix Thomas's pediatrician.

The police and EMT reports, which Conroy had read, included three different versions of who had called the hospital or pediatrician that night. In one version, Thomas had made the call. In another version, Tracy and Eric called together. In a third version, Tracy had placed the call. So who had called and what was the doctor's name? The lawyers had not asked Thomas to answer these questions.

Nor had Devine asked why Tracy was driving after she had fallen. Conroy was also bothered by Thomas's answer that the only witness to the accident was "the deer." He had seen the photographs of the tracks made by the Explorer before it hit the pole. They were not covered by fresh snow. If there had been a deer, why didn't the officers on the scene find its tracks?

On June 28th, Conroy served on Thomas an initial set of thirty-nine interrogatories, asking Thomas to clarify ambiguities and omissions in his deposition.* The submission of interrogatories is standard procedure during the discovery phase of a case.

---

* An interrogatory is a set of written questions about the case submitted by one party to the other party or witness during the pretrial phase of the discovery process. The person answering the questions usually does so under oath and signs a statement declaring that the answers are true.

Thomas failed to respond to the interrogatories within the prescribed thirty-day period. Only after repeated requests did Ford, nearly five months later, finally receive, on November 11th, Thomas's perfunctory answers.

Conroy had asked Thomas for his detailed version of the accident. In reply, Thomas attached a complete copy of the police report and a copy of his deposition. In response to the question about whether he had any previous injuries or conditions that may have been aggravated, accelerated, or exacerbated by the accident, he said, "None."

In reply to other questions about what had occurred that night, Thomas referred Conroy to the reports of the police, medical, and ambulance personnel, and of Dr. Elliot Gross.

That same week the National Highway Traffic Safety Administration released its ninety-three-page final report on the Thomases' accident, but it went unnoticed by the press, which had decided that the case was just another run-of-the-mill wrongful death lawsuit.

The report said that all of Tracy's injuries resulted from her contact with the air bag (in fifteen instances) or the shoulder belt (in three instances) or the knee bolster (in three instances).

The report included information from Thomas's statement that his wife may have received a superficial abrasion to her face when she fell outside her house earlier that night, but gave no indication that any of her injuries were attributed either to that fall or any other mishaps.

Eric Thomas's six injuries were attributed to the deployment of the air bag (in four instances) and the right B-pillar/D ring (in two instances).

"The vehicle's engine apparently stalled during the crash," the report stated, "which allowed the vehicle's interior to cool in the ambient temperature. As a result of the child's exposure to the cold, her [Alix's] fever had dropped to within normal limits." No supporting data substantiated this finding.

According to the report, there were abrasions to the steering wheel rim at the three o'clock sector; the knee bolster showed no evidence of contact with the occupant; and the steering column shear capsule brackets were not compressed. All of these findings indicated that the accident was minor.

"The expanding air bag contacted the chest, anterior neck, and face of the driver which resulted in multiple soft tissue injuries. She sustained a double-bordered parallel contusion over the right scapula, a chinstrap-like contusion with abrasion to the underside of the chin, three parallel contusions with abrasion of the right face, superficial lacerations, contusions and abrasions of the lower lip, ecchymosis between the eyebrows, bilateral subjunctival hemorrhages, and a hemorrhage of the left eyelid. The bag expanded across the anterior neck which probably hyperextended her head. The neck injuries included petechial hemorrhages in the epiglottis and laryngeal mucosa, a one centimeter hemorrhage overlying the right hyoid bone, a 1.5 cm hemorrhage over the posterior cricoid cartilage, extradural hemorrhage of the spinal cord and dura, and petechial hemorrhages of the posterior neck.

"The driver responded to the twelve o'clock impact force by initiating a forward trajectory. Her lower extremities contacted the knee bolster which resulted in abrasions to the knees and lower legs. There was no contact evidence to the bolster. The left side of her head probably contracted the shoulder belt webbing and/or the left B-pillar during the rebound which resulted in left earlobe ecchymosis, a scalp contusion posterior to the left ear, and stippled hemorrhages over the left temporomandibular joint. The medical examiner concluded that the cause of death resulted from blunt force trauma to the neck with asphyxia. The blunt force was associated with air bag deployment."

In other words, the report simply confirmed the findings of the medical examiner, Dr. Gross, and offered no alternative reason for Tracy Thomas's death. For Tom Mellon, this was good news. To Conroy, however, it was obvious that the NHTSA had simply accepted Dr. Gross's conclusions without consulting another pathologist. So if Dr. Gross's analysis was conceivably wrong, the agency's report was meaningless.

That night, Conroy logged on to the NHTSA's Web site. In reviewing its previous reports of air-bag deaths he found references to head injuries, broken necks, and spinal cord injuries, but none to asphyxiation. Could this be the first air-bag case in which a medical examiner had said that a cause of death was asphyxiation?

Yet there was a curious passage in the report that Conroy thought might weaken Mellon's case. It said that Dr. Thomas "initially exited the house with the child to place the child in the forward facing child restraint that was positioned in the left rear of the Explorer that was parked in the driveway. . . . He noted that his wife then exited their residence and walked along the sidewalk to the driveway."

Conroy noted that this account, based on Thomas's statement, was different from the one he'd given in his deposition, in

which he testified to leaving the house with the baby, after
Tracy had left through the front door.

On July 6th, Eric Thomas and his attorney, David DeWeese,
faced Doris and Donald Rose before Judge Max A. Baker in the
family court of Cape May County, New Jersey. Alix, who
would soon celebrate her fourth birthday, was not present.

Judge Baker had reviewed the file and was ready for oral
arguments from both parties. Lisa Radell, representing the
Roses, presented a chart outlining the many times and places
Alix had visited with her grandparents since her birth. Radell
stated that Dr. Thomas disputed only one date and place noted.

On average, during the last three years, the Roses had spent
five days a month with their granddaughter.

Radell requested that the Roses be granted visitation rights
for thirty-six days each calendar year. She said they were not
asking for time during holidays but did want to have extended
visits with Alix in Massachusetts.

DeWeese said that the Roses had spent most of their time
with Alix in Cape May Court House when Dr. Thomas needed
their help after Tracy's death in 1997. During the following
year, he pointed out, Alix had spent only seventeen days exclu-
sively with her grandparents and away from Stephanie and her
father.

Furthermore, he said, Alix's school schedule would limit the
time available for the Roses and she would want to spend time
with friends too. Thomas would place no restrictions on the
time the Roses spent with Alix in Cape May Court House, he
said, as long as reasonable notice was given.

DeWeese did not mention that Eric wanted Donald and Doris not to talk about Tracy in Alix's presence, a violation of the Roses' First Amendment rights.

Judge Baker then said that visitation would not have been an issue if not for Tracy's death, and added that there was a lot more emotion than logic before the court. Baker rejected Thomas's argument that time with the Roses might have a serious impact on the time she spent with his or Stephanie's parents.

The issue was what was good for the child, the judge said. And it was in Alix's best interest to continue to see her natural mother's parents. Every July, Baker said, Alix should spend ten days on Cape Cod with the Roses, and she should also spend four days with them each spring and each fall. He ordered ongoing telephone contact (it was later agreed that the calls would take place each Wednesday at 6:30 P.M.). He also said that if the Roses wanted to travel to New Jersey, they should have unlimited weekend visits as long as Dr. Thomas was given proper notice.

Eric suggested two weeks' notice; the judge agreed.

Baker then asked Lisa Radell to prepare the written order, and after some disagreement on wording, it was signed on August 10th.

After the hearing, Donald walked over to Eric to shake his hand. Thomas pulled his hand back, but Donald leaned in and shook it anyway.

In the corridor, Eric's aunt Minnie said to Doris, "And you call yourself a grandmother?"

As Radell led the Roses away, she told them that they should visit Alix and try to mend fences with Eric's family, who, together with Stephanie's family, were staying at Eric's house.

The Roses were apprehensive but knew it was good advice, and they wanted to see Alix. When they got to the house, Eric stopped them at the driveway and asked them to step into the garage first; he and Stephanie wanted to talk to them privately.

Away from the rest of the family, Eric exploded, "How *dare* you take me to court?" Donald didn't say a word. He knew Doris could answer for herself.

"How dare I?" Doris said, pointing her finger. "You see my husband? He's got more compassion in his little finger than you've got in your whole body."

"I told you this wasn't necessary," Eric replied.

"You asked for this. Not wanting me to talk about Tracy in front of Alix. You *made* us get a lawyer," Doris exploded. "All I wanted was to see my granddaughter!"

Now Stephanie was shouting at Doris: "If you wanted to see Alix, all you had to do was ask me."

"Ask *you?*" Doris replied. "What in the world do *you* have to do with it?"

"Well, I'm her mother now," Stephanie shouted. "Follow me," she said as they entered the house.

In the living room, Eric's aunt Minnie came in from the kitchen and screamed: "Your daughter's dead, forget about it."

Bre stepped between the women. Then Stephanie told Doris she could follow her upstairs if she wanted to see Alix.

Meanwhile, Conroy had scheduled depositions for the officers and emergency medical teams that had responded to the Thomases' accident. He wanted to confirm the statements they had made. These follow-ups to clear up ambiguities and preserve testimony were usually brief and sometimes were taken over the phone to save time.

Conroy assigned his colleague Robert Devine to depose Robert Fitzpatrick on August 12th. He was the veterinarian who first reported the Thomases' accident and the first person to touch Eric Thomas and Tracy at the scene. Conroy wanted to know if Thomas was really unconscious and for how long. He also wanted to know what Fitzpatrick had found when he touched Tracy

Just as important was how long the car had been sitting on the side of the road. Ford's investigators now knew that the temperature in Cape May Court House during the first hours of that morning was about twenty-three degrees. Fitzpatrick, Conroy believed, might be able to recall the temperature inside the car when he first opened the door. With Fitzpatrick's input, Ford could build its own time line.

Sitting in the law offices of a Cape May attorney, Fitzpatrick told Devine he could not open the driver's door but had managed to open the rear door on the driver's side.

"When you touched the carotid pulse on the driver, that means Mrs. Thomas, were you seated in the backseat?"

"Yeah, I was in the back, leaning towards the front," Fitzpatrick answered.

"Did you get a pulse on Mrs. Thomas?" Devine asked.

"She was very cold, and there was no pulse."

"Did you touch the front seat passenger, Dr. Thomas, when you were in the car?"

"Only to see if he had a carotid pulse," Fitzpatrick said.

"Again, touching his neck?" Devine asked.

"Touching his neck."

"Was Dr. Thomas conscious?" Devine inquired.

"Not at the time."

"Did you attempt to rouse the driver by yelling or screaming or moving or shaking or doing anything other than touching the carotid pulse?"

"Once I touched their pulses and in light of her not having a pulse," Fitzpatrick continued, "I went back to my car and made a second call to the 911 operator indicating that I was concerned about injuries at the scene."

Later Devine asked if Thomas had been making any sounds other than those associated with breathing.

"No, he was not."

"Did you see any movement other than . . . chest movement consistent with breathing from the front seat passenger, Dr. Thomas?"

"That's the only motion I saw," Fitzpatrick said.

"Did Dr. Thomas regain consciousness in your presence?" Devine asked.

"No, he did not."

Devine then tried to establish how Tracy Thomas had been belted. The belt was visible across her chest, Fitzpatrick said, and seemed to be in a normal position. The lap belt was below her stomach.

The attorney then asked about tire tracks. Fitzpatrick said that he saw the Explorer's tracks, which he estimated extended as far as he could see.

"Did you notice any yaw marks? Do you know what I mean by yaw marks?" Devine asked.

"Yeah, the sideway swerving type. It seemed to be directly—it did not seem to yaw. To my untrained eye, it just seemed like it was a straight path . . ." Fitzpatrick replied.*

Devine asked the veterinarian if he could establish the distance between the steering wheel and Tracy's abdomen. Six to eight inches, Fitzpatrick said.

Then Ann Walsh of TRW asked by telephone from Chicago, "How about the temperature within the vehicle when you opened the back door for the first time? What was the temperature like in the vehicle?"

"It wasn't cold."†

"For example, could you see your breath . . . while you were in the vehicle, or could you see Dr. Thomas's breath or Alix's breath?" the attorney inquired.

"I didn't—I can't honestly recall seeing any breath in the car."

The deposition ended. It had taken an hour and ten minutes.

Fitzpatrick's answers raised a question: How long would an Explorer, in twenty-three-degree weather with its doors and windows closed, stay warm after its motor had stopped? To answer that question, Ford would have to run some tests.

---

* When Devine asked the question, Ford knew that the Explorer was in two-wheel-drive mode and was equipped with automatic computer-adjusting brakes, which are designed to prevent a car from yawing when the brakes are applied at normal speeds.

† But in an interview for this book, Dr. Fitzpatrick responded this way to the question: Q: "When you opened the back door, it was cool inside. You didn't get a brush of warm air?" A: "It was snowing. It was cold inside. It was a car that had equalized in temperature with the outside."

* * *

Meanwhile, the Roses, who had settled their visitation issues with Dr. Thomas but had not heard from Ford's attorneys, visited the prosecutors in Cape May County.

Doris, Donald, Wendy, and Bre sat on one side of a large table. Investigator James McGowan, Assistant Prosecutor Michael Cohen, and First Assistant Prosecutor J. David Meyer sat on the other side. Across from the Roses was a large mirror, and Wendy wondered if they were being watched from the other side.

The prosecutors said that the case was closed but that if the family had evidence that they thought warranted additional investigation, it would be considered.

The Roses went over everything they had told Detective Webster the previous December, emphasizing statements Tracy had made before the accident as well as some that Eric had made afterward.

Wendy felt that the prosecutors were patronizing her family. When Cohen said he didn't think Dr. Thomas was bright enough to pull off such a crime, Bre walked out.

When they enumerated the many vacations Eric had taken just after Tracy's death, Cohen said he didn't care if Eric had gone out with a thousand women after the accident—it didn't mean he'd killed Tracy.

From there the meeting deteriorated. Someone, imitating Ralph Kramden from *The Honeymooners,* said: "If I killed my wife all the times I said I would. . . ." At that point, Doris lost patience with the prosecutors and also walked out.

On the way out, Wendy found it within herself to make a

joke of her own: "If they find out that Ford is not responsible, then who's going to accuse the deer?"

On August 30th, almost six and a half months after Conroy had retained him, James Benedict, the air-bag expert, came back with his analysis results.

"What I have to tell you, we really can't talk about on the phone," Benedict told him. "I'm prepared to come up and see you unless you're coming down here soon."

"What's going on?" Conroy asked.

"This is very serious," Benedict replied. "We need to speak in person."

Conroy, who was planning to be in Texas three days later, called on Benedict, accompanied by Jonas Saunders, Ford's in-house attorney.

In a small conference room Benedict walked up to Conroy and said, "This is what is going on." He put his hands around the attorney's neck as if to strangle him.

"You've got to be kidding me," Conroy exclaimed.

"No."

Benedict explained that he'd reviewed Dr. Gross's autopsy findings and could find no injuries that Tracy had sustained from the accident that would have caused her death. The only logical explanation for the asphyxiation that fit all the facts was that she had been strangled. Conroy was dumbfounded. Benedict, a conservative expert, was telling him that Tracy Thomas might have been murdered. Conroy had never been involved in a criminal matter before.

Saunders and Conroy agreed to keep Benedict's information to themselves.

Bill Conroy understood that if he pursued Benedict's findings and they proved baseless, his career could be ruined. On the other hand, he could hardly ignore them. He wrestled with his options on the flight home.

As he saw it, his choice now was to advise his client either to settle the case or raise the possibility of murder and risk losing—a potential disaster for Ford and Conroy if they lost. But Benedict was a serious scientist and Ford might be obligated to take his information to the police, in which case Eric could sue the automaker for defamation. The decision to raise the issue of murder would have to be made by Ford's executives.

When Conroy returned to his home in Rosemont, just outside of Philadelphia, he was no closer to a decision than when he'd boarded the plane in Texas. He found his wife in the kitchen and told her what he had learned. She suggested he start reading up on the subject.

At his office the next day, Conroy called Benedict and the librarian at Ford to ask for articles they might have on asphyxiation.

On September 2nd, while Conroy was in Texas, Tom Mellon called Conroy's office. Both Bill Conroy and the firm's senior partner, Joe Pinto, were out. Mellon left a message for Pinto: If Ford didn't settle by the end of the day, Mellon was going to go on national TV the following evening, September 3rd. Pinto returned the call the next morning and told Mellon that this wasn't the way White & Williams did business. Mellon told Pinto that his message must have been misinterpreted. But he did want to settle, he said, and anticipated that the case would be featured on television within a month or two.

When Conroy returned to the office and heard what had taken place, he and Pinto requested an emergency conference with Judge Rosen. A week later, Conroy, Pinto, and Elliott Kolodny, Mellon's co-counsel, met in the judge's chambers. But Mellon wasn't present.

Kolodny told Rosen that there had been a "misunderstanding." Mellon had not threatened Ford. His client, Dr. Thomas, he said, was interested in settling the case and most likely there would be continued media coverage, which would not necessarily help Ford.

Rosen, in his southern New Jersey accent, told Kolodny that it was inappropriate for a litigant to attempt to try his case in the press and he would not tolerate such threats against either party.

Conroy knew that Mellon's message to Pinto was a tactical mistake. It revealed that Mellon was reluctant to go to court. Then suddenly Conroy remembered what, according to Doris Rose, Eric Thomas had told her husband in 1997: "If they ask too many questions, I'm going to drop [the lawsuit]."

With Benedict's findings in mind, Bill Conroy now wanted to know what questions Eric Thomas was afraid of.

SIX

Robert Marshall

It took three weeks for Conroy to receive and read through the literature on asphyxia and strangulation that had been sent to him by Benedict and Ford. Having sifted through the complexities, he now understood why Dr. Benedict had suggested that Ford, before deciding what to do next, retain a world-class forensic pathologist to look further into the matter. It was sound advice.

Conroy and Ford in-house attorney Jonas Saunders knew that they had to tell Ford's executives about the possibility of murder. Conroy also needed Ford's approval to get another expert on the case—and soon. Medical examiner Gross's deposition was scheduled for late October, and Conroy wanted other expert opinions before that took place.

At a meeting in Ford's Dearborn offices, Conroy met with Saunders and several Ford executives.

After going over Benedict's findings and the issues raised in the literature on asphyxia, Ford's executives agreed that the Cape May prosecutors must eventually be told about Benedict's findings. Saunders advised that they should wait for a second opinion, and Conroy was told to retain a forensic pathologist immediately.

On September 23rd, Elliott Kolodny, who was handling the injury portion of Thomas's lawsuit, notified Ford that he needed to know more about its air-bag systems. He listed 143 separate items, involving reams of documents. Request No. 50, for example, asked for all reports, memoranda, letters, presentations, summaries, charts, test results, articles, and correspondence relating to air-bag-inflation-induced injuries that were authored, published, procured, utilized, compiled, and/or retained by Ford. At the same time, Kolodny wrote to tell Bill Conroy that he wanted to depose Ford's engineers concerning the air-bag modules and crash sensors.

Ford thought that the material requested by Kolodny was overly broad, but they undertook a massive and costly search nevertheless. In November 1999, Kolodny was notified that he was welcome to travel to Dearborn and review the materials, since they were too extensive to copy and ship. Ford would then duplicate and send him whatever he needed.

The question raised by Kolodny's aggressive discovery tactics was whether Mellon was trying to get Ford to settle the case. If so, Conroy had no choice but to pursue the possibility of murder, a position that neither Thomas nor Mellon was aware off.

The depositions of police officers and EMT personnel at the scene began on October 9th, and took two months. One by one, Officer Ginyard, medical examiner Lawrence Pratt, EMT workers James Cline and Lisa Schulthies, Officer Robert McHale, Captain William Shea II, Registered Nurse Donna Hess, and Detective Scott Webster would testify under oath about what had happened on the night of the Thomases' accident and during their later conversations with Thomas.

Detective Ginyard, the second officer on the scene, was the first to be deposed. Again, Robert Devine asked the questions for Ford and Ann Walsh appeared for TRW.

Ginyard said he had seen no indication that a deer had collided with the car or was even present.

James Cline, an EMT worker, who hooked up the Life Pack to Tracy Thomas and found that she had no heart rhythm, said the body was just starting to cool down, but he couldn't recall the temperature in the car.

Lisa Schulthies, the EMT medic and Cline's partner, handled Dr. Thomas at the scene. But she too couldn't recall the temperature in the car. She believed that Dr. Thomas was deeply unconscious when she touched his carotid vein with her two fingers.

When asked what "deeply unconscious" meant, she replied, "That he did not respond to any verbal stimulus, he didn't respond to any tactile stimulus, which means touching him didn't wake him up. He was entirely unresponsive." When Ann

Walsh asked if she attempted to apply a painful stimulus, Schulthies said that Thomas had come to before she could do that.*

In late September, Conroy asked his friend Glenn Zeitz, a criminal defense attorney, to recommend a forensic pathologist for the Thomas case. Zeitz, who lived in New Jersey, occasionally represented White & Williams's white-collar clients involved in criminal matters. He had a good track record of getting their clients back relatively unscathed.

Zeitz recommended Dr. Werner Spitz, a leading forensic pathologist, but Spitz lived in Michigan, too far away. Conroy asked for a second name. Zeitz remembered Dr. Michael Baden, from New York, whom he had worked with a few years back.

Baden had performed over 20,000 autopsies. In the 1960s he had been in charge of the pathology investigations into the deaths of President John F. Kennedy and Dr. Martin Luther King for the U.S. House of Representatives Select Committee on Assassinations. In 1992, at the request of the Russian government and the U.S. State Department, he had traveled to Siberia with a team of pathologists to examine the remains of Czar Nicholas and the Romanov family to determine the cause of their deaths.

When Baden returned Conroy's call, he asked who he was and whom he represented. Conroy said he was not at liberty

---

* On October 12th, as these depositions were being taken, the court approved a voluntary dismissal of the lawsuit against Breed Technologies, which manufactured the sensing device that triggered the air bag. The previous month, Breed had filed for bankruptcy under Chapter 11. Tom Mellon, knowing Breed's assets were limited and Ford was the real target, recommended that Thomas dismiss the action against Breed.

to say, nor could he tell Baden if the case was criminal or civil.

But he could send Baden the autopsy reports, the photographs taken at the autopsy, reports of the medical examiner's slides, and the medical examiner's report, with all names and details of the accident deleted.

"Why do you want to do that?" Baden asked.

"I want your opinion. I want your experience," Conroy replied. "I'm going to pay your bill, but for now I don't even want you to know who I represent."

Baden was intrigued. Nobody had ever approached him like this before.

Twenty-four hours after receiving Conroy's package of materials, and on the eve of Dr Gross's deposition, Baden called Bill Conroy.

"She has the classic signs of someone who has been strangled," he said. "The bilateral petechia* in the eyes, in combination with the focal hemorrhaging† in the hyoid and cricoid areas,‡ indicated manual strangulation," he said. Conroy wanted to know if there was anything else.

"The medical examiner's report on his microscopic slides doesn't note any injury to the spinal cord," Baden replied, "so we know her central nervous system was okay, and therefore there was no suffocation or shutting down of her breathing."

---

* A very small, nonraised, perfectly round, purplish-red spot caused by some form of hemorrhaging.

† The escape of blood from the vessels, otherwise known as bleeding.

‡ The hyoid bone is above the Adam's apple, and the cricoid area is the circular area below the Adam's apple.

Baden wanted to know if there were any other documented injuries that he was not aware of.

None that he knew of, Conroy said.

In that case, Baden said, there was no alternative explanation.

Conroy then told Baden he represented Ford and that a claim had been filed that an air bag had caused the death of Tracy Thomas. Baden said that from the little he knew about them, he didn't think an air bag had caused these injuries. Before he could write a report, however, he needed more information.

Conroy suggested that Baden soon meet with James Benedict, Ford's outside expert; Lee Carr, a Ford in-house airbag engineering expert; and a reconstruction expert from Ford so that Baden could get the information he needed for a written report. Meanwhile, Conroy said, he would send Baden an unedited copy of the medical and autopsy files that his firm had obtained to date.

Until a meeting could be scheduled, Conroy decided not to mention Baden's telephone call. Once Baden issued a written report, it would have to be provided to Thomas's attorneys as part of the discovery process.

Medical examiner Elliot Gross's deposition was scheduled for the early afternoon of October 21st, in Cape May Court House. Bill Conroy and Robert Devine represented Ford, and Ann Walsh appeared for TRW. Deborah Romanski, from Tom Mellon's office, appeared for Eric Thomas. Dr. Gross, a courteous and charming man, came alone.

Because Gross's testimony would speak to every aspect of Tracy Thomas's death and would discuss in detail her entire anatomy, Conroy was surprised to see Thomas in the room. Legally, Thomas had the right to be there, but it was unusual for the plaintiff, let alone the husband of the deceased, to be present where sensitive matters—including graphic descriptions and close-up photographs—were to be discussed.

Conroy worried that Thomas's presence might inhibit the witness from expressing himself fully or from using his normal vocabulary to describe his work and findings. He himself, meanwhile, was determined not to reveal Benedict's and Baden's findings.

Conroy preferred to let Dr. Gross tell his story. He first wanted to know his opinion about the time of death. The time of death might also show how long Dr. Thomas was unconscious. In light of what Conroy had learned in recent weeks and his suspicions regarding the "accident," that detail would be an important part of Ford's defense.

Conroy asked Gross if he had tried to figure out the time of Tracy's death. Gross said he hadn't.

"Was there any attempt to get a ballpark range or try and narrow down a time?" Conroy wanted to know.

"Well, the range of time would be between the time she [Tracy Thomas] was last known to be alive prior to the collision and the time that she was pronounced [dead]," Gross responded.*

---

* Gross had been told what Thomas had said: that he left his home at about 12:15 A.M. The medical examiner also knew that the first witness arrived at the scene at about 2:00 A.M.

Conroy took a moment before resuming his queries. Then he asked what had caused Tracy Thomas's death. Gross said that he could not isolate which of the individual injuries had caused her death. However, he said, in his opinion, Tracy Thomas's death came as a result of trauma in part associated with the car's air bag, even though at the time of the autopsy he was unaware of Thomas's claim that his wife had fallen in the driveway prior to the accident.

Conroy then asked the doctor, "What are the causes, in your experience, of petechial hemorrhaging?"

"Well, the most frequent explanation for petechial hemorrhage on a traumatic basis relates to compression of the neck," Gross said. "The explanation is asphyxia, compression of the neck."

Gross added that the hemorrhaging in the eyes could also occur as a result of suffocation, smothering attributable to asphyxia, and the general category of deaths that involved asphyxia, or the interruption of air.

"Why don't you explain to us how the hemorrhage occurs in the eye when it's a situation of neck compression," Conroy prompted.

"Well, it's really not entirely known. There are two explanations that are given, one being that there's compression of the veins that carry blood to the head but without compression of the arteries, which are under a higher pressure. Another is that [when] there is an interruption in oxygen supply, there is damage to the small vessels and blood leaking from them."

In this instance, Gross said, the hemorrhages in the eyes revealed asphyxia, which sometimes occurred as a result of compression of the neck but may also occur from suffocation. He couldn't say which had caused the hemorrhages.

After looking at several autopsy photographs, Conroy asked about the hyoid bone, which is directly above the Adam's apple. There, the medical examiner had discovered a small, one-centimeter (less than half an inch) "focal" hemorrhage, which, he said, could have been caused by ". . . deployment of an air bag, [or] the cover of the air bag, [or] components of it; [or], in a short individual, the component of the restraint system."

Conroy couldn't understand, however, how the inflated air bag pressing upon the area between the chin and neck of a small person could produce focal hemorrhaging in two separate areas.*

Gross repeated that the hemorrhaging at the hyoid bone was from blunt force trauma, but at the time of the autopsy he had not determined why it had occurred.

"How about . . . situations where you've seen hemorrhaging at this area in a non–motor vehicle event?" Conroy asked.

"Non–motor vehicle event, I would think of some blunt force to the neck—karate chop in that area," Gross replied.

Conroy then asked about the hemorrhaging of the cricoid cartilage, a major component of the voice box.

"When you've seen that type of hemorrhaging in non–motor vehicle situations . . . [are] there any scenarios that you've seen where that [occurs]?"

---

* The shoulder belt of a restrained driver, as Tracy Thomas was, stops the upper body motion, while the chin moves to the chest as the body is slowed by the belt. Ford's experts have stated that a tethered air bag could not get under the chin of a restrained driver and cause the injury pattern Gross had documented.

"I think so. Blunt force trauma, such as a karate chop, strangulation," Gross replied.

"And, again, back in February of '97, had you formed an opinion as to what had caused that hemorrhaging at that particular part?"

"I had formed an opinion."

"Blunt force trauma?" Conroy asked.

"Trauma, yes," Gross answered, trying to understand where Conroy's questions were leading.

Gross, rubbing his bald spot, said he considered that the accident had caused the blunt force trauma, which he defined as physical force, but he had not determined that the trauma caused the death of Tracy Thomas.

". . . Did you see any damage to the spinal cord itself?" Conroy asked.

"No, I did not," Dr. Gross replied.

"And as I read your [autopsy] report, is it also fair to say that you found nothing in terms of a spinal cord injury—"

"That's correct," Gross said.

"—that would have explained the asphyxiation here, correct?"

"That's correct," Gross replied.

Thomas, who was at the end of the table, sat quietly, occasionally took a note or two, but showed no emotion, despite the obvious line Conroy was taking.

Gross had now confirmed what Baden had told Conroy: There was no injury to Tracy Thomas's spinal cord that could have led to asphyxiation.

"Let me ask you this question, Doctor: If Mrs. Thomas was presented to you for the autopsy and you had [not] been . . .

given any explanation as to where she had been, if it was [not] an accident, if she was found somewhere—you just don't know—but she's presented with the neck injuries that you've defined for us, and she's presented with the petechial hemorrhaging in the eyes. Given that injury pattern, would that alert you to any potential scenarios that could have resulted in death?" Conroy paused, then added, "I should add . . . the bruises that are depicted on the face, the cut lip, and the bruises you otherwise documented."

". . . Yes, it would," Gross replied after a moment's hesitation.

Thomas seemed uninterested in what was being discussed.

"Would you please tell us what?" Conroy said.

"Some of the other items which I previously mentioned," Gross stated.

"Such as?"

"Strangulation, a blunt force injury to the neck . . ." His voice trailed off.

Conroy now felt that he may have pushed Gross far enough for Thomas and his lawyers to guess Ford's intentions.

"Let's take a break," Conroy said.

Thomas was no longer in the room when they resumed after the break. Conroy had assumed that he had asked to hear the clinical details of Tracy's death so as to obtain closure. But then he remembered that the doctor had remarried and had a second child. Wouldn't that in itself have brought closure? Conroy was puzzled that Thomas sat expressionless at this and subsequent depositions.

Conroy now asked the medical examiner to distinguish between "cause of death" and "manner of death."

The "cause of death," Gross said, "is [either] an injury or a natural cause or a disease—that is responsible for a death." The "manner of death," he said, describes how the death occurred—such as by an accident, by homicide, by natural disease, or by suicide. Sometimes, Gross pointed out, the manner of a given death cannot be determined even if you discover the cause.

Gross added that he had asked Detective Webster if there were any suspicious circumstances surrounding the accident and that the detective had given no such indication in his written report.

"So was it the absence of any suspicious circumstances in the police report that led you to conclude . . . that the injuries had to have occurred in the accident?" Conroy asked.

"That's correct," Gross replied.

Gross repeated that since neither the prosecutor nor the police had indicated any concerns relating to the death, he acted on the information that was available to him.

Gross confirmed that he had no information on air bags when he issued his final report. He knew nothing about the deployment rate of an air bag or how long it would stay inflated before it automatically deflated. He didn't even know the duration of contact between the occupant of the car and the air bag. He had asked for information about these things but got nothing.

Conroy asked about Tracy Thomas's facial injuries.

"Have you formed an opinion as to what caused these contusions on the right side of the face?" Conroy asked.

"No, I have not," Gross replied.

"Do you believe they are . . . scratch marks?" Conroy asked.

"I don't believe they're scratch marks."

"Why not?"

"The skin is intact," Gross replied.

"You [can] have scratch marks that don't break the skin, correct?" Conroy followed up.

"That's correct. Or produced by other—in another way," Gross continued.

"Is it fair to say that you can't rule out the possibility that these are scratch marks? [Do you] agree with that?"

"I wouldn't use the term *scratch marks*," Gross said, then added, "They could be produced [by] . . . strangulation."

"They could be?"

"Yes," Gross replied.

Gross then said that marks like that would be present when a cord or other ligature was used, though he saw no such marks on the neck, which would suggest that no ligature was involved.

Gross said that the injuries to the hyoid bone and neck were "consistent with" an impact from an air bag. Doesn't "consistent with" actually mean "caused by" Conroy asked. Gross said he wouldn't go as far as that.

The county offices closed at five, but Conroy hadn't finished, nor had Ann Walsh asked her questions. Thomas's attorneys were also waiting their turn. The continuation of Dr. Gross's deposition was scheduled for November 8th, two weeks away.

That night, on his way back to Philadelphia along Interstate 76, Bill Conroy thought about Eric Thomas sitting there impassive for most of the day. Conroy could not fathom what he must have been thinking as the medical examiner pored over photographs of his dead wife's tongue and spinal cord. Was Thomas revisiting the scene of the crime? Conroy shuddered.

The next day, with Ford's approval, Conroy asked Glenn Zeitz to assist him in defending the Thomas case. Conroy explained what he'd learned from Gross and that the case was likely to turn into a quasi-criminal investigation. Thomas probably would hire a criminal attorney himself to advise against self-incrimination. Conroy also wanted somebody like Zeitz by his side—someone who knew how a criminal mind worked.

Zeitz was flattered. Most of his clients were criminals: Philadelphia mob boss Ralph Natale; Jay Smith, a high school principal convicted of murdering a teacher and two children; and Robert Marshall, convicted of murdering his wife for the insurance money and the subject of the best-selling book *Blind Faith,* were among the most notorious people he'd represented. Zeitz was delighted by Conroy's call asking him to help defend a Fortune 500 company.

Conroy asked him to act as a consultant, stay in the background, never deal with or speak to Ford, and never appear in court. No one else, outside of Ford and his office, should know Zeitz was involved. If word got out, not only would Thomas's lawyers become suspicious but it would be unseemly that a lawyer who represented robbers, racketeers, and drug dealers was now representing Ford. Only if Thomas retained a criminal attorney would Conroy ask Zeitz to surface.

There are obvious differences between the punishments involved in criminal and civil cases and there are procedural differences as well. In civil cases, defendants are often assumed to be liable unless they can prove otherwise, but this is not true of the Thomas case. It is the plaintiff's responsibility to prove damages. Thus Zeitz's new assignment would require a subtle change in his thinking, but he was looking forward to it.

The first thing Zeitz did was to hire his own private investigator, Alan Hart. Then he studied the files, reports, and photographs that Conroy had sent him, and soon saw that Conroy was on to something.

What U.S. attorneys and D.A.s had been doing to Zeitz and his clients for the last thirty years, Conroy would now have to consider doing to Eric Thomas and his attorneys. Every scrap of paper that might indicate a motive for Thomas to kill his wife would have to be explored.

Zeitz, through Conroy's office, would issue subpoenas for Thomas's gas and telephone bills, credit card receipts, travel records, and accounting records. He asked his investigator, Alan Hart, to try to obtain Thomas's medical history, Department of Motor Vehicles papers, and any civil litigation records, such as possible malpractice claims—and Stephanie Thomas's real property records, medical history, driving records, list of relatives, and prior addresses. Zeitz also came up with a list of people—babysitters, Eric's golfing partners, etc.—who had to be found, interviewed, and/or deposed.

Zeitz would attack Eric Thomas's credibility. If the doctor had something to hide—as everyone does—Zeitz would find it, and if it related to the case, he would use it to discredit Thomas.

* * *

On October 22nd, as the arrangement between Conroy and Zeitz was firmed up, Detective Webster's deposition was taken. The investigating officer's statement was important for both sides. Carol Shelly, from Mellon's office, appeared for Eric Thomas, and Robert Devine and Ann Walsh for the defendants.

Webster stated that after he arrived at the scene of the accident at 2:35 A.M., he was briefed by Officer McHale. Sometime later, Webster walked over to look at Tracy Thomas's body, which was lying on a board next to the ambulance. Lawrence Pratt, the medical investigator, lifted the cover and Webster took the only picture of Tracy Thomas at the scene of the accident.

Devine asked Webster if Thomas told the detective, during the initial conversation at the hospital, that his wife had fallen in the driveway before getting in the vehicle.

"Yes, he said he had taken the child out and prepared the car, and his wife came out afterwards, and she lost her footing and fell in the slush or the snow, struck her face," Webster replied. "He helped her up. She was not injured. She proceeded then to the car and got into the driver's seat and he proceeded to get into the passenger's seat." That raised the question: Had he already put the child in the car before he helped his wife up, or was he still holding the baby?

Webster said he didn't know the answer.

Devine questioned Webster in detail about every line in Thomas's tape-recorded interview, which was taken at police headquarters three days after the accident. At the hospital, Thomas had volunteered that his wife had been having blackouts, but in the taped interview at police headquarters, he wouldn't confirm that statement made at the hospital.

When Webster was asked to relate his conversations with the medical examiner, he said that he and Gross had discussed why Tracy Thomas, with so few injuries, had died.

"He [Dr. Gross] had never handled an incident like this before." Neither had Webster. "It was an unusual accident. It was hard for him to determine exactly what had occurred," Webster said, and added, "He needed more information to piece this together. I remember telling him the background history that I had obtained of the family. At that point, there was nothing negative. . . ."*

"We were all in agreement that the type of accident and the damage that occurred—there should not have been a fatality. It's not indicative of—when you see a fatality, you're looking for major damage. This didn't have major damage."

The medical examiner had told Webster the fetus might have pushed up against her diaphragm. The location of the baby, the seat belt placement and constriction, and the air bag were the only other factors that could have caused her death. But Webster confirmed that he and Gross had had nothing to suggest foul play, so it was ruled out.

Thomas's attorney, Carol Shelly, asked a few closing questions.

"You ruled out foul play," she said. "Is it fair to say that one of the reasons foul play, in your mind, was ruled out was

---

* It was only after the Rose family visited Detective Webster on December 9, 1998, that he was told of some "negative" aspects of Thomas's life. The visit with the Roses was covered later in Webster's deposition.

because the witness, who first came on the scene, told you that Eric Thomas was unconscious?"

"Correct."

"Anybody ever tell you that he [Dr. Thomas] wasn't unconscious or maybe he was faking it?" Shelly asked.

"Nobody ever mentioned that," Webster answered. "Nobody has ever brought that allegation."

"Have you ever uncovered any evidence that Eric Thomas was violent or physical with Tracy Thomas?"

"No evidence of that. No one came forward," Webster replied.

Mellon now knew for sure what Conroy was up to.

Earlier that year, Joe Pinto, Conroy's mentor at White & Williams, had told Conroy that he was planning to retire by the end of the year. Conroy started to think that it was Pinto's presence that had kept him at the firm for twenty years. In fact, Conroy would rather have been at a smaller, more focused firm that specialized in litigation. Now that his heavy schedule for the year, except for the Thomas case, was almost over, he was thinking about making a move. One firm he liked was Ronald Cabaniss's in Orlando, Florida.

Conroy assumed that leaving White & Williams would mean he'd have to ask the court for a time-out so that the other attorneys at the firm could bring themselves up to speed on the Thomas case.

On November 1st, Conroy lunched with Pinto at Bookbinders Seafood House in Philadelphia and told him he'd be leaving the firm. Notifying his clients and transferring the cases could, he estimated, take as long as sixty days. He was prepared to stay on until the end of the year.

Pinto was disappointed. He'd hoped that Conroy would stay at White & Williams and continue to handle Ford.

A week after Conroy had notified his firm and his clients about his imminent departure, Ford told the White & Williams that they wanted Conroy to continue handling their account regardless of where he was practicing. Pinto wasn't surprised. Many clients were now taking their business to smaller, "boutique" practices.

After hearing from Ford, Conroy asked Pinto to help him try the Thomas case, which he believed would go to trial, and Pinto agreed.

During the first week in November, Tom Mellon turned over to Conroy the plaintiff's expert's reports that were due by the end of the year. The first of them was the preliminary report of Randy Pazzaglia, who had reconstructed the accident. No finding as to the cause of Tracy Thomas's death was noted or required. A few days later, William Broadhead issued his report on the restraint system in Thomas's SUV. His report noted that the "sensor system in the subject vehicle fired unreasonably late in the subject collision," and that "available data indicates that the driver airbag system in the 1996 Ford Explorer is overly aggressive."

On November 2nd, Coltharp Engineering Associates, Inc., issued their report on behalf of Thomas's attorneys. Coltharp concluded that "the speed of the Explorer at the point of impact with the pole was 24–25 mph and the change of speed in the Explorer as a result of the collision with the pole was

7-to-10 mph." In addition they stated, "the duration of the collision exclusive of a secondary collision and runout was 0.025 to 0.045 seconds (25 to 45 milliseconds).

The next deposition was taken on November 8th. Again Thomas sat in, this time to hear the testimony of Officer McHale, the first policeman on the scene. McHale confirmed previous depositions. He had found no deer tracks that night.

Tom Mellon then asked, "In this area of Hand Avenue are there many deer?"

"It's known that there are deer in that area, yes," McHale replied.

"Do they [deer] cause a danger in that area?" Mellon asked.

"No. I don't believe they're a danger," the officer replied.

"Are they common in the area?" Mellon asked again.

"I would say it's common, yes," McHale answered.

Mellon then asked the officer if he could distinguish a human footprint from a deer track.

"I think so, yes."

"Is it fair to say that if you had seen anything at all which you believe to be consistent with a deer track, you would have noted it in your police report?" Mellon inquired.

"Yes, I would have," McHale replied.

While Mellon was struggling to establish the presence of a deer, Thomas, sitting at the far end of the conference room, gave no indication of what he was thinking.

Dr. Gross's deposition was scheduled to continue on November 8th. By November 1st, all the attorneys had received transcripts of his deposition to date, and Bill Conroy had sent a copy to Michael Baden, who had agreed to suggest questions that Gross should be asked in the follow-up.

Conroy met Baden at his office in New York, where the pathologist urged him to be much more specific when questioning Gross a second time. Baden suggested certain issues Conroy should press hard on, like how much time was required for pressure to build up in the eyes to cause petechial hemorrhaging, and how long it would take for the pressure to build up in relation to how long the air bag was in contact with the decedent's body. There was also the issue of the relative absence of injuries and what that meant. He should try to get Gross to explain how an air bag could cause a certain injury, how it could make contact with a certain area of the eye. The most important issue, however, was the timing—how the air bag could have caused the death in the fraction of a second that Tracy Thomas was in contact with it.

Conroy himself wanted to emphasize that Gross had little knowledge of air bags when he wrote his final report. He would also use Tom Mellon's own expert, Dr. Jason, to refute Gross. Jason had stated in his report that an injury to the spinal cord had caused Tracy Thomas to die by asphyxia. But Gross had not found any such injury. How could both men be correct? And if there had been an injury to her spinal cord, how could Dr. Gross have missed it?

On November 8th, Bill Conroy and Ann Walsh appeared for the defendants, and Tom Mellon appeared for Thomas, who again sat in on the proceedings, his youthful face expressionless as always. Gross was ready for a tough cross-examination and had brought along Kyran Connor, counsel for Cape May County, to advise him. Thomas had taken a seat in a corner of the room, against a wall. His eyes were focused on Conroy as if he wanted to see exactly how Ford would challenge the medical examiner's findings.

Conroy used Gross's final autopsy report as the basis for his questioning. At Conroy's request, the medical examiner explained how Tracy Thomas had died. During his lengthy description Gross added several details he had not mentioned before—either in his reports or his previous deposition. The first was a contusion on the left side of the tongue; the other was that Tracy Thomas had no natural diseases.

Gross, in a courteous but formal tone, stated that he still considered the cause of death to be "blunt force trauma with asphyxia." However, he could not say whether it was the air bag itself or its cover that had struck the right side of the neck and caused injuries that one would normally associate with a karate-chop mechanism in which a sudden asphyxia occurs.

Gross noted that even though he had not stated that "the air bag caused a sudden compression of the chest or caused an impact on the chest, which could cause a cardiac arrhythmia," it was something that had to be considered.

Conroy asked the medical examiner to go through the injuries that had caused Tracy Thomas's death. Gross said it was difficult to give a precise or simple answer to the question.

"Certainly I would like, as a prosecutor would like, to have a person shot in the presence of witnesses. That doesn't always happen. In this instance, there's a woman who was found and pronounced dead in the car after certain things happened and in which the autopsy discloses certain things [and not others].

". . . All I can do is take what I have and render an opinion. I mean, one can have an impact to the chest which, without any evidence of injury externally, causes a heart arrhythmia."

Gross added that though the autopsy didn't show evidence of hemorrhage to the heart, this didn't preclude the possibility that an impact had caused a cardiac arrest.

Conroy then asked whether cardiac arrhythmia and petechial hemorrhaging in the eyes can occur simultaneously. Gross took a moment before answering, then he moved his chair closer to the table and replied.

"No. And that is one of the reasons why I certified in my opinion [that] the cause of death is a combination [of injuries]. I also can't exclude that the compression—as sudden as it may have been— of an air bag against the chest, may have contributed to an asphyxial component, because of the compression of the chest."

Gross had used the word *compression* for the first time. Conroy waited a few seconds before asking him if the compression had caused Tracy's death. Assuming that the contact between the air bag and Tracy Thomas lasted three seconds, Conroy asked the medical examiner if the air bag could have caused sufficient chest compression to result in traumatic asphyxiation.

At that moment Tom Mellon interrupted, as if he were the medical examiner's attorney.

"Before you answer, Doctor, I'm going to object. . . . We're here on a fact-finding mission, not on hypothetical questions posed to experts. Again, Doctor, you're entitled to answer if your counsel lets you. I'd ask you to keep your statement to facts."

Thomas, still sitting against the wall, seemed not to be paying attention to Gross as the medical examiner repeated that he couldn't isolate traumatic asphyxia as the cause of death. In response to another question, Gross confirmed that the petechial hemorrhages were a result of neck compression, but he couldn't say how the compression occurred.

Conroy now pointed out that in his last deposition, Gross hadn't mentioned compression.

"I agree with you [that] at the last deposition I did not talk about it. I don't know if any questions were asked. But I also believe that I forwarded some additional correspondence to you which I had not in the beginning. And in reviewing that, I did see the statement that I provided through the public information officer . . . it refreshed my recollection that I also considered the compression of the chest as well."

"What I'm hearing, though," said Conroy, "is that the petechial hemorrhaging in her eyes was a result of either pressure to her neck . . . or [to the] chest. It's one of those two, right?"

"No, you're not hearing me correctly," Gross said.

"I'm hearing you, Doctor."

"Objection," said Mellon, interrupting Conroy. "First of all, we're not here to argue. And second, you're not hearing him correctly. It isn't what he said."

"Hold it. You're not going to interrupt," Conroy said sharply.

"Counsel—" Mellon replied, his own voice a pitch higher.

"Just calm down," Conroy responded.

"I do object."

Conroy let it go and addressed some of the issues Baden had raised.

"Doctor, what I'd like to know is, have you formed an opinion whether the petechial hemorrhaging in Mrs. Thomas's eyes was a result of compression of the neck or compression of the chest?" Conroy asked.

"I formed an opinion that there [were] petechial hemorrhages in the eyes," Gross stated. "And petechial hemorrhages are seen in asphyxial deaths, which include suffocation, which include compression of the neck."

"Caused by what?"

"Can be caused by a number of things. It can be caused by strangulation, it could be caused by hanging, it could be caused by blows to the neck, and can also occur with compression of the chest. In this instance, I can't be any more specific [about] the exact mechanism."

With this, Gross admitted that he didn't know the cause of Tracy Thomas's death.

For the first time, Thomas seemed worried. He looked toward Mellon as if to ask how badly their case had been damaged by Gross's admissions. Thomas could not have known where Conroy was heading.

Conroy then asked about the hemorrhaging in the muscles at the back of Tracy's neck. Again, after a lengthy attempt at an explanation, Gross admitted that he didn't know how it had occurred.

"Have you formed an opinion within a reasonable degree of medical certainty whether any of the injuries sustained by

Mrs. Thomas were the result of her physically contacting the cover of the driver's-side air bag?"

"I can't formulate an opinion with a reasonable degree of medical certainty," Gross replied. He could explain various injuries to her face, neck, and internal organs with "a reasonable degree of certainty" but not "a reasonable degree of medical probability or certainty," he said. As he pored over the autopsy photos, the medical examiner repeatedly said he could not identify which objects in the car had caused which injuries and which injuries had caused her death.

"Did you see evidence of a karate chop to Mrs. Thomas's neck here?" Conroy asked, pointing to a spot on one of the photographs.

"The presence of the injuries on the neck are consistent with evidence of a karate chop, which I'm referring to as a blow with the hand held flat against the neck," Gross replied.

"Do you agree that the dynamics of that . . . a force of the side of a hand in a karate chop against the neck, is different than the dynamics of the type of force you would expect to see with an air bag in contact with someone's neck, Doctor?" Conroy asked.

"That, I can't answer," Gross said.

Thomas sat expressionless throughout the questioning.

Later in the deposition, Gross would say that a karate chop could cause either a sudden blockage of the air passages or a sudden cardiac arrest.

By now Mellon was objecting repeatedly and Conroy was telling Gross to keep going "unless Mr. Connor [Gross's attorney] tells us all to shut down."

Conroy then asked if the medical examiner had ever conducted an autopsy on someone who had died from a karate chop and, if so, Conroy wanted to know what Gross had seen.

"I have seen hemorrhages in the neck. In some instances there may have been a fracture of the thyroid cartilage, which would be different than one might necessarily see in a manual strangulation.* I would raise that question. It's hard for me, because this isn't a science, where you can measure everything and reach your opinions based on precise findings. . . . It depends on the circumstances.

"One can see hemorrhages, one may see a fracture, and under those circumstances I might very well say to the police, 'What you might have to consider here is that type of injury.'"

Conroy took a look at his notes, then shifted the topic. Had Gross mentioned any suspicions about Tracy Thomas's death to the police in connection with the hemorrhages?

Yes, Gross replied, "Because it is seen in instances of strangulation."

"Did you mention [to the police] that you were concerned about it?" Conroy asked.

"I mentioned it, yes."

"Was that to Detective Webster?"

"It was, I believe, to Detective Webster. It may have been also to Patrolman McHale. I don't recall exactly, but I did mention this."

---

* The thyroid cartilage is commonly known as the Adam's apple; the cricoid cartilage is the ringlike structure below the Adam's apple. The hyoid bone is above the Adam's apple.

"Do you recall what they said to you in response to that?" Conroy asked.

"I can't tell you exactly what they said, but I did consider in their report the absence of any suspicious circumstances as a basis for my ultimate determinations, considering everything that I had and the circumstances of the death."

At that point Conroy turned the questioning over to Ann Walsh, who revisited the word *compression*. Gross admitted that the air bag "may" have contributed to the compression of the chest. The medical examiner also confirmed that there was no hemorrhaging of the heart or its outer lining or the heart muscle, and that he had seen no external or internal evidence of chest compression.

Gross again confirmed that he didn't see any damage to the spinal cord that would have affected Tracy Thomas's ability to breathe.

"Dr. Jason concludes in his report 'that the mechanism of asphyxia was an injury to the upper spinal cord at the level at which breathing was found causing paralysis from the neck downward, thereby making breathing impossible.'* Did I read that correctly?" Walsh asked.

"Yes, you did."

"Do you agree or disagree with that conclusion?"

"I can't agree or disagree. It's an opinion. It's his opinion," Gross replied.

"Did you see any evidence during your autopsy that there

---

* The plaintiff's (Tom Mellon's) expert who gave a written opinion on May 24, 1999, as to the cause of death.

was an injury to the upper spinal cord which caused paralysis, thereby making breathing impossible?"

"I didn't see any injury to the cord," Gross said, and then added, "I did see extradural hemorrhage, and I did see hemorrhages in the muscles of the overlying spinous processes in that area."

"You did not see any damage to the nerves in the spinal cord, including the nerves that control breathing?"

"There was no—I didn't see any injury to the cord," he said.

Walsh now had an opinion from Gross that differed from that of Dr. Jason, whom Mellon had retained to back up Gross's original finding. This had been one of Conroy's goals and it was now on the record. As if alluding to the discrepancy, Gross would say later in this deposition that he had the last *look* at the body but not the last *say*. He could only give his opinion, as others could give theirs.

As for the air bag itself, Gross could not connect a specific injury with a specific part of the bag. He didn't know how the bag deployed or whether its cover would have struck Tracy Thomas's face.

Walsh then turned the questioning over to Tom Mellon, who took only a few minutes of the medical examiner's time to discuss the meaning of "a reasonable degree of medical probability."

During a break, Conroy called Michael Baden to consult with him about what Gross had already admitted and how he should proceed with the medical examiner. When the deposition resumed, it was Bill Conroy's turn again.

"Let's assume it's manual strangulation, and by 'manual' I mean hands. [If] somebody were to place their hand or hands around someone's neck and [tried] to manually strangle them, can you tell me, Doctor . . . when you would . . . begin to see petechial hemorrhaging in the eyes."

"I would estimate it to be minutes," Gross replied.

"It's not going to happen in thirty seconds, is it?" Conroy asked. "It's going to be more than thirty seconds, right?"

"I just am unfamiliar with any literature on that . . . I would think it would be more than thirty seconds, but I can't—it depends on the force, rapidity of compression. I can't be any more specific than that. I would think it wouldn't be less. I think it would require a little more time. But that's just an opinion."

Conroy knew that Gross's explanation conflicted with how an air bag actually works; when deployed, it remains at maximum pressure for three seconds at most.

"What is it about manual strangulation that creates focal hemorrhaging in the neck? How does that happen?" Conroy asked.

"The pressure on the neck."

Thomas, expressionless as ever, was now staring at Gross. It was more than likely that Thomas understood that Ford was trying to claim he had murdered his wife.

"If you have someone's hands or hand on the neck and they're squeezing the neck, how does that create the focal hemorrhage?" Conroy wanted to know.

"By disruption of the vessels in the soft tissues surrounding them."

Conroy then asked Baden's next suggested question: "Is the hyoid bone located anatomically within the neck in an area that's protected by other parts of the neck?"

"There are muscles surrounding it," Gross replied.

"Were the surrounding muscles also hemorrhaged?"

"No," Gross said. "The hemorrhage was local, as I've described."

"Can you explain to me how an air bag, if it contacted the hyoid bone, could [damage] the hyoid bone itself and not [the] surrounding muscle?"

"I can't tell you exactly how the injuries were produced in this instance," Gross said, sidestepping Conroy's question. "I have said, based on the contusion on [the right side] of the face as well as the hemorrhage about the thyroid cartilage and about the hyoid bone, that [in] my opinion . . . [these wounds are] consistent with an impact from the air bag or . . . [its] cover. That is what I've testified to," Gross explained.

Conroy tried again to make Gross explain how the hyoid bone hemorrhaged if the surrounding muscles did not.

"Can you explain to me why the muscular area around the hyoid bone was not hemorrhaged but the area of the hyoid bone is hemorrhaged if contact with an air bag caused the hemorrhaging? Can you explain that for me?"

"I can't explain it any more than that there was hemorrhage in the skin surface and there was hemorrhage over this focal area," Gross replied.

Conroy, determined to get Gross to answer, rose to demonstrate, by standing in front of Mr. Oakes, the court reporter, with his hands stretched outward and his palms up.

"If I were to put my hands on [the court reporter's] neck and I were to squeeze his neck [with] my hands, and if I were to [also] squeeze his neck at that area, where this hyoid bone had hemorrhaged—could that produce the hemorrhage pattern that you saw and yet not cause the hemorrhaging to the muscles around that area, correct?"

"It could cause him to faint without there being anything internally," Gross responded, again avoiding a direct answer to Conroy's question.

"That wasn't my question," Conroy said, and tried again: "Do you agree that if I placed my hand on Mr. Oakes's neck ... and squeezed at the area of the hyoid bone where the hemorrhaging occurred, where Mrs. Thomas had her hemorrhaging—that I could cause a hemorrhage with my hands, my fingers, if you will, at that area and yet not cause a hemorrhage in the muscular area around it? Do you agree with that?"

"Yes, I do," Gross replied.

"Am I correct that there wasn't hemorrhaging in the muscles around the cricoid cartilage?"

". . . Yes," Gross answered.

Conroy had now gotten Gross to agree that the injuries he'd observed during the autopsy could have been caused by manual strangulation. It was now evident to everyone in the room that Conroy was eventually going to accuse Thomas of murder.

Gross answered the next several questions testily.

"Will you agree, Doctor . . . that in none of the reference materials that you have looked at since your last deposition did you [find] that an occupant died from asphyxiation because of contact with an air bag? Would you agree with that?"

"I would agree that none of the articles mentioned that, yes," said Gross.

". . . Why did Mrs. Thomas die?" Conroy asked. "I'm still struggling with this, Doctor."

"It's a struggle. It's a struggle. I've struggled with it and struggled with it. And I considered everything that I had, and I reached my determination. I think it's a reasonable conclusion in this instance," Gross replied somewhat testily.

Conroy returned to Baden's questions, starting at the top of the autopsy report and working his way down the list of injuries that were present or absent. Was her skull fractured? Were there fractures to the face? To her nose? To her jaw? Was there brain injury?

Gross answered curtly in the negative.

"Would it be fair to say that you don't have the expertise . . . not to be critical of you . . . to express an opinion as to whether the marks are or are not caused by an air bag?" Conroy asked.

"I don't have the knowledge in this particular instance to express an opinion," Gross replied.

This was the answer Conroy was looking for. He was now ready to ask Gross whether he stood by his previous deposition.

"I've given different answers today, and I stand by the ones I gave today."

"Which means that you're—"

Gross cut him off: "As I said, and I [repeat], there were times that I said certain things were consistent [with] the injury to the neck. The contusion would be consistent with an air bag or a lid cover."

"But just so we're clear," Conroy prompted.

"I can't state it with reasonable medical certainty," Gross admitted for the first time.

"That's where I'm going. You're ahead of me," Conroy stated.

"I can't state it with reasonable medical certainty. I don't know exactly how she was struck."

Conroy turned next to questions about unconsciousness.

Gross said, yes, if someone was unconscious for more than an hour and a half, there might be swelling of the brain.

Conroy then asked: "If there was no brain swelling at all, no brain damage at all for someone who claims [to have been] knocked out for more than one and a half hours, would that raise a red flag in your mind as to whether [that person was] unconscious for that period of time?"

"I would consider it," Gross said, sounding uncertain about where this was leading.

"Consider it a red flag?" Conroy said.

"I would consider—I'd be concerned about that, if there was no swelling. If a person were just lying there for an hour and a half, yes. . . . It depends what they were unconscious from."

"Well, a blow to the head. Let's assume there was allegedly a blow to the head that was sufficient enough to render someone unconscious for more than one and a half hours."

"Are we talking about Mrs. Thomas here?" Gross asked.

Ann Walsh answered Gross's question: "No."

Conroy also said, "No."

"I don't—I thought the subpoena relates to my doing the autopsy on Mrs. Thomas."

"It does," Conroy said.

Gross was agitated by the direction his deposition was taking. And Thomas now began looking around the room, at the ceiling but at no one in particular.

"I would want to limit my questioning to that," he said, "unless there was some order otherwise. I don't want to go into a whole avenue of questioning that's unrelated to the autopsy."

"It's up to you if you don't want to answer it," Conroy told him "Just make the record clear that you're not going to answer the question."

" . I do not wish to spend my time or the county's time on questions that are unrelated to the autopsy."

"Let me try and make it a little more relevant for you," Conroy offered. "You spoke to Mr. Thomas after the accident. . . . One of [the] things you considered [in] . . . your investigation was your discussion with Mr. Thomas, correct?"

"I can't say that I considered it or not."

". . . It was important to you to know the circumstances of alleged injuries to [Mr. Thomas] in this vehicle and what happened to him in the same accident with an air bag deploying and also wearing a seat belt and sorting out what may have happened to Mrs. Thomas? . . . Did you consider that at all?" Conroy asked.

"I considered it, yes." After a pause, Gross added, "I don't know what injuries he had, nor did I explore it."

"Did you know that he claims he was knocked out from this accident?"

"I didn't know. No, I did not know at the time, either." Then he reconsidered. "Well, I think that the police reports do reflect that there may have been some unconsciousness."

"Doesn't it seem unusual to you," Conroy continued, "given your experience, that one could be unconscious for an hour and a half, [after] being hit by an air bag, and yet not have a bruise on [one's] face, glasses still intact, hat still on, not even a blemish on [the] face from the air bag and . . . no swelling of the brain in later examinations? The CAT scan is negative. Would that at least raise a concern in your mind that something might be unusual with the whole scenario?"

Mellon objected. Thomas's eyes were now fixed on Gross.

"I can't answer that question. I didn't examine Mr. Thomas," Gross finally said.

Mellon continued to object and Conroy asked the question differently. Mellon objected again.

Conroy tried once more: ". . . And there's a CT scan done at the hospital that evening and it comes back negative. There's no evidence of swelling of the brain. There's no claim of brain damage. There's no abrasion on the individual's face. . . . Given that scenario, given your experience, doesn't it seem unusual, given the absence of injuries as I've defined it, for a person to be unconscious for one and a half hours?"

Again Mellon objected that this was beyond the scope of the subpoena and Gross repeated that he wasn't prepared to answer the question.

Conroy then said that he would ask the judge for a ruling. Meanwhile, he asked the medical examiner's attorney, who hadn't spoken all day, whether Gross should answer. But before Connor could speak, Dr. Gross repeated that he would not answer such questions.

Finally, Connor spoke up: "I think what the doctor . . . is

trying to say to you [is that] Ford Motor Company has plenty of money to hire its own expert and ask [him] what he thinks. . . . The doctor works for us. He doesn't work for anybody else."

In reply, Conroy said: ". . . It's beyond me, quite frankly, that a medical examiner will be looking at what happens to one person in a car . . . who dies and then . . . ignores what happened to the other person, whether [there is] anything suspicious about that person as well."

Conroy's strategy was now in full view: Look at Tracy Thomas, he was saying, with her facial injuries supposedly caused by an air bag, and then look at her husband, who claims also to have been knocked out by an air bag but doesn't have a mark on him.

Ann Walsh then stated Conroy's question more clearly, ". . . If you had known that Dr. Thomas was unconscious for an hour and a half, and if you had known that he had no facial injuries of any kind, would that have been another unusual circumstance of this accident?"

Mellon objected, but Gross replied: "My investigation was limited to the investigation of Mrs. Thomas's death," he said, and for another ten minutes the group argued about whether it was Gross's responsibility to consider the condition of the other occupant as well when he made his findings.

Finally Gross said, "Based on my findings, I considered the death initially as suspicious. I conveyed it to the police. I think I said this. Do I then carry out my own criminal investigation? No. That's handled by the police and it's handled by the prosecutor.

"And if somebody else comes up with it a year later, two years later, I would refer them to the police and to the prosecutor and they in turn would come to me."

When Dr. Gross completed his deposition, Thomas, who had been sitting expressionless throughout the afternoon, rose and silently left the room.

While Conroy was deposing Dr. Gross, his consultant Glenn Zeitz was rereading Eric Thomas's deposition and had some questions about Tracy's fall. Had she fallen on her face? Does that explain the injuries?

Zeitz also wondered why Tracy Thomas, after her fall, had driven the vehicle. He himself had gone through three pregnancies with his wife. Each time, as her pregnancy progressed and she got touchier, he became a little more tender, a little more protective. Zeitz didn't believe that the reason for Tracy's having taken the wheel was that she liked to drive. If he had to go to the hospital in the dead of winter, with snow on the ground and with a sick child, he'd say, "Look, honey, do me a favor; get in back with the kid. I'm driving."

Something else bothered Zeitz. When Dr. Fitzpatrick, the first witness, got to the car, with the windows closed and the engine off, he saw both parents motionless in the front seat and a relatively calm baby in the backseat. That was bizarre. Why wasn't the baby crying or exhibiting any signs of anxiety? Conroy told Zeitz that he too wondered about this.

On November 11th, three days after Gross's second deposition, Conroy and Zeitz met for four and a half hours. Conroy said that Gross had now contradicted Mellon's outside expert,

Dr. Jason, on the subject of the spinal cord injury. There was no such injury, therefore Tracy Thomas could not have died from suffocation caused by an injured spinal cord.

If the case went to trial it would boil down to a battle of the experts. Some, like Dr. Jason, would argue that the air bag had caused her injuries, which had caused suffocation and death. Others, like Baden and Benedict, would claim that those injuries had never occurred and therefore that the air bag could not have killed her.

Zeitz thought that if the case went to trial, Ford would win on the strength of its experts' testimony.

Conroy wasn't so sure. Zeitz hadn't factored in that Eric Thomas was a leading citizen in Cape May Court House, which would be important.

They agreed that their best strategy was to attack Thomas's credibility. From now on, they would treat Eric Thomas as though they were dealing with a defendant in a criminal case.

Zeitz told Conroy about a fifteen-year-old case he'd been thinking about lately. His client, Robert Marshall, had given different accounts to the police and other parties about when he had pulled his car over to the side of the Garden State Parkway and how he got knocked on the head by a blow from behind and how he was unconscious when his wife was shot and killed by an unknown person. Marshall had been convicted of having his wife killed for insurance money so he could continue another relationship.

Conroy was intrigued and agreed that they should explore the relationship between Eric Thomas and his present wife,

Stephanie. They would send Thomas a second set of interrogatories concerning his romantic life before, during, and after marriage to Tracy. He would by law have to respond under oath.

The lawyers also agreed that they would track down Stephanie Thomas's previous husband, Sean Haley, and interview him—if he was willing.

SEVEN

Relevant Questions

By November 24th, Bill Conroy had left White & Williams and joined Ron Cabaniss, with offices in Wayne, Pennsylvania, a thirty-minute train ride from Philadelphia. Within a year he would partner with Campbell, Campbell and Edwards in Boston.

Conroy may have been in a new office, but he was still representing Ford on the Thomas case and deciding whether to recommend that Ford commit to a defense based on the theory that Tracy Thomas had been strangled manually.

Despite Conroy's growing suspicions, it was still a risky move. Ford would accuse Thomas not simply of misstating facts, but of having been directly involved in the death of his wife. The charge, whether proved or not, would cast a shadow over Thomas for the rest of his life. The ramifications for Conroy and the automaker were just as serious. Conroy knew he'd better be right before he mounted such a defense, but in truth, he had no idea what had happened that night between the Thomases. The only thing he was sure of was that the air bag hadn't killed Tracy.

Whether he was guilty of murder or not, Thomas had clearly made misleading statements in his deposition. Earlier in the week, Conroy had received Thomas's medical and chiropractic records, which he showed to Zeitz. The reports noted that Thomas had been treated for osteoarthritis of the cervical spine on December 6, 1996, two months before the accident, yet during his deposition, when he was asked "Have you had any neck injury before February 9, 1997?" Thomas's answer was "No." Also, in his reply to Ford's interrogatories, Thomas again denied that he had any preexisting conditions and said that he hadn't sustained any injuries before the accident. Why would he lie about something that could so easily be checked out?

If Thomas had killed his wife, Zeitz wondered how it was done. He speculated she'd been placed in the SUV after she had been killed. Or was there an altercation between Eric and Tracy in the vehicle that caused the Explorer to run into the utility pole, and then she was strangled while she sat in the driver's seat?

Could whatever have happened that night been so repugnant to Eric Thomas that he had somehow submerged his memory of the events?

Early in December, Conroy received a letter from Tom Mellon confirming the dates for some upcoming deposition and addressing some questions that had been raised during Dr.

Gross's deposition. Though Conroy had refused to meet informally with two of Mellon's experts, Mellon remained "willing to have both [his] experts present their point of view of the subject of foul play" to Ford.

Mellon described the factors that he believed were inconsistent with foul play. For one thing, Tracy's facial injuries were consistent with the "tethered" air bags that were in the Explorer. In February 1992, Mellon noted, the NHTSA stated that "the presence of tethers significantly affected the maximum displacement, which, in turn, had an effect on the type of facial contact the bag produced. Untethered bags tended to engulf the dummy's face and create a sliding or slapping motion. The tethered bag contacted the low jaw and chin areas while not producing contact patterns above the upper jaw."*

Tracy Thomas's injuries were consistent with the air bag striking beneath her neck, Mellon said. He also noted that there was no evidence of a karate chop or similar injury, because there was no significant bruising. The hemorrhages on the back of her neck and stipple hemorrhages on the muscle underneath were consistent with Tracy's head hitting the head restraint and were evidence of hyperextension of the neck. "The hemorrhage on the dural sac is indicative of a distraction injury which was caused by a rapid hyperextension. This is inconsistent with any possible theory of strangulation," Mellon wrote.

---

* The outmost edge (the face part of the air bag closest to the driver) of an inflated tethered air bag is ten inches from the steering wheel. The inflation rate is such that the bag is fully inflated before the driver can contact it, assuming the driver is more than ten inches from the steering wheel.

He ended by noting that there were no defensive wounds, which indicated that there had been no struggle. "In the final analysis, I certainly want no part in representing Dr. Thomas if he is indeed responsible for this tragic occurrence; however, my best efforts suggest otherwise," he wrote.

The court set December 17, 1999, as the cutoff date for factual discovery and the taking of oral depositions. It had been almost a year since the action began, and Mellon and Kolodny still hadn't received from Ford all the discovery materials they had asked for. Conroy, meanwhile, was still awaiting Thomas's responses to Ford's initial subpoenas, including his phone records and Tracy's insurance policy numbers.

As Conroy's suspicions hardened into theories, and knowing what his expert reports would say, he suggested to Ford that the company fully commit to a defense based on the theory that Thomas had killed Tracy. In reply, Ford asked Conroy if he could deliver the case for them and Conroy said yes. Ford told him to proceed as he wished.

Conroy was particularly concerned that Ford's possible defense not hit the media. That meant getting the experts' reports nailed down in writing as soon as possible, though the rules governing evidence required him to turn the reports over to Thomas's attorneys immediately upon receipt.

Mellon got his expert reports out first and in mid-January forwarded them to Conroy—the second set to be entered into evidence after the initial report from Dr. Donald Jason. Mellon sent along four new reports. The first was written by Taras Rudnitsky, an engineer, who had personally designed, tested, developed, validated, and certified air-bag systems for General Motors. In his fifty-eight-page document, Rudnitsky noted defects in the air-bag system of the Thomases' 1996 Explorer. For one, the system allowed unwarranted deployments and risked causing injury or death. Rudnitsky concurred with other reports that said the Explorer's air bag was unreasonably aggressive. He also pointed out that "data from Ford's own crash tests of 1996 Explorers indicates that Ford failed 5 out of 7 tests in one test configuration mandated by the government for driver crash protection."

A second accident analyst, Richard Reed, concluded his report as follows: "It is my opinion, based upon the information I have reviewed to date, that the fatal injuries sustained by Mrs. Tracy Thomas resulted from her interaction with the air bag system in the 1996 Ford Explorer on February 9, 1997," and added that "Mrs. Tracy Thomas would have survived the collision with minor or no injuries had the driver-side air bag system in the 1996 Ford Explorer not deployed as a result of the crash on February 9, 1997." His report also mentioned several supposed defects in the design and manufacturing of the Explorer's air-bag system.

Wayne Ross, M.D., P.C., in a preliminary report dated January 6th, stated, "In rereading Dr. Elliot Gross' deposition, it is quite clear that the defense counsel and their experts contend that this is a homicide. By way of this, they implicate Dr. Thomas as the perpetrator. Nothing could be further from the facts." In his opinion, it was "quite clear that the circumstances of death are due to a sequence of factors related to the motor vehicle accident—collision with object—with air bag deployment—to a restrained driver." The petechial hemorrhages in Tracy Thomas's eyes, he said, were related to the body organs' inability to get and/or use oxygen, due to the spinal cord injury.

The final report in the packet was submitted by Dennis Shanahan, M.D., M.P.H., on January 7th. He found that "Mrs. Thomas's fatal injuries were a direct result of her head and upper torso being impacted by the inflating driver's side air bag. Had she not interacted with the deploying air bag, she would have survived the crash with minimal injuries such as abrasions and contusions."

The battle of the experts had begun. If the air-bag system was defective—and this was uncertain—did the air bag kill Tracy Thomas? At the heart of that debate was the question, Was there a spinal cord injury? For if there was not, then the air bag, defective or not, could not have been the cause of death.

Meanwhile, the discovery disputes, despite attempts by both sides to resolve them, were hopelessly bogged down. The cutoff date of December 17th for discovery had come and gone, and six weeks later, on January 31st, the two parties found themselves in court before Judge Rosen for a status conference. The tension was high and the meeting quickly spiraled out of control.

The attorneys for both sides had provided the court with copies of their written communications, and on the morning of January 31st Mellon had faxed to the court, at the last minute, a letter listing the items he believed Ford had not yet responded to.

In the meeting with the judge were Tom Mellon and Elliott Kolodny for Thomas, Thomas Hinchey and Bill Conroy for Ford, and Ann Walsh for TRW.

Hinchey had been involved in the case from the beginning. His job was to ensure that Ford responded properly to discovery requests and that the other side did the same.

Mellon began by asking the court to commit Ford to a date when the rest of the discovery material would arrive. He had recently received four boxes of material, he said, but Ford's crash-test records, including photographs and videos, were still missing.

His team needed to view the videos to see what happened to test dummies under conditions similar to those in which Tracy Thomas had died.

To make matters worse, Ford wanted $16,000 before releasing copies of the tapes. This inflated cost was curtailing reasonable discovery, Kolodny said. He and Mellon thought that price was outrageous.

Tom Hinchey replied that Ford had produced "voluminous" discovery materials in the last month and a half and they were now simply waiting for Kolodny to pare down his list to a reasonable length.

Judge Rosen suggested that Kolodny view the original tapes and narrow down a list of those he still wanted, so as to reduce the cost.

Hinchey objected. Ford didn't want to ship the original tapes to Kolodny, he said, for fear of losing them.

So it went back and forth for an hour until Rosen halted the bickering and asked for a list of the tapes and where and how they were stored. The court, he said, would determine a proper method and a reasonable fee for reproducing them for Thomas's attorneys.

Rosen was eager to move ahead to the depositions. Conroy said he wanted to depose the Rose family and Teresa Bridge-Jackson, who had been the first doctor to see Eric Thomas at Burdette Tomlin Memorial Hospital. Bridge-Jackson had failed to show up for her deposition. As for the Roses, they had agreed to a date around the holidays, but were so distraught about missing their daughter at Christmas that they asked for a postponement until after the first of the year. Here it was the end of January and nothing had been scheduled yet.

The judge wanted to know what contribution the Roses would make.

Tracy Thomas's parents had found Eric Thomas's behavior unusual after the accident, Hinchey said, and Ford believed that this contradicted Thomas's own claim of grief.

Judge Rosen agreed that the Roses' depositions should be taken; otherwise, he could see grounds for a later claim of reversible error.

Kolodny argued that taking such a deposition from the Roses was improper. But if it happened, he said, he would ask the court to limit the uses of the information obtained.

Tom Mellon added that "what's behind the story . . . is that [Conroy] is positing that . . . Dr. Eric Thomas . . . killed his wife."

This was the first time Mellon acknowledged in open court that he knew the defense Ford was considering. Conroy had not been deterred by Mellon's letter in December claiming that foul play didn't belong in this case. Now Mellon was putting the issue before Judge Rosen, perhaps hoping the judge would nip it in the bud.

"The reason that ... Dr. Bridge-Jackson [and] the Roses are [going to be deposed]," Mellon continued, "is not to understand the emotional distress of Dr. Thomas. It's to ... develop the groundwork for ... a theory of homicide ... by Ford's counsel, so [did I hear] a proffer [that that is Ford's intention]? * If we stick to that proffer, all is fair, all is reasonable."

"All right," Judge Rosen said, his voice rising. "I've heard enough. They [Ford] have a right to [pursue] whether they feel it goes to the damage issue [and to pursue] a theory as to how Mrs. Thomas died.

"They have a right. We're talking about a death here. It's crucial to both sides of this case. This is not a slip and fall, and they have a right to develop that, and I'm going to permit it, and I would be doing the same for you guys," he said, pointing to Mellon and Kolodny, "if there was someone—some witness whom you needed. This is not a game. I'm trying to get it over with, but is that all, and then you're done."

All through the judge's statement Thomas sat quietly, his eyes fixed on Judge Rosen.

Hinchey added that based on the discovery material he had received, he still expected that a second deposition from Dr. Thomas may be needed.

But Judge Rosen was more interested in knowing if Mellon's previous statement was correct: Was Ford's defense based on the theory that Eric Thomas had killed his wife?

---

* A proffer, in legal terms, is a verbal or written offer to the court that evidence will be produced to the court at some time in the future or at trial.

Hinchey said he couldn't comment, since Ford was still investigating statements by the medical examiner and the police in their depositions.

"It's a serious case," Rosen said, "and it's going to be resolved, and it seems to me if you're proffering that kind of extremely . . . serious allegation, that you've got to . . . say this is where we're going—or cast it aside so these gentlemen on the other side can properly prepare."

"Judge," Hinchey replied, "we, like the medical examiner and like the police, are investigating it. That's the best I can tell you. Our reports are coming out in the beginning of March— our expert reports. Now, when the reports come out [we'll know where we are], but until I have the whole deck of cards—"

"I'm going to hold you to that day," Rosen interrupted.

"I understand," Hinchey told him. "And we're prepared to deal with it, Judge." Conroy didn't look up, not wanting to give the court any indication of Ford's intended defense.

Judge Rosen said that if Ford's allegation was supported by their experts' reports, he would give Thomas's attorneys time to respond. He repeated that the issues raised were extraordinary and serious. If new information came up in the additional discovery, then everyone would have the opportunity to respond.

There were also more mundane issues to be settled—specifically, the cost of taking expert depositions scheduled for dates between March 3rd and March 30th. There were approximately seventeen of them—more experts than available days. Who was going to pay for the experts' preparation, testimony, and travel time?

Mellon said that he wasn't paying for Conroy to question his experts for six hours about a homicide. But he was willing to pay for the experts Mellon wanted to question, if the plaintiffs decided to question them.

"You pay for his," Judge Rosen responded. "He'll pay for yours.... Let's not get too exotic here."

Rosen was also sensitive to the preparation and travel costs involved, but, he said, "You know, we're not talking about a minor case . . . and what's at stake here is, number one, a dead human being, but number two, serious liability issues for an automobile manufacturer, and more serious allegations of intentional taking of a life, and . . . everyone's going to get a full opportunity to explore this case or none of us would be doing your clients a service."

Judge Rosen asked both sides for a list of their experts, where they lived, when they were needed, and the costs associated with their depositions. Rosen himself would determine reasonable costs and would also extend the deadline for expert testimony accordingly, he said.

To the evident surprise of the attorneys, Rosen then asked if law enforcement was still looking into the case.

"No," Mellon replied. "Absolutely not, Your Honor. Law enforcement closed the books a week after this accident. Any representation . . . or suggestion otherwise is disingenuous," he said with mounting indignation.

Rosen asked everyone to remain calm.

When Mellon ended, Hinchey said the case hadn't been closed. It was simply inactive.

"Well, I'd like a representation on this record as to where the information came from," Mellon demanded. "Who the officer is, and who the D.A. is. I think that's critically important because we're using the federal process—"

"Hold," Rosen said loudly.

"—to slander a doctor," Mellon continued.

"Whoa. Whoa. Whoa. Whoa!" Rosen had now raised his voice. "No one's slandering anyone. I'm trying to find out what's going on."

". . . We are taking the reputation of this man and saying he murdered his wife. These are not lightly taken allegations. Now, if counsel thinks there's an ongoing investigation, we ought to have on the record who that police officer is or that D.A. is, on the record."

Rosen was determined to cool things down. "I'm not sure, you know, [that in] homicide cases, there's no statute of limitations, and there—and—"

Mellon interrupted to say that there was no investigation.

"And cases—homicide cases are technically never closed," Rosen said. "Because there's no statute [of limitations]." Then, turning to Hinchey, the judge asked if there was in fact an ongoing investigation.

"What I do know from discussions with Detective Webster," the attorney replied, "is that they're not finished looking at it yet."

Mellon then announced that he would have an affidavit to the court within forty-eight hours disproving Hinchey's statement. Rosen said that would not be necessary.

But Mellon refused to sit down and accused Hinchey of being "disingenuous," "mendacious," and "downright unprofessional."

Rosen halted Mellon's diatribe and reminded him that if Ford felt it had a legitimate defense based on good-faith information, Hinchey was obligated to pursue it, so those characterizations were uncalled for. Mellon, chastened, murmured his agreement. Rosen was clearly impatient to move on.

The entire case would move on, Hinchey replied, if Dr. Thomas would finally respond to the supplemental discovery requests that had been issued on November 2, 1999, three months earlier. Ford was waiting for Dr. Thomas's phone records, insurance policy numbers, car-lease information, dental practice appointment schedule for the eight-week period after the accident, and his home-loan applications. The defense wanted to know if the facts supported Dr. Thomas's claims.

Then almost as an afterthought, Judge Rosen asked: "Was there any sort of marital . . . any sort of divorce going on or anything of that sort?"

"Not that I'm aware of," Hinchey replied.

"Absolutely nothing," Mellon stated flatly, as if he had been insulted. "They were very happy. They had a sixteen-month-old. She was in utero six months. There's not even a hint of discord—not a hint of discord found by anybody."

Tom Mellon's aggressive reply surprised Bill Conroy, who had sat through most of the meeting in silence. Conroy was now more determined than ever to look into Eric Thomas's personal life.

Two days later, on February 2nd, Ford submitted its supplemental interrogatories to Thomas. Zeitz and Conroy had been working on these questions since November and formulated them on the basis of information from their investigators, including interviews and conversations with the Rose family. Since they might never get another chance to depose Thomas, Zeitz was ready to put the doctor against the wall. The questions were aggressive:

1. During the six months following the accident, please identify the dates and locations of each vacation and/or trip that you took outside the State of New Jersey.

2. With respect to each trip and/or vacation . . . please provide the following information: a) the purpose of the trip and/or vacation; b) the individuals with whom you traveled on the trip and/or vacation; c) the individuals with whom you visited during the trip and/or vacation; d) the location where you stayed during the trip and/or vacation; and e) whether you played golf during the trip and/or vacation, and if so, the number of times you played golf and the location during each trip and/or vacation.

3. With respect to the $200,000 life insurance amount you recovered for the death of Tracy Thomas, please provide the following information: a) the date when you applied for this insurance benefit after the accident in question; b) the date when you received the life insurance policy check; and c) a detailed statement of how the life insurance money was spent by

you, including the individuals and/or entities to whom you made payments with the money received from the life insurance company.

4. Please state whether you and/or Tracy Thomas borrowed any amount of money from any source before the accident in question to assist in the purchase of the Callaway Dental Practice.

5. If you answered in the affirmative to the preceding interrogatory, please provide the following information: a) the name of each person from whom you borrowed money, and the amount of the loan; b) the date each loan was repaid by you; c) the source of the money to repay each loan.

6. With respect to your relationship with Stephanie Haley Thomas, please provide the following information: a) identify when you first met Stephanie before the accident in question; b) describe the nature of the relationship with Stephanie from the time that you first met her up until the time you married Tracy Thomas. This should include in your statement of whether you were romantically involved with Stephanie and if so, the circumstances, before you met Tracy; c) state whether you had any contact with Stephanie from the date of your marriage to Tracy up until the time of the accident in question. If the answer is yes, please identify the dates of such contacts

and the purpose for them; d) please state when you last spoke to Stephanie before the accident in question, where the conversation took place, and the purpose of the conversation; e) please state when you first spoke with Stephanie following the accident in question, where the conversation took place, and the purpose of the conversation; f) during the first six months following the accident in question, identify each date and location that you physically met with Stephanie and the purpose of the meetings; g) please state when you first became romantically involved with Stephanie following the accident in question.

7. Please identify all motor vehicle accidents investigated, known, and/or relied upon by your experts wherein a person sustained injuries which they claim are substantially similar to Tracy Thomas' injuries because of an air bag. Your response should include the date of the accident, the vehicle involved, the injuries sustained, and an identification of the specific documents in the expert's possession on each such accident.

In January 2000, the Cape May County attorney asked Ford for information on air bags. When Bill Conroy learned about this request, he assumed that Dr. Gross might be thinking of amending his findings. Conroy, not wanting to make the same mistake Ford had made by not supplying air-bag information to the police and the medical examiner just after the accident, told the county attorney he'd be happy to demonstrate how air bags worked. On February 16th, about three years after Tracy Thomas died, Conroy and Ford's experts and engineers found themselves standing in a garage next to Dr. Gross's office.

A Ford engineer set up a portable demonstration unit that included a steering wheel and an air bag. By previous agreement, there was no discussion of Tracy, her injuries, or death. This was simply a fact-finding mission so that Gross could witness the function and deployment time of an air bag.

The medical examiner wanted to know how fast the bag fills with air and how the air leaves the bag. Could the bag remain inflated longer than intended? Gross was clearly preoccupied with the duration of deployment—that is, the time between inflation and deflation.

The experts took Gross through everything, step by step—including how the air bags were folded and what they were made of. They explained the volume of air in a driver's bag compared with that in the passenger's bag and how the person's body or head hitting it actually helps to push the air out through its vent holes. Then they told him that even if contact wasn't made, the bag would deflate in three seconds, because of its venting. As fast as it fills, one of the engineers said, it empties. But the force with which the occupant hits the bag contributes to the speed at which it deflates.

When the demonstration was over, Dr. Gross viewed two videotapes showing air-bag deployment that Conroy had brought with him. The medical examiner also reviewed some photographs and other materials that Ford's people had brought. The pictures showed the smearing effect of the bag on the skin, as well as the different types of injuries.

What Bill Conroy didn't know was that a week later, the medical examiner would also meet with Tom Mellon, Elliott Kolodny, and plaintiffs' experts Dr. Donald Jason and Dr. Wayne Ross. This would be the first meeting between Jason, who had said that Tracy Thomas's death was caused by a spinal cord injury, and Gross, who had actually removed and examined Mrs. Thomas's spinal cord and had stated several times in his depositions that there had been no injury to the spinal cord.

During his professional career, Dr. Gross had occasionally changed his mind in light of new information. Conroy had no idea if the medical examiner planned to amend his autopsy report now that his findings were the central issue in the case. In a perfect world, Conroy thought, Gross would now change his report to support Ford's position. At the worst, the medical examiner would be a bit less positive in his findings.

When Conroy left Gross's office on February 16th, he drove to the Cape May County prosecutor's office. Since the matter of foul play had been discussed in open court, Ford and Conroy thought they should inform the local prosecutor of Benedict's and Baden's findings. Also, if there was a chance to reopen the investigation, now was the time to move. Conroy had looked at the law and assumed that his conversations with the prosecutors were privileged and protected.* He knew, however, that if

---

* The law protects from forced disclosure certain statements made between people, including those between husband–wife, priest–penitent, and attorney–client.

Thomas learned of the meeting, he might bring an action against Ford for defamation. He could not be sure how the court would rule.

The meeting took place in the office of Acting Cape May County Prosecutor David Blaker, a big man, who was almost as tall as Conroy.* Also present were Detective Webster and Kyran Connor, the attorney who had represented medical examiner Gross at his second deposition. Conroy began by saying that he had information he believed they didn't have and that as an officer of the court he was obligated to tell them what he knew. Treading carefully, Conroy said he would outline the information he had, which was, he believed, different from Cape May's investigation. Some of the differences, Conroy was careful to say, may simply indicate an unintentional miscommunication.

One discovery Ford had made, he said, was that Detective Webster had told him that at the time of the accident, Dr. Gross had never discussed petechial hemorrhaging of the eyes, which he now understood was relevant. And if the police had had this information at the time of their investigation, they might have looked upon Tracy's death differently. Moreover, there were the inconsistent statements Thomas had made on a variety of issues, which Conroy now outlined.

When he had done this, he came to the main reason for his visit: Conroy revealed that Ford had obtained expert opinions, whose findings were that Tracy Thomas had not died as a result of the auto accident but was strangled.

---

* David Blaker was appointed by the governor of New Jersey but never confirmed by the state's senate.

Conroy was particularly careful not to express his own opinion of what might have happened or to criticize the police investigation. He presented only the facts he possessed.

The Cape May Court House team said nothing. Everyone in the room was probably aware that if Dr. Thomas failed to respond to Ford's questions and asserted his Fifth Amendment protection against self-incrimination in this civil action, but he would not only severely jeopardize his case, but he would probably lose it. It was also true that Eric Thomas had exposed himself to an investigation by an entity—the Ford Motor Company—with more money, a wider range of tools, and more far-reaching resources than the local police.

As the meeting was about to break up, Blaker asked Conroy if Ford would share their investigative information with the prosecutor's office. Conroy said he saw no reason why they wouldn't.

When Conroy returned to his office he found on his desk the documents he had requested from Thomas's insurance carrier, the Great West Life and Annuity Insurance Company. That same afternoon, he called Glenn Zeitz to tell him he'd uncovered some important new information.

In his deposition, Thomas had testified that he and Tracy had taken out a life insurance policy two months before the accident and that Tracy's death benefit was $200,000. Now Great West's documents revealed that Tracy's benefit was originally $150,000 and, just a month before the accident, had been increased to $200,000. But that wasn't all. Conroy saw for the first time that Thomas had in fact received $400,000 from his carrier in June 1997, not $200,000 as he had testified, under a provision that doubled the value of the policy in the case of accidental death.

Eric Thomas had misrepresented a material fact.

The next day, Prosecutor Blaker called Bill Conroy to ask for copies of Ford's depositions and investigative reports. Conroy took the opportunity to tell him the new information he'd found in Thomas's insurance records.

It was during this period that the Roses began calling Conroy's office to say that the Cape May prosecutors had not been helpful and they hoped that Conroy would give them more satisfaction. Like Thomas, they had no idea that Conroy had just met with the prosecutors. Conroy assumed that they wanted to know what his investigation had turned up. It was difficult for him to keep it from them, but he also knew that he had to protect his case. Plus, he wanted to avoid giving anyone reason to accuse him of trying to manipulate the family. So he said little and let them do most of the talking.

The Roses repeated that their son-in-law had told Donald six months after the accident that he would drop the lawsuit against Ford "if they ask too many questions." Now, more than ever, Conroy wondered what questions Thomas was afraid of being asked.

The court had set the first week in March as the final cutoff date for discovery. Conroy's experts' reports were due just before the deadline and were all issued on March 2nd. The technical reports came from Gregory Smith, a senior mechanical engineer; Joseph Wills, of Ford's design analysis department; James Boland, also from Ford; Mark Novak, director of engineering processes and practices at Breed Technologies; and Jeffery Pearson, an engineer with TRW. Collectively, the engineers and accident reconstructors stated that the assertions provided by Dr. Thomas's experts did not represent the facts in the case and that the design and construction of the crashworthiness system of the Explorer—including the air-bag restraints—were reasonably safe, reliable, and effective.* The air bags, they said, were not dangerous or defective.

Robert Mendelsohn, M.D., concluded on the basis of Dr. Gross's finding that there was no swelling of the spinal cord, no impingement on the spinal cord, and no fracture or dislocation of the cervical spine. Trauma to the C2-C3 cord was most unlikely and the dural hemorrhage found overlying C2 and C3 of the cervical cord would not have affected Tracy Thomas's ability to breathe. Therefore, respiratory arrest did not account for her asphyxiation.

James Benedict, the first physician whom Bill Conroy had contacted and the first one to raise the possibility of strangulation, stated that his findings were based on notes and photographs taken during the inspection of the impounded vehicle on May 25th and October 15th of 1999, and on an accident reconstruction conducted by Greg Smith and Lee Carr of Ford.

---

* The crashworthiness doctrine imposes liability on the manufacturer not for causing the accident, but rather for failing to minimize the injuries or even increasing the severity of the injuries sustained brought about by a cause other than the alleged defect.

Benedict outlined in detail the condition of Tracy Thomas's spine and then listed her injuries. He noted that the lack of oxygen [asphyxia] could not have been caused by a spinal cord injury, since he, like Dr. Gross, saw no evidence of such an injury.

In Benedict's opinion, what killed Tracy Thomas were significant biomechanical forces applied to her neck—forces that were not associated with the air bag or the restraint system. The air bag was designed to be fully deployed for considerably less than one second and that at least thirty seconds of significant pressure on Tracy's neck were necessary to produce petechial hemorrhages in the eyes consistent with asphyxia.

Benedict could find no connection, he wrote in his report, between the hemorrhaging in the eyes, the focal hemorrhaging noted by Gross on the back of the neck, and the focal hemorrhaging overlying the greater horn of the hyoid bone and a fully inflated, or almost fully inflated, air bag. In addition, he could not attribute the marks on Tracy Thomas's face to the air bag or its cover, which showed no signs of impact.

Benedict closed by stating: "My time is billed at $500 per hour. For an eight-hour deposition, the fee is $4,000. Reimbursement for reasonable travel expenses to and from the deposition, if required, would be additional."

His bill would serve notice to the plaintiffs that the cost of taking expert witness depositions would be substantial.

Dr. Michael Baden's report was also dated March 2, 2000. In it, he noted that he had reviewed the autopsy report, photographs of the scene and autopsy, microscopic slides, ambulance reports, police investigation reports, the death certificate, deposition testimonies, the plaintiff's complaint, and the plaintiff's experts' reports, including those of Dr. Jason.* He had also visited Carr Engineering, Inc., in Houston, he said, to study airbag deployment.

Baden listed the facts of the accident and noted that during the autopsy, Dr. Gross had removed the posterior portion of the cervical spine and had later confirmed that there was no spinal or skull injury, as well as no chest or abdominal injury.

He could state with "a reasonable degree of medical certainty," that the injuries sustained by Tracy Thomas were a result of "traumatic compression of the neck at the hands of another."

Like Benedict, Baden said that Tracy's neck would have to be compressed for many seconds before venous blood returning to the heart ruptured capillaries and caused petechial hemorrhages. He noted that "air bag deployment, which takes less than one-tenth of one second from start to finish, cannot compress blood vessels long enough to cause petechiae to form nor to cause death from asphyxia, which is the inability to breathe in air and oxygen."

Baden also referred to Dr. Jason's report, which gave the cause of death as "an injury to the upper spinal cord." Gross's findings, and Baden's own review of microscopic slides, showed no spinal cord injury. Baden discounted Dr. Wayne Ross's findings, which also assumed a spinal cord injury. Dr. Gross's finding of "blunt force trauma with asphyxia" was the incorrect starting

---

* A year later Baden amended this statement to say that he had reviewed "photographs of the microscopic slides."

point for other findings of the plaintiff's experts, which were therefore flawed as well.

In conclusion, Baden stated again, "In my opinion, Mrs. Thomas died of compression of the neck by the hands of another."

Ford's defense was now in the open for everybody to see. As Glenn Zeitz said, the tables had turned. Eric Thomas was now the defendant and Ford the prosecutor. The case was no longer about an air bag killing Tracy Thomas; it was about Dr. Thomas having killed her and faking an accident to hide the crime.

EIGHT

Out in the Open

By the end of the first week in March, Tom Mellon had received the reports of Ford's experts and understood what awaited his client. It was now clear to Mellon and Thomas that Ford had not been fishing for a defense when it took Dr. Gross's deposition.

Eric Thomas must have by now learned the lengths to which defendants in product-liability lawsuits would go to avoid a jury trial. Defense attorneys had been known to accuse plaintiffs of paying attention to the car radio at the time of the accident, turning to talk to someone in the backseat, or watching a pretty girl walk by. In most cases, challenging the plaintiff's character was a crucial part of a defense. If they could refocus attention away from the product and toward the plaintiff, they would be halfway there with a jury and the plaintiff might be ready to settle or drop his case before trial.

But Mellon and Kolodny continued to believe in Thomas's innocence, and were willing to risk their reputations and the substantial sums needed to pursue the case, which they had taken on a contingency basis. Their firm had already spent over a hundred thousand dollars on the Thomas case and was prepared to spend more.

When the attorneys met in Judge Rosen's courtroom on March 10th for a scheduled settlement conference, everyone knew there would be no settlement.

Eric Thomas, who had now read Ford's experts' opinions, arrived with his attorneys. He was dressed, as always, in a dark blue suit and white shirt. He gave no indication of how he felt about Ford's defense, although he knew by now that Bill Conroy had visited the Cape May County prosecutor and implicated him in the death of his wife.

Mellon, just before he came to court, had sent Rosen, by fax, a motion for a protective order, requesting that any information containing allegations of wrongdoing, misdeeds, or foul deeds by Dr. Thomas be sealed by the court so that the information would not be available to anyone outside the courtroom (other than law-firm colleagues and various experts). This was Thomas's first appearance at a court hearing, and most likely it was meant to underline the seriousness of Mellon's request.

At two P.M., the courtroom was sparsely populated. Only those who had to be there were present and there were no members of the press.

Addressing Judge Rosen, Mellon reiterated his request that the court determine which parties outside the lawsuit would be free to discuss or disseminate the defendants' experts' findings. Conroy, who had only now been handed Mellon's motion, objected. He wanted to review it before responding, he said. The court set April 7th as a date to hear oral arguments on the proposed protective order. Mellon now objected, pressing the court to grant his "little bitty motion" without delay. Judge Rosen refused. The session had barely begun and the courtroom atmosphere was already tense.

Mellon told the court that Dr. Thomas was planning to amend his initial pleadings to include a cause of action involving defamation and/or conspiracy to interfere with his civil rights. He was also considering a cause of action for Ford's falsely reporting a crime, as well as ethical violations.

His client was a "minority" resident of Cape May Court House, Mellon said. Conroy, acting outside judicial procedure, had made public certain allegations against Dr. Thomas when he visited the local prosecutor the previous month, hoping that they would bring charges against him. Ford, Mellon said, was cloaking itself with judicial immunity while trying to intimidate his client. If Ford's position leaked, it would be devastating for Dr. Thomas. In fact, he declared, it was Ford's intention to destroy Dr. Thomas long before the case ever got to a jury.

Rosen patiently told the agitated attorney to relax while the court heard from Ford's attorneys.

Conroy was firm in his response. He was going to develop this case as he saw fit, he said bluntly. He would be asking many more questions, which he had a right to do. He didn't care how his actions were characterized or what names he was called—he was going to get his job done. He was going to investigate Dr. Thomas's charges against Ford and he would not allow a motion that tied his hands.

And so it went, back and forth, between the two attorneys. Time and again, Rosen had to ask Tom Mellon to lower his voice during his presentation. When he was finally able to make himself heard, Rosen pointed out that Dr. Thomas's allegations against Ford had been made public, as was his right, because it was in the public interest to know that a complaint had been lodged against a product. Moreover, he had made serious allegations against the defendants. Just as Dr. Thomas had a right to make his assertions, the defendants had a right to assert those defenses that had a legitimate basis. And the experts' reports that had been presented to the court served as such a basis. Furthermore, Rosen pointed out, if Mellon was correct about Ford's motives and the defendants' position turned out to have been false or without merit, there were legal remedies available to Dr. Thomas.

Rosen would place his own set of documents under seal, he said, because he had the power to do that. However, since he wasn't going to rule today on the motion for a protective order, he would not order anything else to be sealed.

Mellon was now extremely upset. His voice rising, he said that Cape May Court House "is a very small community. It's a very tight-knit community. Everybody knows everybody. This man is a minority in a very small community. If you don't seal these expert documents for those who are in and out of this courtroom . . . somebody is going to get them. . . ."

Judge Rosen interrupted to say he thought "the cat was [already] out of the bag."

"Well, we [too] think the cat's out of the bag," Mellon replied, "but we don't need that cat going to the news-papers. . . . And we don't want anybody further sued for defamation."

Rosen then pointed out to Mellon that there were First Amendment issues to be addressed and an entire body of jurisprudence to be reviewed. If this were a matrimonial issue or a child custody matter, he said, he would have a lot more authority with regard to sealing, but not in this case. "I'm sure other people who have this vehicle [the Explorer] would like to know [if there is a problem with] it," he added.

"Absolutely," Mellon agreed. "We don't want that sealed."

Rosen pointed out the lopsided logic of Mellon's wanting to air his client's position and at the same time suppress his opponent's defense. ". . . Their expert feels . . . there is no defect, that the air-bag system worked fine and . . . this was a homicide. It's not pleasant. It's not nice. But . . . you're going to have to address this, because there is essentially in federal courts . . . a presumption that this type of material cannot be sealed without showing good cause."

Conroy rose to say that Dr. Thomas had been presented to the public as a perfect plaintiff and now Ford had the right to present its own view of him. When he referred to Tom Mellon's initial "public relations campaign," his voice rose several notches above his usual conversational tone.

Again, Judge Rosen called for everyone to calm down.

Rosen then suggested that in time, a *jury* would decide this case.

Mellon immediately replied, "Are you suggesting that based

upon their defense of homicide, we just let a *jury*"—and here he mimicked Rosen's southern New Jersey accent—"decide and we do nothing for six months or a year?"

"Now, if you continue to mimic me, you will be sitting in jail," Rosen admonished.

"No, no, no, no, no. I'm sorry. I apologize," Mellon said, realizing he had gone too far.

"You know what, Mr. Mellon?" Rosen replied. "In thirteen years I've never had a lawyer get up and mimic me." The judge was working hard to control his own emotions.

In the next few minutes Mellon found himself apologizing to Rosen eleven times, saying repeatedly that he was completely sincere in his apologies and had great respect and fondness for the judge.

"I'm not sealing this record," Rosen said finally and decisively. "I don't believe I have the authority . . . let's move this case forward."*

With that, he turned to disputes about outstanding discovery. Mellon noted that he had just received another 32 boxes, maybe 150,000 pages, from the defendants—and all without an index. His team had been riffling through box after box trying since January to figure out what was contained in those 150,000 pages.

In response, the defendant's attorneys said that the discovery requests by the plaintiffs were so voluminous that it was

---

* Dr. Thomas's attorneys never formally refiled the motion to seal the expert reports and documents and no hearing was held on April 7th. Instead Thomas amended his lawsuit to file the defamation claim.

almost impossible to respond within the time the court had allotted.

Each side suspected the other of deliberately preventing proper discovery. Mellon, who in January had been eager to end Ford's discovery, now wanted more time himself. He said he needed until July 1st to supply the rest of his experts' reports and to take additional depositions of Ford's experts now that he knew their line of defense.

Rosen scheduled new dates for the remaining procedural matters through the end of 2000. Conroy would have another forty-five to sixty days after July 7th to depose anyone he wished, and the Roses' depositions would have to be taken during that initial period. By the end of the year, the court wanted in hand all the Daubert challenges, dispositive motions, and motions in limine.*

After almost three hours of nonstop argument, Mellon wanted another word: "I need to say again, because I want to do it, I have an absolute, one hundred percent, heartfelt, sincere apology—"

---

* In situations where a dispute issue generates expert testimony from numerous sources, the trial court has a right to evaluate the proposed expert testimony and eliminate that which falls short of the standards of reliability.

In this case, with "dispositive motions," the judge was referring to those that would affect the entire case—i.e., motions to dismiss or motions for summary judgment.

Through motions in limine, a party can request that the court prohibit opposing counsel from referring to or offering evidence on certain matters. The party usually does this because they believe reference to the matter would be highly prejudicial and could not be tempered through a judge's instructions to a jury.

"Oh, forget about it," Rosen muttered, trying to leave the bench.

"No, I've got to say it, though—apology."

"Don't worry about it. It's not a big deal."

"Well, it is to me," Mellon said.

"Counselor, none of us are perfect human beings . . ." Rosen replied, "and it's not a big deal. I just want to give you a date to come back." After the short meetings with the attorneys from both sides, he set May 3rd for the next status conference.

After losing the motion to seal Ford's incriminating reports, Mellon's first order of business was to try to rebuild his client's credibility. Since Ford was in effect charging Thomas with murder, Mellon decided to use a standard police investigative tool. It was a huge gamble, but Mellon felt he had no other choice. He would have Eric Thomas take a polygraph examination. In federal cases and in almost all the states, the results of polygraph tests are not admissible unless both sides agree to its evidentiary purpose. Polygraphs are not scientific and have not been recognized as a reliable tool. However, a favorable result would boost his client's position and help Mellon himself sleep better at night.

Within a week, the lawyer asked his client to take a "friendly polygraph." It would be protected by the attorney-client privilege, Mellon knew, and would only be for the benefit of Thomas and his attorneys. The polygrapher's knowledge would also be protected by the privilege. Eric Thomas readily agreed. He understood that if for some reason he failed the examination or it was inconclusive, no one in a position to use it against him would know. And if the results did become known, they would not be admissible in court.

If Thomas passed the test, Mellon planned to offer the Cape May County prosecutor the opportunity to review the results or administer a second test to his client.[*] Mellon was sure that when he passed that second test, the police would have no reason to doubt his client.

More important to Mellon, however, was the spin value of telling the media that Thomas had passed a polygraph. He could then go on the offensive: Look at what Ford is attempting to do to my client. He's passed. He's not lying. Ford is irresponsible. They're to blame for the death of this man's wife and now they're conducting a smear campaign. They're defaming an innocent man just to save themselves money.

A successful examination of Thomas might even force Ford to rethink its defense and bring everyone back to the settlement table. Mellon knew that Judge Rosen would be delighted by that.

On April 7th, Thomas sat before William L. Fleisher, a certified polygrapher for many years. Fleisher would administer a single-issue test, the type that was normally used when a subject was involved in someone's death. He knew that Thomas was suing Ford and alleging that the air bag in the car had killed his wife, and he knew Ford's defense was that Thomas had murdered her. It was not his job to judge the polygraph subject. His job was

---

[*] Innocent persons have often failed a polygraph test and guilty people have been known to pass the examination.

simply to determine whether Thomas responded with a truthful answer or not when he asked the most relevant question: Did you kill your wife?

The machine would use three sensors—one to Thomas's thorax, to measure any changes in respiration, inspiration, and expiration; a second for galvanic skin response, to measure the combination of sweat gland and brain activity; and a third, the cardiograph, to measure blood pressure, blood volume, and pulse changes. The variations in these measures would then be charted as questions relevant to the case and control questions were asked. After taking into account many variables, the truth or falsehood of Thomas's answers would be determined.

Thomas had been given a pretest interview in which he was asked his name and age, the type of discharge he had received from the service, if he had slept soundly the previous night, and how many hours he had slept. When asked if he was on medication, he said he was taking a muscle relaxant, Flexoral, as needed.

Thomas was then asked:

HOW DO YOU FEEL ABOUT BEING INTERVIEWED?
  Kind of frustrated and . . . because I know what happened and it's ridiculous for them to say that I was responsible for my wife's death.

DID YOU EVER THINK ABOUT DOING SOMETHING LIKE THIS?
  Killing my wife? No. No.

IN YOUR ENTIRE LIFE DID YOU EVER?
  Think about . . . hurting my spouse? No. Not even once. No.

DID YOU?
Cause Tracy's death? . . . No.

IN YOUR ENTIRE LIFE, DID YOU EVER?
Cheated . . . somebody. No.

WHY DO YOU THINK SOMEONE WOULD DO SOMETHING LIKE THIS?
I have no idea. I really don't. If things weren't right in the marriage, I don't know.

IN YOUR ENTIRE LIFE, DID YOU EVER TELL A LIE TO GET OUT OF TROUBLE?
No.

DID YOU LIE TO ME ABOUT WHETHER OR NOT YOU DID THIS?
No.

Just after three P.M., Fleisher asked Thomas to sit in the examiner's "motion chair," which was designed to determine if deliberate movements were being used by the subject as a countermeasure.

Once he was seated in the chair, Thomas was asked to close his eyes. Among the many questions asked of Thomas, two stood out.

DID YOU CAUSE TRACY'S DEATH?
No.

REGARDING TRACY'S DEATH, DID YOU CAUSE IT?
No.

Then Fleisher left the room. Passing Mellon and his investigator, David Warren, in the waiting room, he said, "I have to score the charts, but it looks like he passed it."

A score of +6 or higher is considered to be truthful; −13 is considered deceptive. When Thomas's charts were collated, his overall score was +16 on a scale of 21. There was no indication of deception.

Tom Mellon was pleased.

In the report he issued later, Fleisher stated: "Dr. Thomas can be eliminated as a suspect in the death of Tracy Rose Thomas."

NINE

The Bomb

On April 10th, Bill Conroy filed a motion to compel Thomas to respond to Ford's requests for supplemental interrogatories and documents.*

Conroy was frustrated by Tom Mellon. The second set of interrogatories for Thomas had been served on February 8th and were supposed to have been answered by March 9th. When they didn't arrive, Conroy wrote to Mellon. He wrote again on March 16th and again on March 17th. Conroy informed the court that Thomas's attorneys had not responded to his letters. Finally, on March 30th, Mellon advised Conroy that they had prepared responses, but it was Thomas's position that certain

---

* In civil cases, a formal request that the court direct some act be done in favor of the applicant.

documents Conroy had requested were privileged. Conroy told the court that when he asked Mellon to send him the answers and any documents that were not privileged, Mellon ignored the request; nor did Mellon provide a log of what he and Thomas considered privileged. Finally, Conroy filed his motion for Thomas to respond.

The next day, April 11th, Captain James McGowan of the Cape May County Prosecutor's Office, who was also a certified polygrapher, received a phone call from the acting Cape May prosecutor, David Blaker, to discuss a polygraph examination Dr. Eric Thomas had just taken.

Blaker told McGowan that Tom Mellon had asked if the police would be interested in reviewing the tapes and charts of Thomas's polygraph. McGowan responded that it was the policy of the department not to review somebody else's results; if Mellon wanted, the police could administer their own test to Thomas.

The next day, McGowan was called by Detective Webster. Webster said it was the medical examiner's opinion that the air bag had caused the death of Tracy Thomas, but if someone didn't know all the facts, it would be possible to conclude that manual strangulation or a blow to the neck—like a karate chop—was the cause. These factors should be taken into consideration if Thomas was to be given a polygraph examination.

McGowan called Mellon and they set a date of April 18, 2000, for Thomas's polygraph.

Two days later, on April 14th, Medical Examiner Gross sent a letter to Bill Conroy and Tom Mellon regarding the death of

Tracy Thomas. In it he wrote, "Each of you, on behalf of your respective clients, has asked me to review my findings in the above matter. Those findings are contained in the autopsy report which I finalized on April 8, 1997—and in the amended certificate of death filed on that same date."

Gross detailed the meetings he'd had with both attorneys and their respective experts earlier in the year and outlined the material he'd reviewed.

"I have the impression," Gross wrote, "that on the one hand, Mr. Conroy hopes that I will adjust my opinion, at a minimum, so as to exclude the possibility that the air bag contributed to this death, while, on the other hand, Mr. Mellon hopes that I will adjust my opinion, at a minimum, so as to conclude that the microscopic slide unequivocally demonstrates objective injury to the decedent's cervical cord.

"Several very capable medical, engineering and legal minds have taken a turn to figure out just how Mrs. Thomas died. But none of us was there when it happened. And so all that any one of us can do is apply his or her own best professional judgment to the known facts.

"In such a case, it is not the province of the Medical Examiner to reach conclusions about the precise mechanism of death that are not virtually compelled by the available evidence. Reaching for such conclusions is not the appropriate posture for a Medical Examiner in our public health system.

"It is my view that my certification of the cause and manner of death (as amended) in this case continues to be a responsible determination of the issues of importance to the public, based on reasonable medical probability. . . .

". . . The arguments that have recently been made to me do not provide me with a sufficient substantial basis to consider changing my findings or amplifying on my deposition testimony."

Once more, Gross stated that "blunt force trauma with asphyxia" was the cause of death.

When Eric Thomas arrived at the Middle Township Police investigative offices on April 18th for his second lie-detector test, he was suffering from allergies and taking Claritin. The medication would not interfere with the test results, he was told.

As in the earlier polygraph, Thomas was asked a number of pretest questions, some of which would be used as controls— where the answer was known to be a yes or a no—and others where the answer was not known. During the administration of the exam, the control questions would be interspersed at random with the relevant ones.

Thomas was asked "Are you a friend of Dominic Lanzar?" as a control question.

"No," he replied.

"Did you strangle your wife?" and "Did you strike your wife across the neck?" He said no to both questions.

"Have you now told the entire truth regarding your wife's death?"

This time, Thomas answered, "Yes."

Thomas left after the examination without waiting for the results. Shortly afterward, McGowan told Tom Mellon that his client had passed the test.

The attorney had reason to be pleased on several counts. First, this police-administered test could not be challenged as a "friendly polygraph," and Mellon also knew that the Cape May Prosecutor's Office would now have a hard time justifying reopening the investigation of the Thomas case. Moreover, the test results provided Mellon with another asset. Tom Hinchey, Bill Conroy's colleague, had told Judge Rosen that Ford was considering asking the court for permission to redepose Thomas. Lack of candor would form the basis for any additional depositions that were requested. Now Mellon had up his sleeve the perfect reason to object to any such request from Ford: two positive polygraph results.

A week later, Tom Mellon received a letter that sealed things.

OFFICE OF THE PROSECUTOR
COUNTY OF CAPE MAY

May 2, 2000

Thomas E. Mellon, Jr., Esquire
Mellon, Webster & Mellon
87 North Broad Street
Doylestown, PA 18901

RE: Fatal Accident Investigation
    Tracy Rose Thomas Inv. File No. 97–058

Dear Mr. Mellon:
    Enclosed please find a copy of the single page "Polygraph Examination Report" of Captain James McGowan dated April

18, 2000 which concludes that there was "no deception indicated" by your client's responses to the relevant questions. This
conclusion serves to corroborate our previous and continuing
determination that there exists no credible evidence of criminal culpability on the part of your client or any other known
individual(s) with respect to the tragic death of his wife, Tracy.

Consequently, our above-referenced investigation file
remains closed.

If you have any questions or concerns regarding this matter, please do not hesitate to contact me.

> Very truly yours,
>
> [signed]
> J. David Meyer
> Acting First Assistant Prosecutor

The letter was a treasure. Not only could Mellon use it in
court if need be, but it would also prove useful if Ford's defense
ever hit the newspapers.

The same day that the Cape May County prosecutor's letter
was sent to him, Tom Mellon responded to Ford's supplemental
interrogatories on behalf of Eric Thomas. To a number of them
he replied that the question "inquires into matters that are neither relevant nor likely to lead to the discovery of admissible
evidence. To the contrary, the sole purpose of this interrogatory
is to harass, intimidate, and inflict emotional distress upon the
plaintiff." He then proceeded to respond to those questions he
deemed relevant, with details provided by his client.

To the question about Thomas's relationship with his present wife, Stephanie, Mellon said that Dr. Thomas had dated Stephanie in high school and that their relationship afterward was as friends. Between the time of his marriage to Tracy and Tracy's death, Dr. Thomas occasionally spoke with Stephanie on the telephone, and Eric and Tracy Thomas would occasionally see Stephanie at church when they went to visit Dr. Thomas's parents in South Carolina. Dr. Thomas did not recall any specific dates.

Dr. Thomas did not recall the last time he spoke with Stephanie before Tracy's death, but he and Tracy did speak to Stephanie at church in South Carolina.

After Tracy's death, Dr. Thomas spoke to Stephanie when she and her mother called him to offer their condolences. At no time during Tracy's life did Dr. Thomas have an affair with Stephanie. The suggestion that there was an improper relationship between Eric and Stephanie is false.

Dr. Thomas began his romantic relationship with Stephanie in the summer of 1997 [six months after Tracy's death].

Dr. Thomas was unable to provide Ford with the specific dates of his travels.

Understandably, Conroy and Zeitz were not happy with these responses, which raised more questions than they answered, but they soon got the break they were looking for. While he was preparing for another case in Baltimore, Bill Conroy heard from his investigator that Stephanie Thomas's ex-husband, Sean Haley, had been located in Austin, Texas.

Conroy called Haley and explained that he was representing the Ford Motor Company in connection with a lawsuit that had been filed by Dr. Eric Thomas and that he wanted to speak to him about the breakup of his marriage. Haley, who was the acting director of the high school enrichment program at Huston-Tillotson College, said that he was reluctant to discuss the matter, but he would listen to the attorney's reasons for wanting the information.

Conroy knew from his investigator's report that Haley, thirty-three years old, had married Stephanie Arrington in May 1995 and that they were divorced in February 1998. Haley had an undergraduate degree from Morehouse College and a master's from the University of Texas, and Conroy assumed he was African American.

Conroy felt that Haley, perhaps without knowing it, had information that was valuable to Ford's defense. Thomas had just stated in writing that he became romantically involved with his present wife in August 1997, almost six months before Stephanie and Haley were divorced. And then there was the eager way Tom Mellon had responded to Judge Rosen's question about the state of the Thomases' marriage, saying how great it was.

Conroy pointed out to Haley that he was not obligated to talk, given spousal-immunity laws. He was just interested in the time line of their relationship and was curious to know if he'd ever heard of Dr. Thomas before he and Stephanie divorced. Haley said he'd think about it.

A few days later, he called Conroy back. Though it was painful for him to talk about it, it was true that Stephanie had had an affair with Thomas and he had spoken to Thomas about it, Haley said. He added that Stephanie had admitted to him that the affair had begun before the death of Thomas's wife.

Conroy told Haley he'd be in Austin the following month. They agreed to meet in late June.

Meanwhile, in Baltimore, Conroy had another Ford case to try. This one involved an unrestrained female passenger, eight months pregnant, who had been ejected from an Aerostar van, which then landed on top of her. Afterward, her husband had held her hand and prayed as passersby tried to lift the van from her. She and her baby died an hour later. Conroy knew that the defense would be difficult, since the jury would be impressed by such images.

A truck had broadsided the minivan. Ford argued that the Aerostar was not prone to rollover and that the truck driver was responsible for the accident. The plaintiffs had filed one lawsuit against Ford and another against the driver, who was from out of state and whom the plaintiffs were unable to serve or find. The case therefore focused on Ford. Conroy, knowing how money could change the lives of survivors, had offered a settlement of over a million dollars, but it was rejected. He had no choice but to go to trial.

While Conroy was in Baltimore on the Aerostar case, Judge Rosen held a status conference between the parties to the Thomas case. On May 19th, James Pickering joined Tom Mellon and Elliott Kolodny for Eric Thomas, who was again present. Thomas Hinchey appeared for Ford.

Once again, just before the hearing, the plaintiffs faxed a motion to the court. Thomas wanted to amend his complaint against Ford. Hinchey received his copy of the motion and its contents for the first time as he entered the courtroom.

As the session began, Judge Rosen read aloud the cover letter that accompanied the documents he and the defendants had just received.

The letter and the motion noted that Thomas was seeking to add several causes of action—including intimidation, intentional infliction of emotional distress, trying to instigate a criminal investigation, defamation, and punitive damages. The correspondence also noted that Thomas had passed two polygraph examinations, showing that he was not involved in the death of Tracy Thomas. Furthermore, Dr. Gross had issued a supplemental report, dated April 14th, confirming his original findings, and the Cape May County Prosecutor's Office had written, on May 2nd, that "there exists no credible evidence and criminal culpability on the part of your client [Thomas]. . . . Consequently, our above-referenced investigation file remains closed."

"Boy, I would love to settle this case," Rosen remarked, then said that he would deal with the motion in due course. Meanwhile, the judge informed the parties that presiding judge Stephen Orlofsky wanted the case ready for trial without delay.

The same old issues were then raised: Ford hadn't produced an index for the discovery material the plaintiffs had just received. Sidestepping the charge, Hinchey told the court the plaintiffs hadn't informed Ford which of Ford's experts they wanted to depose, nor had anyone from Mellon's office visited Ford's reading room, where most of the discovery was available.

Kolodny responded that they had been kept busy dealing

with the foul-play allegations Ford was making outside of the litigation process; because of those, his office hadn't been able to furnish Ford with their final experts' reports. The May 31st deadline was just around the corner, but they needed more time.

"No," Rosen told him. "You're done with discovery as of today. Let me tell you, this system is broken. It's going too slow and it's costing too much. You are all going to be working—and I'm not kidding you—you're going to be working day and night on this thing. . . . You owe that to your clients, everybody, the plaintiffs, and the defendants."

Kolodny noted how much work his team needed to do—digest the thirty-five boxes of documents in the discovery material before they could take depositions from Ford's in-house personnel. This was impossible to do without an index.

"You know," Rosen replied, "there are some courts that take three, four, five, six, seven, eight years to get a case ready. This is not one of them."

". . . That is not what I'm used to," Kolodny said. "I am not used to a defendant who produces thirty-five boxes of documents without an index."

Hinchey then admitted that the discovery material provided to the plaintiffs had no index. Rosen gave Ford until close of business on the following Tuesday, May 23rd, to provide the index.

Kolodny added that he would then need months to review all the discovery because of the "highly technical" nature of the case, and they might find that additional material was needed. He told the court that he hadn't taken even one deposition in over a year because the plaintiffs didn't want to go on a fishing expedition.

Hearing the argument on both sides, Rosen agreed to extend "fact discovery" until the end of August and final expert reports until October 13th. "Let's get this show on the road," he said again.

Rosen then moved on to the only other outstanding issue—the motion to add defamation to the complaint. "So you definitely do not want to consider filing this as a separate action?" he asked.

"And have two separate juries determine whether or not Ford's allegation that my client is a murderer—[have] my client go through that twice and allow Ford to present this defense—" Kolodny sputtered in outrage.

"Do me a favor," Rosen replied. "Save the drama for when the movie is made, not in here. Okay?"

"I understand, Your Honor. I apologize, Your Honor."

Judge Rosen then asked what the statements and letters attached to the motion were all about. The defendants were seeing the polygraph test results and the prosecutor's letter for the first time, Hinchey said, and had no previous knowledge of their existence.

"If the county prosecutor and the medical examiner have closed this out, where are you going with this thing?" Rosen asked him.

"Your Honor, that was my point," Hinchey responded. "We are hearing about it for the first time now . . . at twelve to five."

"I'm not asking for a definitive conclusion," Rosen asked, "but I want to know what this case is about. I really would like to know. . . . And I want it over with. And I know, for the record, [Thomas is] agreeing with me by the shake of his head. And I understand that. That's what my concern is. It's not just that I sit up here and like to make people's lives miserable. If I wanted to do that, I could be a dentist and drill holes—"

The laughter that exploded in the courtroom reflected the tension among the participants.

"But there's a reason for it," Rosen continued. "And the reason is that people deserve their day in court. And, darn it, I'm going to make it happen. I wish I could help you settle this. But it doesn't seem to be in the cards."

Ford would have until June 20th to file its response to Thomas's motion to amend his complaint. On July 18th, Judge Rosen would hear oral arguments before ruling on the matter.

Conroy and Zeitz knew that the polygraph results meant trouble if the case went to trial. At some point before jury selection or after the jury was impaneled or even during the trial, somebody associated with the plaintiff's case would surely make the jury aware that Thomas had passed two tests. It wouldn't matter how many instructions the judge gave to the jurors to disregard what they had heard. You can't unring a bell, Zeitz told Conroy.

Zeitz also knew that the polygraphs would insulate Tom Mellon from the perception that he was presenting a fraudulent claim to the court, even if Ford could show that Thomas lied.

The immediate problem for Conroy was that whenever he tried to impeach Thomas's credibility with Rosen, Tom Mellon would say that his client had passed two lie detector tests even if the results were inadmissible at trial.

But Zeitz was sanguine. Many of his clients had passed polygraph tests, he said, and told Conroy not to worry: Whatever water we're taking in our boat now, we'll bail out later.

Conroy knew that he had to deal with the reality of this setback and at the same time move forward with the science and continue to look for Thomas's misrepresentations. If they stayed the course and went after Thomas's credibility, the chances were that the case would never come to trial.

Conroy then turned his full attention to the Aerostar case in Baltimore, and saw there the kind of success that sometimes made his job heartbreaking: the jury found in favor of Ford, and the plaintiffs—who had rejected a settlement offer of over a million dollars—were awarded nothing.

On June 20th, Bill Conroy filed Ford's response to Thomas's motion to amend his complaint. At the same time, knowing that he would soon take Sean Haley's statement, he withdrew his motion to redepose Thomas, reserving the right to file it at a later date. Now that the discovery cutoff date had been moved to the end of August, there was time.

"Ford intends to renotice these depositions after its discovery and investigation [are] complete," Conroy told the court, "and the issues of the redeposition of Dr. Thomas and deposition of Stephanie Thomas are ripe for consideration by the Court."

Conroy wanted Haley's sworn statement in hand first, because if Thomas lied about his relationship with Stephanie, his misrepresentations would give the court additional reasons to grant his request to redepose Thomas.

To prepare for Thomas's defamation claim, Conroy consulted with Jonas Saunders, Ford's in-house general counsel. Saunders wanted to retain a First Amendment specialist and Ford's first choice was Floyd Abrams, he said.

Abrams, who ran his practice from New York City, was legendary. He had argued more cases before the Supreme Court of the United States involving freedom of the press than any other lawyer in American history. He represented the *New York Times* in the Pentagon Papers case, *Time* magazine in libel cases brought by Scientologists, and CBS in defense of a copyright suit brought by the descendants of Dr. Martin Luther King Jr., and at CNN's request, he had headed the investigation into the network's controversial story that nerve gas was used on American defectors in 1970.

When Floyd Abrams agreed to represent Ford, the stage was set for oral arguments on what could be the most important motion of the Thomas case. If the court allowed Thomas's new claims, Ford would not only become the defendant once more, but the case would be on a fast track to trial. The issue of whether the air bag killed Tracy Thomas would now sit side by side with Thomas's allegations that Ford had resorted to reprehensible tactics designed to hide the cause of her death.

★ ★ ★

On June 23rd, Bill Conroy, with the usual group of attorneys, was back in court for another status conference. Judge Rosen wanted to make sure that there were no problems with discovery or anything else that would prevent the case from moving forward.

Elliott Kolodny reported that progress had been made in discovery but said that there were new troubles ahead. In the winter of 1999, Ford had introduced dual-stage air bags.* Since Thomas's lawsuit claimed that his SUV lacked certain safety features, Kolodny wanted to know if this technology had been available at the time the plaintiff's vehicle was manufactured. If it had, Kolodny knew that that fact alone would indicate that Ford knew its air bags were causing unwarranted injuries.

Ford's answer, which finally arrived on June 12th with a caveat, lacked the proper verifications: ". . . that the matters stated therein [were] not within the personal knowledge of the deponent, the person making the verification." Kolodny needed to depose the proper people during the first two weeks of August but he didn't know who they were, he said. He wanted to know if Ford was slowing down the train on purpose.

Judge Rosen ordered Ford to supply the names of the people with direct knowledge.

---

* An air bag that deployed at different speeds, depending on the force of a car's impact and the position and weight of the person sitting in the car's seat.

Next, Kolodny said that he planned to be in Dearborn, Michigan, the following week and wanted Ford to produce for him the original negatives and/or photographs, not Xerox copies, from *every* crash test report he reviewed. Hinchey told the court that the Ford reading room did not have original photographs, only Xerox copies. There were perhaps thousands of photographs at issue. Only after Kolodny made his selection from the copies could Ford obtain the originals and make photographic prints for him.

Kolodny was now agitated. "You know, you have an odd way of practicing law by ranting and raving," the judge told Kolodny.

"It's not ranting and raving, Judge, it's frustration. It's absolute unequivocal frustration about the way we've . . . been treated by defense counsel."

"And I don't like it," Rosen interjected.

Hinchey then said that Ford didn't have originals; they had only negatives. If Kolodny wanted original prints, he'd have to pay for them.

When Judge Rosen asked where the negatives were, Hinchey said he didn't know. Neither he nor Conroy had ever reviewed the photographs at Dearborn.

It was clear that both sides were playing with words in order to advance their position or to stall the discovery process.

The court ordered Ford to supply the location of every original negative by the close of business the following Monday.

Next, Tom Mellon complained that the plaintiffs were still

missing indexes for some thirty-five boxes of material, amounting to over 100,000 pages. He said that he was entitled to identification of all those pieces of paper.

Hinchey reminded the court that he had said they had not compiled an index.

"But [can you say], for example, that box fourteen is responsive to interrogatories six, nine, and twenty-two?" Rosen asked him.

"No, sir," Hinchey replied. "I spoke to Ford, and they said we can give you an index of Bates numbers.* That's all it's going to be is Bates numbers."

"You can't respond to document requests and interrogatories by saying, 'Here's eighteen boxes,'" Rosen told Hinchey, who finally agreed that by the following Friday they would go through all the boxes and identify what was in each box and what it pertained to. After saying that that would be satisfactory, the judge brought up correspondence from both sides relating to the polygraphs Thomas had taken.

Upon hearing about the polygraphs, on June 1st, Conroy had filed a third set of interrogatories on Thomas, as well as a formal request for the plaintiffs to produce all documents related to the polygraphs. Mellon had replied that he would turn them over only if Ford agreed to stipulate to their

---

* An organizing system used in discovery in which each piece of paper or each article is given a number before it is turned over to opposing counsel. The number can be used when referencing a document during court proceedings.

admissibility, since it was unclear whether or not they would be admissible.

Judge Rosen seemed to take the defendant's side on this.

". . . I'm just not aware of a rule of law or an evidence rule that says discovery is limited to what's admissible," Rosen told Kolodny. "Believe me, in a way I wish there was such a rule, because ninety percent of what you guys get in depositions and interrogatories and documents will never see the light of day at trial."

He continued to argue, but in the end, Kolodny agreed to provide Ford with the information about the polygraph.

Conroy was pleased. He would now have the material he needed to depose the polygraph examiners. If Thomas had lied about any known facts during the course of the test, then the value of the polygraphs would be nil.

". . . I don't want them disclosed to anyone other than you and your experts," Rosen told Ford's attorneys. "In other words, to no third parties. Obviously, you need to show them to an expert, that's fine. [But] I don't want them disseminated," he added, addressing all the parties to the lawsuit.

Conroy pointed out that the polygraph results and the letter from the prosecutor's office were attached to the papers previously filed with the court and were never placed under seal—the cat might already be out of the bag.

The court asked the parties to do their best to "sit tight on them. You can use them, but I don't want them disseminated to any non-third parties, that's all."

Despite the evident hostility in his courtroom, Rosen was still looking for a settlement. "Is it worth anyone's time to try to have another settlement conference on this, or is everyone still dug in?" he asked. "And I really have to look to Ford on this."

"Dug in, Your Honor," Bill Conroy replied.

"Dug in?" Rosen repeated.

"Yes, sir," Conroy confirmed.

When the hearing was over, Conroy asked to meet with Judge Rosen and Tom Mellon in chambers.

Even in cases where Conroy felt his defense was one hundred percent correct, he would normally offer a settlement in order to avoid the cost of a trial. Here, however, since Ford was not prepared to offer a cent, Conroy felt some explanation was due Rosen, if only to convince the judge that there was no hope of a settlement. Mellon said he couldn't understand why Ford had taken this unusual position. His client hadn't done anything to cause the accident—Dr. Thomas wasn't the man he was being made out to be. Conroy didn't respond. He did, however, ask Rosen to get the case to trial and not waste the court's time trying to get the case settled.

Glenn Zeitz was eager to hear what Sean Haley had to say. Their plan was not to depose him but to take his sworn statement, so that the plaintiffs wouldn't have to be notified. The statement could be used later in support of a motion, but it wouldn't be admissible at trial. If Haley's information was valuable, however, then a deposition, where both sides would be present, would be needed, and that could be used at trial.

Before Conroy left for Austin to take Haley's statement, Zeitz reminded him to read the divorce documents to see what the financial settlement had been. Had Stephanie been willing to sacrifice a lot to get out? Or were there financial incentives for her to leave Sean Haley and marry Eric Thomas?

As he walked into the offices of an Austin law firm that he'd retained as a place to take Haley's statement, Conroy was introduced to a good-looking, well-dressed, soft-spoken young man. To Conroy he looked like the baseball player Darryl Strawberry. For this meeting, Haley had brought along his brother, Anthony, a local attorney.

After shaking hands and exchanging pleasantries, they got down to business. "Did there come a . . . time before Stephanie filed for divorce that she informed you that she was seeing someone else?" Conroy asked.

"Yes," Haley replied curtly.

"When, [did] Stephanie [first] indicate to you that she had been seeing someone else?"

". . . It was approximately in the month of February of '97."

Stephanie Haley had lost no time after Tracy Thomas's death to abandon her own marriage.

"And in response to her saying that, what—if anything—did you do?" Conroy prodded.

"Initially [I] asked how long this had been going on . . . she [said] a short while and I then looked for some old telephone bills. . . . I had started with February [1997], and I actually worked back past . . . beyond October [1996]," Haley told the attorney.

"And when you looked at these phone records, what did you find?" Conroy asked.

"Consistent calls on a daily basis. . . ."

Conroy then wanted to know if Haley had found anything besides the record of phone calls.

He'd found a business card, he said, and it listed the same numbers he'd found on the old phone bills. The card was in the name of Eric Thomas.

After that discovery, Haley sat down with his wife for a serious talk. Stephanie talked about some of her business trips before February 1997, and acknowledged that she and Eric had met on several occasions in various locations throughout the country. She mentioned Boston and some other cities.

Just before their second anniversary, in May 1997, Stephanie asked Haley for a divorce. That was when he called Thomas to confront him. He first asked Thomas not to call his home anymore and then asked that he step aside and give him and Stephanie a chance to work things out in their marriage. Thomas agreed to stop calling the house, but he said it was up to Stephanie to decide between Sean Haley and himself.

By then, of course, there was no turning back. Tracy Thomas had been dead for a few months, and Stephanie was ready to take her place.

Conroy probed a bit more. ". . . Do you recall Stephanie saying anything to you about the accident?" he asked Haley.

". . . I recall [that she] mentioned . . . a phone call . . . as we were both in bed—and she began to cry. And I asked her what was happening, what was wrong, and she mentioned that a friend of hers had been in an accident. And she was . . . distraught by it . . . crying."

"Did you later . . . learn who this friend was?"

"Yeah. I later asked her again—once I had found out that

she was involved in an extramarital affair . . . —if Eric Thomas was . . . in the accident, and she acknowledged that [he was] one of the individuals."

Conroy decided not to pry anymore. The young man was obviously in pain. Haley gave Conroy the name of a friend of Stephanie's, Carlisha Brown-Robinson, who was upset about her leaving Sean for Eric.

Conroy was not sure that he needed Robinson's statement; the phone records Haley had mentioned would probably be enough. Anthony Haley promised to send copies of his brother's relevant phone records to the attorney.

Conroy knew he could now challenge Thomas's credibility. Thomas had stated under oath that he hadn't had any outside sexual relationship while he was married to Tracy. If Haley was telling the truth, then Thomas had lied under oath. That meant Ford could now attack his credibility not only on this issue but on others: Tracy's fall in the driveway, the drive to the hospital, the deer in the road. Conroy knew that if he could prove Thomas had lied about one matter, everything else he said could be questioned, particularly by the jury.

Similarly, Conroy could destroy Thomas's claims of loss of consortium, emotional distress, and mental anguish. How could the loss of Tracy be distressing when Thomas was having an affair with Stephanie? Why would he sue Ford for mental anguish?

Conroy had been convinced from the start of the civil action that Thomas's performance as a grieving widower and single parent was a sham. And now, with Sean Haley's testimony, he could convince a jury.

That afternoon, upon returning to his office, Conroy wrote Mellon and Kolodny that he now planned to call Sean Haley as a witness. He suggested that Haley's deposition be taken in the near future but did not reveal that he had taken Haley's statement or what he knew.

Sean Haley had given the Ford team a lot to work with. Now they had to track Stephanie's business trips and see if they matched the times and locations of Thomas's trips in the months before and after his wife's death. Doris Rose's date book and calendar might come in handy, since she had often stayed in New Jersey with her granddaughter while her son-in-law was away.

Ford now had good reason to pursue Thomas's travel and credit card records, telephone bills, and checks.

It was also clear that Conroy now had to redepose Eric Thomas, and also depose Stephanie Thomas. Conroy's motion to redepose Thomas would say that he had lied in his interrogatories about his neck injury, about the proceeds of Tracy's life insurance, about his wife's fall before she got into the SUV the night of the accident, and about the history of his relationship with his present wife, Stephanie.

Conroy was sure Tom Mellon would oppose the motion. When he did, Conroy would file a brief in reply and attach Sean Haley's statement.

Glenn Zeitz saw that the pieces were now falling into place. Taken separately, none of them was enough to damage Thomas's case. The fact that he'd increased the amount of Tracy's life insurance just before the accident didn't mean anything by itself. That he'd had an extramarital affair with the woman who was now his wife was also not important in itself. Thomas's false claims about his neck injury may reveal a bit of greed yet didn't point to homicide. But all these facts combined with the expert testimony that Tracy Thomas had died not from an air bag but from manual strangulation— Zeitz felt they had something like a nuclear bomb. Sooner or later, it was going to make headlines.

TEN

Additional Charges

Early in the morning of July 5th, as Doris Rose was preparing to leave for New Jersey to pick up Alix for one of their scheduled visits, the phone rang. It was Eric.

Lately he'd been calling her "Mamma D." again, as he did when Tracy was alive. Today, his voice was like a little boy's.

"Mamma D.," Eric said. "Can you find it in your heart to forgive me?"

He sounded so strange that Doris wasn't sure it was Eric. "Who is this?" she asked.

"Eric," he replied, and then repeated, "Can you find it in your heart to forgive me?"

"How far back do you want to go?" Doris asked her former son-in-law. "Forgive you for what?"

Eric repeated his question several times, and each time, Doris said, "Tell me what you want me to forgive you for and we'll see."

Eric didn't answer.

Finally, Doris said good-bye and hung up. That was the moment when she remembered how Tracy had loved to dress Alix in floral dresses that matched her own.

That same week, Bill Conroy wrote to Elliott Kolodny saying he wanted to take a videotape deposition of Stephanie Thomas. In addition, he asked to schedule a redeposition of Eric Thomas. With Sean Haley's statement in hand, Conroy decided to contact Stephanie's old friend Carlisha Brown-Robinson, whose phone number he'd just received from Anthony Haley.

She confirmed what Haley had told Conroy and agreed to a deposition. Now Conroy was ready to put Eric Thomas's truthfulness to the test. In his letter, he asked Kolodny to respond by close of business on Friday, July 7th, so that the appropriate arrangements could be made. Kolodny did not reply.

Meanwhile, the two sides continued to wage a fierce battle over discovery, flooding Judge Rosen with motions to compel this or that. Conroy demanded that Mellon respond to his third set of interrogatories, and Mellon complained that he still had no firm idea which Ford people had personal knowledge of air-bag tests, so he couldn't request the proper depositions. With another discovery cutoff date imminent, Judge Rosen ordered both sides to act responsibly.

Amid this back-and-forth wrangling, another important date loomed—July 18th, the day Rosen had set for oral arguments on Thomas's defamation complaint. Bill Conroy met Floyd Abrams for the first time that day. They'd been talking for a month, but only by phone.

For fifteen months the media had ignored the Thomas case. There was brief coverage at the time of the accident in local papers and again when the lawsuit was filed. But on the morning of July 18th, Renee Winkler, from the New Jersey Courier Post, showed up. She routinely scanned court dockets as a good source of potential stories and had noticed that Floyd Abrams was approved by the court to appear on behalf of Ford. Abrams's presence in the New Jersey courtroom intrigued her.

Elliott Kolodny and James Pickering appeared for the plaintiffs, while Bill Conroy and Abrams appeared for the defendants. Mellon was not in court; he was involved in jury selection in another case.

Judge Rosen had read all the briefs, affidavits, and papers relating to the amended complaint and now wanted to hear oral presentations.

The issue was fairly straightforward. Thomas, in addition to suing Ford for causing Tracy's death, now claimed that the company had defamed him and intentionally caused him emotional distress by telling the Cape May Court House prosecutor that he had murdered his wife. The claim was simple, but the legal complications were not. At issue were complex rules regarding what lawyers may or may not do in the process of defending their clients. Much of the upcoming debate would be about what lawyers call privilege.*

Conroy had gambled by going to the prosecutor in February with new information. Ford had approved his actions and he himself had looked into the law and thought he was covered by privilege, but he'd known at the time that if Thomas objected to his actions, it would be up to a court to decide if he'd acted within the law. Now it was time to face Judge Rosen and let him decide.

Elliott Kolodny began by stating that when Conroy and Ford's engineers met with both Dr. Gross and the Cape May County prosecutors on February 16th, Ford lacked a good-faith basis for alleging that Thomas had murdered his wife. Ford's intent in accusing the doctor of murder, Kolodny said, was to deter him from proceeding with his lawsuit and to cause him undue emotional distress.

Ford's actions were not protected by privilege, Kolodny continued, and cited a previous case to illustrate that Ford had only a qualified privilege with respect to reporting potential crimes to authorities.

Rosen asked Kolodny what specific acts of Ford's were defamatory to Dr. Thomas.

---

* An attorney is usually afforded an opportunity to pursue a legal strategy free of the possibility of being held liable for a tort such as slander or defamation. This is referred to as an "absolute privilege." In cases where courts have placed limits on what an attorney can do or say in pursuing a legal strategy, it is referred to as a "qualified privilege." Where an attorney holds only a qualified privilege, he may be disciplined by the bar association or even in some cases sued for actions taken in pursuing a particular legal strategy.

All of them, the attorney replied.

"The fact that they presented a dog-and-pony show to prosecutors, to the police department, to the medical examiner alleging that Dr. Thomas murdered his wife are defamatory acts in our view," Kolodny said. "Unfortunately, because we haven't had any discovery here, I have only been able to allege the bare minimum. . . ."

"I understand," Judge Rosen replied, "but I want to know, since you are talking about a privilege, what is it precisely that you feel violated the privilege."

Kolodny said that prior to the February 16th meetings, Ford had already deposed the medical examiner and the police officers. These additional meetings weren't necessary for Ford to prepare its defense.

Then Rosen asked: For the sake of argument, if Ford said it had evidence that Dr. Thomas had murdered his wife, "why would that not be covered [by] the litigation privilege?"

Kolodny didn't answer. Instead, he told the court that Ford hadn't met even the threshold of privilege, because its allegations were neither reasonable nor necessary. Besides, he added, "the litigation privilege was completely inconsistent with the Ku Klux Klan Act," which should also apply to Ford's actions in this matter. The KKK Act, Kolodny pointed out, referred to intimidation.

The Civil Rights Act of 1985 also deals with the issue of conspiracy, so, Judge Rosen asked Kolodny, who, according to the plaintiff, were the conspirators here?

". . . Ford's employees, Ford's attorneys, Ford's experts. . . ." Kolodny replied.

"Are you claiming that this is racial?" Rosen asked bluntly.

"No, no, I'm not claiming that Ford's conduct is racially motivated," Kolodny said. "I am not saying that Ford has done this to Dr. Thomas because Dr. Thomas is a black man living in a predominantly white community. But I have argued in my brief that on the damages side the Court does have to take into account . . . the unfortunate factual situation in our society that when a black man is accused of murder, it is significantly and qualitatively different than [if] a white man is accused of murder."

Rosen wanted to make sure he understood Kolodny's claim. ". . . Like it or not, the adversarial system can be—and this is an understatement, especially if you are a witness or a party—can be unpleasant at times. . . . There are tort cases I see all the time where someone, a plaintiff, claims injuries and the defendant comes back in a counterclaim and says this is a fraud, this is phony, you are not injured. Would this rise, to your view, to the level of a civil rights violation?"

Kolodny skirted this question too and at the same time broadened his position. "If the allegation is, . . . Your Honor, [an attempt] to intimidate someone into dropping the lawsuit, it is actionable. . . . It is not typical for a multibillion-dollar corporation to accuse a man of murder after a thorough investigation by a federal agency [NHTSA], charged with investigating this specific type of accident, [who also] said it's not murder, it's the air bag. We have a medical examiner in this case who isn't your normal medical examiner . . . a ten-year veteran, the [former] chief of New York's medical examiner's office. . . ." Not wanting to be pinned down, the attorney instead tried to make the judge see how unfairly his client was being treated.

The judge repeated his question. ". . . Putting aside the defamation now. I'm talking about the federal civil rights statute. You believe that's actionable . . . because it's aimed at intimidating a party in a lawsuit?"

Kolodny repeated. ". . . Let's assume . . . that the Ku Klux Klan went into Dr. Thomas's office and destroyed it, and Dr. Thomas sued . . . for damages, and . . . the Ku Klux Klan threatens Dr. Thomas: If you don't drop your suit, we're going to do something . . . Is that actionable under 42 U.S. C 1985? You betcha. You betcha. Is what Ford did here identical? . . . I can't answer that question at this stage of the game. With due deference to Mr. Conroy, I am not prepared, and I am not, so the record is clear, accusing him of targeting Dr. Thomas because he is black. The effect, however, . . . of Mr. Conroy's actions is much more significant because . . . in our society a black man accused of murder in a predominantly white community has a heck of a lot more to be nervous about, and those baseless allegations are that much more intimidating."

Rosen replied that cases under the Ku Klux Klan Act were those in which attempts were made to intimidate a witness from going to court or testifying. Usually they involved threats like "You are a dead man—that kind of stuff." How had Thomas been "intimidated" by Ford, Rosen wanted to know.

Kolodny replied that if Ford's actions forced Dr. Thomas's attorneys to spend large amounts of money addressing the carmaker's charges, then that in itself was an injury and could force Dr. Thomas to withdraw his claims.

"The mechanism of intimidation engaged in by Ford," Kolodny said, "was defamation and intentional infliction of emotional distress. They didn't say, 'Hey, we're going to lynch you, Dr. Thomas, unless you drop this case.' They said, 'We're going to make these allegations of murder.' Now, what does that do to somebody in Dr. Thomas's case? It makes you think really, really hard . . . [it] causes you sleepless nights." With that, he finished his presentation.

Rosen noted that any allegation can be offensive and hurtful, but wasn't that the nature of the adversarial system? It was important to remember that Dr. Thomas's charges against Ford were also offensive and hurtful.

Floyd Abrams then rose to address the issues of conspiracy and intimidation implicit in the 1985 Ku Klux Klan Act. Kolodny's view of that statute, Abrams said, "is one which would federalize virtually every unpleasant act or charge that is made in our . . . sometimes very painful courtroom proceedings."

The Ku Klux Klan Act of 1985 stated that both conspiracy and intimidation had to be present, Abrams continued, and neither of those had been involved in Ford's actions toward Dr. Thomas. Furthermore, it had never been held that to say something which causes a witness or a party to a suit emotional pain is intimidation.

Rosen then clarified Kolodny's position. ". . . He's not just saying things in the lawsuit are causing pain," he told Abrams. "It's going to the prosecutor to initiate a criminal complaint [with the intention of frightening him]."

Abrams replied: "Suppose Ford in this case—putting aside the allegations made by the plaintiff—had said that the plaintiff was for some reason responsible, not for murder or anything like that, but responsible for his wife's death because he mistreated her in the car, because of malpractice." What if, he said, Ford had said Dr. Thomas himself had really been driving, that the accident was his fault, and these allegations were untrue? Abrams asked whether this fell under the Ku Klux Klan Act. "Yet such charges might deter someone from suing or lead someone to ask, 'Who needs this lawsuit if I'm going to be accused of that?' That's part of our legal system. Lawyers say things, lawyers make charges; and when they're wrong, they pay for it."

Abrams then elaborated the remedies available to any litigant who felt unjustly accused. "If anything Ford had done or [said] in this case of the [kind] alleged here . . . is found by the jury to be totally untrue, [and] unwarranted, with [no] basis at all, the jury will . . . treat Ford [accordingly]. There is a weapon, there are sanctions . . . available, but the sanction is not another lawsuit. The sanction is not another claim under a federal statute, [one] which has to be read narrowly."

Turning to the question of the legal privilege involved in Conroy's visit to the district attorney and the medical examiner, Abrams claimed that Conroy's was absolute—not qualified. "[In] case after case," he said, ". . . the good goes with the bad. . . . All sorts of things are swept into the realm of what is protected, including things we think are worth protecting and things we think are not worth protecting."

Abrams noted that Judge Orlofsky, who would ultimately hear this case, had said in another case "it is because we want lawyers to be free and litigants to be free to assert their theories, half of which in most courts and maybe more than half will be wrong, that we provide a very broad level of legal protection."

"And an absolute privilege means we do not consider motive," Abrams explained, and added, "You asked Mr. Kolodny a number of . . . hypothetical questions, and he responded by [referring to] particular facts that you were presenting to him. [But] the facts can't matter. The answers can't be different. As a matter of law, an absolute privilege protects absolutely."*

Privilege "extends to all statements and communications that have anything to do with the pending legal case," Abrams said. He agreed that obviously "Ford would benefit if a criminal prosecution arose in the same case about the same issues, about the very core issue in the case," and supported Ford's defense.

But what was really going on here, Abrams claimed, was "an effort to prevent lawyers from doing their jobs, to prevent full and complete activity by counsel, which is protected by the absolute privilege."

Rosen nodded, acknowledging Abrams's point, but said that Dr. Thomas was claiming that Ford had exceeded its own investigation. It had taken a further step, encouraging law enforcement authorities to affirmatively charge him criminally, and "that goes beyond the original intent of the privilege." The judge asked Abrams to respond to that issue.

---

* Whatever is to be ascertained or decided by the application of statutory rules or the principles and determinations of the law, as distinguished from the investigation of particular facts.

The law offered other avenues for dealing with misconduct, Abrams replied. Bar associations and juries that gave punitive damage awards were alternatives to "opening up the privilege."

"The bar," he said, "must be free to act as vigilant, zealous defenders of their clients."

Posen then asked, "What was the purpose of going to the prosecutor or the medical examiner?"

On that matter, Abrams deferred to Bill Conroy, who had not yet spoken.

"The medical examiner, Elliot Gross," Conroy said, "wanted certain information that dealt with the mechanics of how air bags operated." Conroy was referring to a request made to him in a letter from Kyran Connor, county counsel at the time to the medical examiner.

Conroy stated that the purpose of the meeting he had later that day with the prosecutor was to tell him what he'd learned through depositions in this case—that the medical examiner had said he had given Webster evidence which the detective in his deposition said was never communicated to him.[*] This information, Conroy said, seemed serious and he felt he had to alert the prosecutor's office.

"I had [also] consulted with experts," Conroy said, "who gave me their view of what had happened." He could not withhold the information, he said. If he didn't go to the prosecutor with the information, he told the judge, then he'd be accused at trial, "'If you thought this was so important, why

---

[*] Referring to the "petechial hemorrhaging" in Tracy's eyes.

didn't you go to the prosecutor with it?' I felt I had an obligation to do it."

Kolodny then told the court he believed that Ford would never present this defense to a jury, in which case there would be no opportunity to ask the jury for punitive damages.

As he sat in Judge Rosen's courtroom, Bill Conroy believed he'd done the right thing by going to the Cape May prosecutor. By now, it was almost as if Tracy Thomas had become his client. He had evidence of a crime and his duty, as an officer of the court, was to inform the D.A.

Having listened to both sides, Judge Rosen told the attorneys that they would hear from him soon.

Renee Winkler filed her story that same day. It broke in the local *Courier Post* the next morning, and other Eastern papers picked it up.

FATAL CRASH OR MURDER?
N.J. DENTIST, FORD DIFFER

When a Feb. 9, 1997, accident claimed the life of Tracy Thomas and her 6 month fetus, her husband, a Cape May Court House dentist, sued Ford Motor Co., claiming airbag deployment caused the tragedy.

Ford is fighting back in a nontraditional way: It claims Tracy Thomas, 37, died of manual strangulation and names her husband as the suspect.

While finger-pointing is almost standard in civil cases, especially those alleging product defects, Dr. Eric Thomas's lawyers argue Ford's claims are so outrageous they are slanderous.

At a hearing Tuesday before U.S. Magistrate Judge Joel Rosen, attorney Elliott Kolodny, representing Dr. Thomas, asked permission to amend the 1999 wrongful death lawsuit to include counts of defamation and intentional infliction of emotional distress.

To support the automotive giant's allegations, local defense attorney for Ford, William J Conroy, contacted the Cape May County Medical Examiner's Office, the Cape May County Prosecutor and the Middle Township Police, suggesting they reopen the case and amend the established cause and manner of Tracy Thomas's death.

One of several experts retained by Ford, forensic pathologist Dr. Michael M. Baden of New York City, reported hemorrhages in Tracy Thomas's eyes and neck were inconsistent with airbag injuries, but were consistent with manual compression of the victim's neck.

That finding was echoed by other medical experts, including Dr. James V. Benedict of San Antonio, Texas, who said an exploding airbag would generate force to the victim's body for "less than the blink of an eye" while the pressure needed to cause the injuries found on Tracy Thomas's body lasted at least 30 seconds.

Floyd Abrams, lead counselor for Ford, said, "The key to the case is the cause of death. If false charges are made, there are remedies available."

Immunity from liability for lawyers preparing a case is broad and essential to investigation, Abrams said.

COURIER POST Staff
July 19, 2000
By Renee Winkler

Because a transcript of the proceeding was not immediately ordered by the parties, no reporter who picked up Winkler's story knew of the references that Thomas's attorneys had made to the civil rights act of 1985.

CRASH DEATH WASN'T MURDER. PROSECUTORS TELL FORD CO.

The Ford Motor Co. wants to be able to tell a jury that a pregnant Cape May Court House woman was murdered here in 1997, not killed by a defective airbag as her husband has claimed in a federal lawsuit.

But prosecutors here said Wednesday that the death of Tracy Thomas, 37, and her unborn fetus remains an accident, despite Ford's attempt to have them reopen the case.

"There's no credible evidence of any criminal culpability, either on the part of Dr. (Eric) Thomas or any other individual," First Assistant Cape May County Prosecutor J. David Meyer said. "We have told Ford that and they're aware of our position."

"We intend to put on extensive evidence showing that the airbag played absolutely no role in Mrs. Thomas's death," Ford's spokeswoman Susan Krusel said.

At a Tuesday hearing before U.S. Magistrate Joel Rosen in Camden, Thomas's attorneys asked to amend their lawsuit against Ford to include charges of defamation and intentional infliction of emotional distress.

Such a ruling could leave Ford open to punitive damages during a jury trial. However, a judge's approval is needed because lawyers typically are immune to such claims.

Floyd Abrams, lead attorney for Ford, argued Tuesday that "the key to the case is the cause of death."

"If false charges are made there are remedies available," Abrams said.

. . . Still, in what [Tom] Mellon said was an attempt to resolve the issue, Eric Thomas volunteered to undergo two polygraph examinations.

He passed both, Mellon said, including one administered April 18 by the Cape May County Prosecutor's Office.

THE PRESS OF ATLANTIC CITY
July 20, 2000
By W.F. Keough

Tracy's sister, Wendy, was confused when she read in the morning papers that Ford was accusing Eric of murder. Neither Ford's lawyers nor the prosecutors had called to warn her of this possibility and she didn't know what to think. But when her mother heard about it, it seemed to her that justice would now be done.

Until the story broke, life had gone on as usual for Cape May Court House and Eric Thomas. He still saw patients, played golf, went to parties and professional meetings, and participated in the life of his community. There was now a pool behind their home, and Stephanie tended to the children. She was also expecting another child. The Court House community seemed to have accepted Stephanie easily, and if anyone gave a thought to the events of February 9, 1997, it was with sadness, but certainly not suspicion. Tracy Thomas had died tragically in a car accident, and her husband had gone on to make a life for himself and his daughter—things like that happened in many families.

The initial reaction to the stories in the press was disgust that Ford would go to this length to win a case. Some people didn't want to go on the record, but others spoke freely. Bill Cottman, a member of Thomas's country club, said, ". . . When a large company takes on an individual like that, I think it's patently unfair. If a guy doesn't have the wherewithal to fight, he's got to lose." When Barbara Callaway, the wife of the dentist who had sold Thomas his practice, read the article in the *Press of Atlantic City,* she went to Thomas's house and told him she didn't believe a word of what she'd read. "It's not fair [of Ford]," she said.

Tom Mellon was happy to see this criticism of Ford.

Within a week the national media were calling the principals in the case, requesting interviews. The Roses found ABC pushy and told NBC that they couldn't talk until after they'd been deposed, but there was no date for that yet.

FORD AIRBAG-DEATH CASE
PLACES OLD NEMESES IN OPPOSITION

Ford Motor Co.'s assertion that a crash victim died not from a defective airbag but at the hands of her husband has prompted the plaintiff to cry slander, which is promising to turn a garden-variety product liability case into a defamation suit.

What's more, the case puts at odds two medical forensic experts who have butted heads before: Michael Baden and Elliot Gross, who have espoused diametrically opposite views of the cause of death in the case.

* * *

In 1979, Baden was the New York City medical examiner when he was demoted by Mayor Ed Koch over alleged incompetence, and Gross was named as his replacement.

Amid the controversy, Baden alleged that with Gross at the helm, the medical examiner's office misplaced bodies and organs and took payoffs from funeral directors. Baden filed suit in federal court against the city over his firing, but the U.S. Court of Appeals upheld the city's right to fire him in 1980.

Later, Baden voluntarily left another job as medical examiner in Suffolk County, N.Y., after he was quoted in an article on "high tech homicide" that appeared in *Oui* magazine. That article was later retracted by the publication.

Baden gained fame when he testified as an expert witness to help exonerate O.J. Simpson of murder charges. He was also called in to consult on an investigation of the death of John Belushi and on the murder trial of British nanny Louise Woodward.

Still to come in the case are depositions from the victim's parents, who live in Massachusetts and are expected to describe Eric Thomas's behavior after the accident, Conroy said at a status conference last January.

In March, Magistrate Judge Rosen denied a request by the plaintiffs to seal materials containing the allegations of wrongdoing in the case. He found that the product liability dispute is a matter of public interest.

NEW JERSEY LAW JOURNAL
July 31, 2000
By Charles Toutant

Baden, who at the time was the director of the Forensic Science Unit for the New York State Police in Albany, told Conroy that his findings in the Thomas case had nothing to do with his past dealings with Dr. Elliot Gross. He added that when Conroy first sent him the autopsy information, he didn't know who the victim was, much less who the medical examiner was. And he was not told either of these things until after he gave the attorney his finding of "manual strangulation."

But doubt now clouded Baden's findings, and Conroy knew he'd have to look for another pathologist as backup. Werner Spitz had been Glenn Zeitz's first choice, but there was a risk. What if Spitz sided with Dr. Thomas's experts? Conroy decided to stick with Baden for the time being.

On August 3rd, Bill Conroy wrote to Elliott Kolodny that while Kolodny hadn't returned his calls, Ford would provide seven of Ford's employees for depositions between August 7th and August 11th. In addition, he wrote, the videotapes of sled tests* and the index of discovery documents Kolodny had requested while in Dearborn on June 29th and 30th were also ready. After the plaintiffs reviewed the videos, Conroy said, he would be open to discussing the matter of supplemental depositions.

---

* A sled test whereby a certain part or system of a vehicle is placed on a rail and accelerated for a distance and crashed into a fixed barrier. In the case of evaluating air-bag components, Ford uses only the portion of the vehicle forward of the B-pillar to evaluate the crush characteristics of the front of the vehicle and how the air bag and seat belt perform under different speeds and angles.

Earlier, in July, Kolodny called Doris Rose to enlist her support in her ex-son-in-law's suit against Ford. He offered to send her pictures of children who had been killed by air bags. Doris refused his request.

A little later in August, Mellon sent a letter directly to Doris and Donald Rose. He identified himself as counsel to their granddaughter, Alix Rose Thomas, "regarding the tragic death of her mother and your daughter . . ." He did not mention that he also represented Dr. Eric Thomas. He told the Roses that he wanted to tell the court the complete story of Tracy's life, from childhood through her adolescence, her adult years, everything up until the time of her death. He asked for their help so he could present to the court a sympathetic portrait and win a judgment for the benefit of their granddaughter. He asked to meet with them. With the letter, he sent what he characterized as "information," which he asked the Roses to consider. This information included the Cape May prosecutor's investigation report, the Cape May County coroner's report, and the two lie detector tests. "As you will see," he wrote, "all the documents hold that the tragic death of your daughter, Tracy Thomas, was due to an air bag accident. There are no other reasons whatsoever."

The Roses saw through his ploy. When they read the letter, they wondered if Mr. Mellon had accidentally omitted the fact that he also represented Eric Thomas. They had to deal with Eric because he was the father of their beloved Alix, but if they'd had a choice, they would forget he existed. Donald knew that what Mellon really wanted was for him and Doris to be sitting on his side of the courtroom when the case came to trial. That would never happen. The Roses did not respond to Mellon's request.

By the end of that week, Eric Thomas and Elliott Kolodny had appeared on ABC's *Good Morning America*. Ford's charges against Thomas were making news, and ABC aired a segment on the controversy, using footage of Thomas at the scene of the accident taken shortly after he filed the lawsuit, as well as new footage of Alix. On camera, Thomas said he was sure that the air bag had killed his wife and unborn baby. The network also showed a letter from Ford which said that their experts had confirmed that Tracy Thomas had died "of compression of the neck at the hands of another. In short, she was strangled."

Elliott Kolodny refuted that, saying, "These allegations are foisted upon [Dr. Thomas] by a multibillion-dollar corporation against one lone individual out in Cape May County. And it's tough."

"Did you love your wife?" ABC asked Dr. Thomas on camera.

"Yes."

"How hard has this been for you?"

"Life has been turned upside down," Thomas replied. "It's a—it's a tragic acc—tragic accident that I don't have the language, the vocabulary, to explain to you what this had done."

Two days later, on August 9th, Bill Conroy filed a formal motion to redepose Thomas. For Conroy, this was now the most important motion before the court. If the court granted his motion, Conroy felt that with a little push, Thomas would withdraw his suit. He worded his motion carefully.

At the time of Thomas's first deposition, Ford did not know certain material facts, Conroy said. Meanwhile, Thomas had been less than truthful about several things in his previous deposition: a preexisting neck injury before the accident; the state of his marriage to Tracy Rose Thomas; his involvement in an extramarital affair; his claim of loss of consortium* and mental anguish; the amount of life insurance he actually received after Tracy Thomas's death; and the date he returned to work after the accident. In addition, Conroy wanted to ask him about the polygraph tests he had been given.

Shortly after appearing on *Good Morning America,* Elliott Kolodny went to Dearborn to view the videotapes of crash tests and to take the depositions of Ford's most knowledgeable persons on air-bag deployment.

He found, however, that with one exception, the employees provided by Ford were either unprepared or had no knowledge of air bags. Kolodny wondered why Ford was not responding fully, ethically, or properly to discovery. Not until June 2000 had Ford looked for the documents he'd requested in December 1999. Time was being lost, and it was costing his firm money.

But he did make one interesting discovery. According to

---

* The relationship and all of the accompanying benefits enjoyed by a married man and woman.

one Ford employee he deposed, the Explorer was failing its government-mandated crash tests. Kolodny also believed he'd uncovered evidence that showed neck-injury patterns in short-statured women that resulted in death. Another Ford employee testified that there were problems late in the design stage of the driver's-side air bag and he wasn't sure what had been done to correct them. Kolodny knew these issues all required further investigation.

TREAD FAILURES LEAD TO RECALL OF 6.5 MILLION FIRESTONE TIRES

The company [Bridgestone/Firestone] that makes Firestone tires said today that millions of tires it had produced since 1991 seemed unusually prone to flinging off their treads, sometimes with catastrophic results. Facing 50 lawsuits, 46 deaths, 80 injuries and a federal investigation, the company said it would provide free replacements for the 6.5 million tires still on the road.

Of the tires affected by the announcement today, about two-thirds came new on Ford Explorer sport utility vehicles and Ranger and F-150 pickup trucks, Mercury Mountaineer sport utilities, as well as Mazda Navajo and B-series pickups.

THE NEW YORK TIMES
August 10, 2000
By Matthew L. Wald

On August 14th, upon his return from Dearborn, Kolodny appeared before Judge Rosen to ask the court to compel Ford to provide document and videotape discovery.

Conroy replied angrily that Ford had "produced—I can't tell you how many documents."

"Let's move on," Rosen told him. "When is [Kolodny] going to have the remaining documents?"

"This week," Conroy replied.

Kolodny then told Rosen about the corporate designees he'd been given. He'd asked for air-bag systems experts but got two deponents—one for driver, one for passengers—who would speak only about air-bag modules, not about air-bag systems.

Kolodny added that Ford's designees had no documents, and didn't know where to get them.

Rosen asked Conroy to provide the court with an affidavit concerning the nature of Ford's document search—how it was conducted and who was involved.

The argument suggested that a vicious cycle was in motion. At the plaintiff's request, Judge Rosen would instruct Ford to do something, then Kolodny would try—and fail—to obtain what he wanted and would then report back to the court. Rosen would address the issue at another conference, would again order something to be done, and again Kolodny would try and fail. They were getting nowhere with discovery.

Kolodny then complained that videotapes were missing. Earlier, on June 29th and 30th, he and one of his experts had gone to Dearborn to examine some tapes, but Ford gave him only tapes that showed Explorers running into walls. What he needed and had asked for were "sled test" videos, which showed small-size dummies in relation to steering-column problems.

"I need those videotapes," he exclaimed. "They're absolutely crucial. I will state unequivocally on the record, my experts cannot complete their analysis [without them]." Kolodny wanted all of them, he said.

"When you [say] all," Rosen asked, "what does that mean? All for this model vehicle? All for this model air bag? All for what?"

"I want all the videos associated with the reports that they [Ford] have already produced," Kolodny explained. Since Ford had produced documents without an index, he said, he couldn't give the court a list of the tapes he needed. That was why he was asking for all of them. Only by obtaining every tape could he determine if Ford was hiding any.

"This is a game," Kolodny said angrily.

"Remain calm," Rosen told him. "I'm telling you, the next thing I'm thinking of doing is appointing a special master. . . . We'll get through this."*

Ford seemed to be stonewalling, though incompetence on Ford's part may also have been a factor.

However, one problem was now obvious: Was it possible that Mellon's firm was simply too small to go up against a giant like Ford? Mellon had gone very public with his lawsuit early in the game, perhaps hoping to force Ford to settle. He was now finding out how determined the automaker was not to settle.

---

* A person (usually a judge or any attorney) appointed by the court to oversee an act or process pertaining to a particular issue.

ELEVEN

A Bad Truth Is Better
Than a Good Lie

A week later, on August 21st, Elliott Kolodny filed a motion for sanctions against Ford based on his frustration in Dearborn and his belief that the automaker had no intention of cooperating fully with air-bag discovery requests.

That same week, after realizing that the media were on Thomas's side, Conroy went to Dearborn, not to deal with Kolodny's discovery requests, but to meet with Susan Krusel, of Ford's public affairs staff, and with senior members of the office of the general counsel.

Conroy told them that if Ford allowed itself to be pounded in the media for the next few months and didn't respond assertively, the entire community from which a jury pool would be drawn would be polluted. Regardless of the evidence, Ford could lose the case.

As a result, Ford abandoned its "no comment" policy, and issued press releases stating its position at the time. Mysteriously, parts of depositions and inside information, which advanced Ford's positions, were leaked to reporters. One leak was Dr. Gross's deposition, parts of which were then reported in detail. By the end of August, the basis for Ford's defense had been fully reported in the media.

Mellon responded by revealing the polygraph tests as evidence of Thomas's innocence and by telling the *Courier Post* that "Dr. Thomas is a vulnerable person. And Ford, instead of defending [its case], engineer against engineer, takes the lowest road and makes accusations of homicide. This is an outrage."

That same week, Bill Conroy learned that Mellon had begun consulting with Carl Poplar, a well-respected criminal attorney with thirty-five years of experience. This meant that Conroy, to keep Mellon on the defense, now had to reveal Zeitz before Poplar appeared in court. Conroy knew that Poplar would surely appear at a hearing concerning Conroy's request to redepose Eric Thomas.

On August 31st, Judge Rosen handed down his ruling on whether Dr. Thomas could amend his initial complaint to include defamation. At issue was whether Ford's actions in approaching prosecutors were protected by the litigation privilege or whether Ford had entered into a conspiracy to intimidate Dr. Thomas into dropping his lawsuit.

Rosen stated again that the court recognized the potentially devastating effect of Ford's defense on Thomas. However, the court also recognized the potentially destructive effect of Thomas's allegations against the automaker when he charged Ford with "wanton and willful disregard" for the consequences of its conduct, design, manufacturing, and sale of its Explorer. Rosen would not attempt to arbitrate the facts of the case but would deal only with the question of privilege.

The judge promptly denied Mellon's request to add a cause of action against Ford for intimidation and violation of Dr. Thomas's civil rights under the KKK law. Ford had not gone directly to Thomas and tried to bully him. And in going to the medical examiner and the prosecutors, he said, Ford had not presented the information by way of intimidation, threat, or violence.

As to the claim of "intentional infliction of emotional distress," Rosen said that Thomas's attorneys had presented enough facts to let a jury, not the judge, decide the issue.* He therefore allowed Thomas's request to seek monetary damages for emotional distress.

The crux of the defendant's issue was the litigation privilege, which, Rosen noted, was over six hundred years old. Under New Jersey law, Thomas had sufficiently stated a prima facie claim of defamation [an action that "is false and is injurious to the reputation of another or exposes another person to hatred, contempt, or ridicule, or subjects another person to a loss of good will"] and Ford had not contested it, because they believed that the privilege protected them. But, in his opinion,

---

* Known as a "prima facie burden."

Ford didn't have an absolute privilege, though it might have had a qualified privilege, Rosen said. In New Jersey, absolute privilege had been limited to situations in which the court had the power both to discipline persons whose statements exceeded the bounds of permissible conduct and to strike such statements from the record. Because this court didn't have control over an alleged abuse and the power to sanction Ford, Rosen would allow Thomas's claim for defamation; only a jury could decide the issue and damages to Thomas. Mellon could now file an amended complaint.

Bill Conroy was devastated by Rosen's opinion. The tables had turned again. Ford was once more a defendant. What loomed on the horizon, if Conroy had been wrong in going to Dr. Gross and the prosecutors, was the issue of punitive damages. For the time being, Conroy would appeal the ruling to the presiding judge. He believed that Rosen had failed to consider all the relevant case law related to absolute privilege.

On September 5th, Tom Mellon filed a brief opposing Ford's motion to redepose Thomas. In it, Mellon denied Ford's allegations of inconsistencies in Thomas's statements and stated that "at no time during Tracy's life did Dr. Thomas have an affair with Stephanie." He charged Ford with having no evidence, no basis on which to make such a statement, and no witnesses. Conroy could see that Mellon actually believed his client.

Before replying, Conroy first had to respond to Elliott Kolodny's motion requesting sanctions against Ford for delaying discovery. Conroy stated that Ford's initial discovery had been completed within the deadlines the court mandated and that only later did they discover additional documents that should have been given to Thomas's attorneys. Conroy provided affidavits showing that the plaintiffs arrived in Dearborn seven months after Ford invited them to the company's reading room and that even then, they didn't review documents but only videotapes. The plaintiffs had no grounds for requesting sanctions, Conroy stated.

After sending that reply, Conroy turned to his response to Mellon's opposition to Ford's redeposing Eric Thomas. In drafting his answer, Conroy repeated his claim that Thomas had made conflicting statements about the night of the accident. To support his claim of an extramarital affair with Stephanie, Conroy now enclosed Sean Haley's "sworn statement," which, "flatly contradicts Dr. Thomas's version of events in terms of when, before and after the accident, Dr. Thomas was actively calling and seeing Stephanie, including weekend trips together before the accident." Stephanie Thomas's close friend Carlisha Brown-Robinson, whom Conroy planned to depose, would corroborate Haley's statements, Conroy stated. Stephanie had told her—before the accident—that she was seeing Thomas.

Bill Conroy had now laid all his cards on the table and could imagine the scene when Mellon called Thomas on the carpet. Would Thomas continue to lie to his attorneys? Would they continue to believe him?

A status conference was scheduled for the next day, September 12th, with Mellon and Conroy present. Judge Rosen raised the matter of redeposing Thomas.

Conroy told the court that according to his experts, the

injury pattern on Tracy Thomas was not consistent with air-bag deaths at slow speeds. He noted the petechial hemorrhaging in the eyes and the consolidation of injuries to her throat and larynx areas and said that the medical examiner had not previously documented his suspicions of some of the injuries. Second, the family had expressed other suspicions to the police before Ford was involved in the case. Also, only when Ford took their depositions were some of the reservations of the police about the case revealed.

Conroy then raised the issue of Thomas's misrepresentations during his first deposition. He had withheld information about back pain he had suffered a month before the accident. He had mischaracterized the nature of his relationship with Stephanie prior to the accident, and Ford had uncovered a different chain of events from what Thomas had described in his interviews and depositions. Sean Haley, Stephanie's ex-husband, had identified certain trips during which she joined Thomas prior to the accident and this information had been corroborated by Stephanie's close friend Carlisha Brown-Robinson. Both of them would testify to these facts, Conroy said. Ford now had to establish the truth about the relationship. At a minimum, Conroy said, the issues surrounding the relationship went to Thomas's claim for loss of consortium.

Conroy asked the court's permission to depose Sean Haley and Carlisha Brown-Robinson and the polygraph examiners. They wanted to know under what circumstances the tests had been administered, why they were done, and if the examiners had had all the relevant information before conducting the tests.

Conroy summed up by saying that because of the extraordinary nature of this case—the fact that Ford was challenging the conclusions of both the medical examiner and the police—they had a right to get to the bottom of it.

Tom Mellon replied that thorough investigation by the NHTSA, the police, and the medical examiner had concluded that the death of Tracy Thomas was consistent with the deployment of the Explorer's air bag and had identified no other cause of death. He told Judge Rosen that Conroy was making too much of some small inconsistencies in some of Thomas's tangential statements.

Mellon accused the automaker of arrogance. "Ford has decided to bury Mellon, Webster and Mellon and to bury Dr. Eric Thomas," Mellon told the court, by taking more depositions, spending more money, and causing more delay. "I can't match them, Your Honor, I'll tell you right now," Mellon said. "Now, everybody in Cape May Court House knows that [Thomas is] an adulterer/murderer. . . . Ford knows inconsistencies are for cross-examination, the great engine of our litigation process. Trials are really not the presentation of evidence, they're about cross-examination."

Then, to Conroy's surprise, Mellon consented to Conroy's request to depose Sean Haley and Carlisha Brown-Robinson. Mellon believed that their statements—along with those of the Rose family—would expose "the utter silliness of what's happened heretofore [and] make an official record of it for all time," he said.

"I understand the Roses, I truly do," Mellon continued. "Tracy was their shining star. Her death was horrible. They can't believe it could [have been] a little car accident. Mrs. Rose quit her job to move in with Eric. She was going to take charge, she was going to be the new mom. . . . They don't bring [their suspicions] to the attention of anyone for a year and a half [until just before] Stephanie, the new wife, adopted Alix, their treasured granddaughter. This is nothing more than a bitter family feud. But that's no reason to take Eric's deposition. Let the Roses speak for themselves."

The court granted Ford's request to depose Sean Haley and Carlisha Brown-Robinson. Rosen said he would rule on the Thomas depositions at the end of the hearing.

Addressing the issue of the polygraph examiners' depositions, Mellon said that if Ford agreed to the admissibility of the tests, then a deposition would be proper and he wouldn't object. But why take a deposition of someone who would never testify in the courtroom? Why take a deposition of someone who had no relevant evidence?

In closing, Mellon pleaded, "I just wish there was something I could say powerful and convincing [enough] to stop this madness. If [Dr. Thomas] gave an inconsistent statement, being human, let them fully exploit that inconsistent statement at trial, but for God's sake, give Dr. Thomas some peace."

Rosen then listened to Elliott Kolodny's complaints about how Ford was still responding to discovery.

To make his point, he told the court that when he was in Dearborn, a Ford employee had admitted there were problems late in the design phase of the driver-side air bag, and Kolodny said he believed Ford was withholding that information. He'd since learned that the Explorers' air-bag vent holes were to be thirty millimeters in size, but Tracy Thomas's SUV air bags, when investigated by NHTSA, were only thirteen millimeters in size. If this was true, the decrease in vent-hole size from thirty millimeters to thirteen millimeters could have increased the force of impact by about eighty-one percent. Kolodny wanted to know why Ford had not shared this information with NHTSA investigators and why its corporate designee didn't know about this problem when deposed. Kolodny felt he'd uncovered important evidence in support of his clients' claims.*

"We're all ... aware of other cases of Ford withholding documents," Kolodny told Rosen. "The ignition-switch litigation in California, the tire fiasco that's going on right now involving the Explorer—there have been allegations that Ford is withholding documents."

After Kolodny made his point, Mellon asked Rosen for an unequivocal order for Ford to provide the documents relating to the vent-hole issue. Rosen agreed and ordered Ford to produce the person who was most knowledgeable on the subject.

After a short recess, Rosen ruled on the remaining matters. "The decision whether to permit a witness to be redeposed is discretionary," he began. "In this case, I think it would be an abuse of my discretion not to permit a limited redeposition of Dr. Thomas.

"Was this an accident?" Rosen continued. "Was this a homi-

---

* In an interview for this book, Ford stated that the design specification for the driver-side air bag is thirteen millimeters and not thirty millimeters as suggested by Kolodny, and that NHTSA did not consult Ford on the design specifications before they issued their report. Eric Thomas's experts did not make the claim in any of their reports that Kolodny stated in open court.

cide? There are serious questions about the condition of the decedent before the incident, the circumstances surrounding it, and certain matters pertaining to the personal lives of these parties, which frankly I wish, in a perfect world, we did not have to get into. However, Ford is defending this case and it will be for the jury to decide ... whether or not this death, this tragic death, was caused by Ford and a negligently designed product or whether the decedent died at the hands of her husband. I don't know.

"I know this. The issues here are incredibly important. . . . Number one, the nature of [Dr. Thomas's] relationship with his wife and his current wife. Number two, what happened that night when she left the house. Did she fall? Were the marks on her face caused by the air bag? Why was she driving? A jury has got to have the full facts in this case. And I believe, in light of the record that's developed here, it would be [an] abuse of my discretion not to permit a redeposition, limited only to the areas noted in Ford's brief and limited to four hours, and it will occur in this court house."

There was another reason he granted the redeposition, Rosen said.

"I recently ruled . . . that plaintiff could proceed on the defamation claim and Ford would have a good-faith defense, qualified immunity. Well, certainly now that that issue is in the case, they have the right over and above what I've already noted to develop facts to determine whether there was a good-faith basis for . . . making these accusations against Dr. Thomas. This is a new issue in the case that broadens the scope, in my view, of discovery. The plaintiffs want to pursue their claim of defamation. Ford opposed that, but I said yes they could. Now, at the end of the day . . . this is an extraordinarily serious case. There is a dead human being. It's a tragedy no matter what happened. . . . Both sides [should have] a reasonable opportunity to develop the record."

The court ordered that Eric Thomas's deposition be taken within thirty days, but no later than October 11th, and that all discovery relating to the deposition be completed forty-eight hours before the deposition.

Conroy and Mellon agreed that Stephanie's deposition would be taken after Thomas's. Finally, Rosen granted Conroy's request to depose the polygraph examiners, because it went to the issue of Thomas's credibility. The Roses' depositions would follow.

The next day, the local headlines read "Ford to Reopen Deposition of Dentist."

In Judge Rosen's courtroom the previous day, Mellon had surprised Conroy by admitting "Yes, [Dr. Thomas] was in Boston, and, yes, by coincidence Stephanie was there and so [were] Tracy and Alix and they had lunch together." Zeitz believed Thomas had fabricated the meeting and was digging himself a deeper hole.

Zeitz was eager to confront Thomas. Ford didn't have an eyewitness to the accident and there wasn't a confession, but Zeitz believed he'd found a motive—the insurance money. And there was opportunity. Ford also had witnesses who would contradict Thomas's sworn testimony and there were experts whose testimony supported Ford's strangulation theory. Zeitz saw the Marshall case all over again, where his own client had been convicted of having his wife murdered to benefit from insurance proceeds and to cover an adulterous relationship. But this time Zeitz was on the other side.

Hoping to launch a preemptive strike against Thomas's attorneys, Conroy asked Ford for permission to bring Zeitz out into the open. He believed Carl Poplar was also waiting in the wings, and he wanted to set the stage for the next round of depositions. By letting Mellon and company know that Ford had hired Glenn Zeitz, Conroy would show the plaintiffs that Ford was taking its homicide defense seriously. Ford told Conroy it would let him know shortly.

Meanwhile, on September 13th, Tom Mellon filed Thomas's amended complaint, which dealt with defamation. Two days later, on September 15th, Bill Conroy filed his notice of appeal to Judge Rosen's August 31st opinion allowing the amended complaint. It was now up to presiding judge Orlofsky to rule whether a jury would hear Thomas's additional claims.

In the next several days both sides filed motions and replies to the various issues before the court. One of them was Ford's response to the plaintiffs' motion for sanctions against them for discovery violations.

That same week, Ford gave Bill Conroy the go-ahead to cut Glenn Zeitz loose, and on September 21st, Conroy informed Mellon that Zeitz would now be involved in the case. In that letter he raised the issue of separate counsel for Stephanie Thomas at her deposition, since her interests might prove to be different from Thomas's. If he had killed Tracy, having the same attorney would taint her.

During this flurry of legal activity, the public relations war between the two parties continued. Since the beginning of September, Tom Mellon had been talking to reporter Emilie Lounsberry of the *Philadelphia Inquirer* about an exclusive interview with Thomas. Lounsberry had known the attorney since the 1970s, when Mellon was chief of the criminal division of the Eastern District of Pennsylvania. Mellon had also been considering allowing *60 Minutes* or *20/20* to break the story, but Lounsberry's interest made him decide to forgo the network news shows in favor of someone he knew.

Mellon wanted to lay out his defense—not only to win public support for his clients' claims, but to restore, as best he could, the positive image of Thomas he had started with. Potential jurors, who would be drawn from the local community, should know the full story, not only what they might hear in the courtroom. In light of the media interest, Mellon expected a front-page story.

The plan was for Lounsberry to conduct an exclusive, unrestricted interview with Thomas at his home and then the two of them would visit the site of the accident. Mellon felt that Lounsberry would do a comprehensive piece and expose Ford's tactics.

Mellon was present at the interview but did not interrupt or coach his client. Lounsberry asked the same questions several times in different ways and found Thomas's answers to be consistent.

The evenhanded article included these paragraphs.

In a bold defense, Ford asserted that Tracy Thomas was strangled, and that the air bag had nothing to do with her death.

The company also contends that at the time, Eric Thomas was having an affair with his current wife, whom he married in July, 1998.

In a three-hour interview with *The Inquirer* last week, Eric Thomas said he had nothing to do with his wife's death and he was not having an affair.

"I can honestly tell you that I did not kill my wife," he said, sitting at the kitchen table of his two-story colonial a few miles outside the tiny town of Cape May Court House. "I can tell you the air bag did."

"You don't know what other people are thinking," [Thomas] said, sitting between his current wife, Stephanie, and Mellon. "I'm living a fearful life because I feel someone out there will believe all this foolishness. It's embarrassing. . . . There's a dark cloud, and sometimes it seems like it's getting darker."

Eric and Stephanie Thomas said they were not romantically involved at the time of Tracy Thomas's death. They married in July, 1998, 15 months after Tracy Thomas died.

"There was nothing romantic developed until months after the accident," said Stephanie Thomas, 34, who is now six months pregnant with the couple's second child.

Lounsberry also quoted Mellon, Conroy, Kolodny, Gross, Baden, NHTSA officials, and the Roses, and the paper ran several color photographs. The article referred as well to additional interviews, court documents, and transcripts of depositions that had been taken to date.

Nevertheless, Mellon was upset when he read the story while attending his son's varsity soccer game. This was not what he had expected.

The next day Mellon sent Lounsberry an eight-page letter outlining the many reasons he was unhappy with her story. He said he had expected her investigation to expose Ford, that he felt she lacked objectivity. He criticized her for failing to mention exculpatory evidence, such as Thomas's having passed two polygraphs. He pointed out that she neglected to tell her readers Ford had lobbied for the prosecution of Thomas with the prosecutor's office; that the medical examiner and the prosecutor had written letters denying the need to reopen the case; that the Atlantic City Medical Center established CPK enzymes present at triple the normal count in Thomas—indicating a very traumatic event to his muscular system; that the doctor was diagnosed as being unconscious; that there was a bitter relationship between the Roses and Thomas and his present wife; that Ford had not provided proper discovery in the case; and that Thomas's experts had identified the air bag as the cause of death.

For his part, Conroy couldn't understand why Mellon had allowed his client to do this interview. He didn't need more publicity. It was sheer madness, Conroy thought, for Mellon to let his client deny the affair in view of Sean Haley's sworn statement. He had gained nothing, and he had put Thomas in harm's way.

When Zeitz saw the *Inquirer* picture of Mellon and Thomas at the accident scene and then read the story, he was sure Mellon hadn't consulted Poplar, who would have forbidden this kind of interview. Zeitz himself counseled his own clients to write on a yellow sticker "Silence is a friend that will never betray you" and place it where they couldn't miss seeing it every day. If this were a criminal case, Zeitz knew that a grand jury could subpoena Lounsberry and ask for her notes. Zeitz and Conroy discussed what parts of the interview they could use at the Thomases' upcoming depositions.

On September 28th, the day after Lounsberry received Mellon's letter, Glenn Zeitz appeared in Judge Rosen's court for the first time.

Because of the heated and acrimonious nature of the case, Mellon and Kolodny were now communicating with Conroy only via letters. But they were happy to see Zeitz, whom Mellon had known for years. They'd occasionally been on opposite sides of several cases; they had also encountered each other after Mellon left the U.S. Attorney's office.

Now, finally, Mellon had an opponent he could talk to.

Zeitz disappointed him. "My entry into the case is not a wholesome development—it's a bad development for your client," Zeitz said. He was sure, he continued, that Ford would prove that Thomas was lying about the affair and that he'd been lying to his attorneys.

Mellon repeated "I don't believe that, I believe Ford smeared him."

"We're going to prove it," Zeitz replied. "I'm trying to give you a heads-up as someone who knows you. I've been on this case for over a year, and you're being led down the primrose path."

Mellon was shocked to hear that Zeitz had been present behind the scenes for that long.

When court convened for the scheduled status conference, Tom Hinchey sat in for Bill Conroy, who was out of town on another case. Tom Mellon appeared alone for Dr. Thomas.

As usual, Mellon had sent the court a memo listing the issues he wanted to cover. Also on the agenda was Ford's motion for the court to reconsider its order requiring the appearance of Ford's designee, Jennifer Gilhool, on the size of the vent holes. That issue was raised first.

Hinchey said that Ford felt Gilhool's appearance would violate the "work product doctrine," since she was also an attorney in Ford's Dearborn office.[*] In fact, Bill Conroy had actually volunteered Gilhool on September 12th, and the court had accepted. But Ford was now withdrawing the offer because the court's written order was so broad that it seemed to cover Ms. Gilhool's mental impressions and thought processes.

Rosen was upset. If his order was inartfully drafted, he said, why didn't they just drop him a note? "Don't kill more trees with three more inches [of paper]," the judge said, referring to Ford's motion on the subject. "I apologize; [the order] was to permit counsel for the plaintiffs to question her about a document search, to be sure that we have all the documents.

"You're not trying to shield documents by sticking a lawyer

---

[*] The discovery process requires the parties to a lawsuit to exchange certain documents pertaining to the disputed issue or issues. Each side prepares a list of documents they request the other side produce for their review. Exempt from this list are any documents prepared by a party's attorney in anticipation of litigation. This includes his or her notes, working papers, memoranda, or similar materials.

in a role that any other Ford executive can handle, are you?" Rosen asked.

Of course not, Hinchey said, as if it had never occurred to Ford to do such a thing.   .

Then Tom Mellon told the court that on September 12th, the same day Kolodny had raised the vent-hole issue, a federal magistrate in California had held Ford in contempt for its failure to produce documents after years of litigation.

Hinchey said he wasn't going to allow the proceeding to invade Ford's work product. If the judge wanted to question Ms. Gilhool in his chambers, that was acceptable to Ford, he added. That seemed to settle the matter for the moment.

Next on the agenda were the depositions of Eric and Stephanie Thomas. Mellon requested a postponement from the court-ordered date of October 11th until the 20th or 27th.

This angered Rosen, who demanded that Thomas appear for his deposition on October 11th. All the other depositions— of Sean Haley, Carlisha Brown-Robinson, Ford's employees in Dearborn, and the polygraph examiners—were to proceed after the Thomases'. "In other words," he said, "I want this over with."

Eric Thomas, who had been listening quietly to these arguments, now turned his attention to Glenn Zeitz, who addressed the court for the first time, setting the stage for a head-to-head battle with Tom Mellon.

"I don't want to give comfort to the enemy. I just think Mr. Mellon may have missed one item on his list, which is the defendant's [Ford's] insistence on new representation for Stephanie Thomas." Mellon's law firm was representing both

Thomas and his estate, he pointed out, but in New Jersey, "you can't represent a driver and a passenger [in the same accident]."

He explained that if Stephanie Thomas was going to be asked questions whose answers might be in conflict with her husband's, that could cause potential problems. "I'm going to be participating in these depositions of Dr. Thomas and his wife— that's why I wanted to raise [the issue]."

Mellon quickly agreed that Stephanie should retain new counsel.

Rosen concurred. "I think it's a wise idea," he said. ". . . It makes a whole lot of sense."

Zeitz also requested that Eric and Stephanie's bank records, credit card statements, and phone records be produced before their depositions. Rosen ordered the documents produced forty-eight hours in advance.

The attorney raised another issue. "There is a period of time [where] there's no spousal privilege, obviously before they [Dr. Thomas and Stephanie] got married, and there's a period of time where there is a spousal privilege," he said.*

Zeitz believed the Thomases would assert the privilege for both periods. He wasn't asking for a ruling now, but he wanted to know that the judge would be available to rule when required during the depositions.

---

* The law protects statements between a husband and wife, made during the time of their marriage, from forced disclosure. These statements cannot be forcibly produced during discovery, nor can a spouse be compelled to testify against the other.

"I'll be here," Rosen said. "Barring an act of God, I'll be here October 11th."

As eager as he was to try this case, Zeitz knew that a monumental mess was on the horizon for the plaintiffs. Stephanie was about to get her own attorney. Now Alix's rights were also an issue. Would she be properly represented by her father, who was being accused of killing her mother? Zeitz suggested to the court that a guardian ad litem be appointed to protect Alix's interests.*

With these details addressed, the session ended.

After court recessed, Rosen held one of his usual conferences in chambers. Seeing that Mellon was on better terms with Zeitz than with Conroy, the judge suggested that the two attorneys meet for some off-the-record talks—perhaps about settlement. Rosen still hoped that the case would come to a peaceful end.

During the short conversation that followed, Zeitz said to Mellon, off the record, "I only have to prove an affair and the defense will win. I don't have to prove murder. The affair is enough." Mellon at first denied that Thomas had been romantically involved with Stephanie before Tracy's death and then added that if the charge was true, he'd drop the suit and sue his client for his own fees and costs. Mellon followed up with a letter to Zeitz.

---

* A special guardian appointed by the court to represent an infant, ward, or unborn person in a particular litigation. The guardian ad litem exists only for a specific litigation action.

LAW OFFICE
MELLON, WEBSTER & MELLON

September 29, 2000

Glenn Zeitz, Esquire
Centre Square West
Philadelphia, PA 19102

RE: Thomas vs. Ford Motor Company, et al.

Dear Glenn.

I am pleased that Ford finally has a lawyer that I can talk to regarding this extraordinary case. Ford needs an educaticable [*sic*] captain at the helm.

To follow this metaphor, this case is a Titanic that is absolutely going down. . . .

In any case, please be sure not to become Captain Smith, the commander of the Titanic who was responsible for the spectacular loss. Stated otherwise, protect your reputation. Don't let Ford "off the case" on you as the responsible captain.

Please remember that everything we said yesterday is "off-the-record" as per Judge Rosen's suggestion. Accordingly, please note I am not sending correspondence to any other counsel. I will do so only when it is "official" business.

With regard to the "affair," Ford needs a discriminating lawyer to travel to Austin, Texas, as well as to do the depositions of Eric and Stephanie. An experienced, discerning criminal lawyer, like yourself, will be able to separate gossip and collateral nonsense from hardcore proof.

As Judge Rosen directed, I will pledge our full cooperation regarding any and all information pertaining to Eric and

Stephanie. Likewise, I respect your promise to do the same . . . although it is my understanding that you have no statements, documents, telephone records or anything else whatsoever regarding Carlisha Brown-Robinson and Sean Haley. PLEASE CONFIRM THIS IN WRITING.

I look forward to spending time with you next week to share "off-the-record" impressions. In the final analysis, this case is going to be all about the medicine including, but not limited to, forensic pathology. Don't let Baden's stardom and blunderbuss lead you astray.

Looking forward to our first meeting. Best regards.

Very truly yours,

[signed]
Thomas E. Mellon, Jr.

Zeitz replied to Mellon's letter.

LAW OFFICES
GLENN A. ZEITZ

October 2, 2000

Via Facsimile
Thomas E. Mellon
Mellon, Webster & Mellon
87 North Broad Street
Doylestown, PA 18901

Re: Thomas vs. Ford Motor Company, et al.

Dear Tom,

I appreciate your *pledge* of full cooperation.

I also appreciate your statement to me that should we prove the "affair" you will drop the lawsuit and sue your client for your costs, since he lied to you. I know that you will honor that *pledge* also.

Rest assured that no one is leading me astray!

Very truly yours,

[signed]
Glenn A. Zeitz

After Zeitz's appearance in court was reported in the press, Carl Poplar called him to say that he was now Eric Thomas's personal attorney. He suggested they meet on October 4th.

The two criminal attorneys' relationship went back thirty years. Zeitz considered Poplar, a balding, gray-haired man in his sixties, to be honorable, ethical, and capable. Since both of them toiled in the criminal courts, the two men had much in common, and in fact, in the past, had referred clients to each other.

During their lengthy conference at his office, Poplar told Zeitz he hadn't known about the Lounsberry interview until he read it in the *Inquirer*. In fact, he hadn't yet met Thomas— he'd only consulted with Tom Mellon on the phone.

Zeitz believed him. Poplar had always shunned publicity. Zeitz, who spoke freely, felt comfortable enough to tell Poplar: "Your dog has fleas, and sooner or later you're going to get fleas on yourself, because you don't have control of your client." Thomas had serious credibility problems, Zeitz said, and as a courtesy to his old friend he brought Poplar up to speed on Ford's case. He told Poplar about the insurance money and about the likelihood of an extra-marital affair between Thomas and Stephanie. Carl Poplar listened quietly, taking notes from time to time.

Perhaps unconsciously repeating what he'd said to Tom Mellon, Zeitz's final words to Poplar were: "You're on the *Titanic.*"

"Let's wait, and let me see," Poplar replied.

The next day, October 5th, Bill Conroy finally received Sean Haley's phone records.

Perusing them, Conroy discovered that Eric and Stephanie had spoken to each other more than 140 times in the three months preceding Tracy's death, a staggering number. That fact alone might put their case over the top.

The next day, Conroy and Zeitz met, and as Zeitz was describing his meeting with Poplar, Conroy handed him Sean Haley's telephone records. There, as clear as day, was the evidence of an ongoing relationship between Eric and Stephanie before Tracy's death. Not only were there many phone calls between them from October 1996 until February 9, 1997, but seven of them had been made the day of the accident.

Zeitz couldn't understand how Eric Thomas could have made such a mistake. He had to have known that sooner or later this evidence would surface. Then again, from long experience, Zeitz knew that clients were often blind to the obvious when they were trying to hide something.

If Poplar had not been an old friend, Zeitz would have sandbagged him instead of sharing this devastating information.

Instead, Zeitz immediately called Poplar and suggested they meet again.

Before meeting with Zeitz on Friday, October 6th, Poplar met with Eric Thomas for the first time. He learned that day that a lawyer named Gregory Miller might represent Stephanie Thomas. Poplar, now officially Thomas's personal attorney, instructed Tom Mellon not to produce, for the time being, Thomas's telephone, credit card, and banking records, which Conroy was due to receive on Monday, October 9th. Mellon should tell Conroy and the court that he was delaying delivering until Poplar had the chance to review the documents. Poplar also told Thomas that he needed more information before he could properly advise him. Next, Poplar would have to ask the court for a time-out to get himself up to speed.

On Saturday, October 7th, Poplar met Zeitz in his office. By then, Zeitz had highlighted in yellow each phone call from Stephanie to Eric.

"Look at these," Zeitz told his friend. "I want you to see where we are. We're going to be able to establish in the upcoming depositions that your client has been lying about his relationship with Stephanie prior to the accident."

Poplar said nothing about the records, but he did tell Zeitz that Stephanie was considering being represented by Greg Miller, who had formerly been with the U.S. Attorney's office in Philadelphia.

Poplar also told Zeitz that he would be asking the court for an emergency meeting on Tuesday, October 10th. He needed time to confer with his client before his deposition, which was

scheduled for October 11th, and would request a postponement. No doubt Miller would want one, too, if he decided to
represent Stephanie.

Zeitz sympathized. He knew that Poplar was being asked to
clean up the elephant's cage after it had taken a dump. Zeitz had
been there before and knew what it felt like.

The next day, Monday, October 9th, Conroy met with Zeitz
to prepare for the emergency court hearing. An hour later,
Zeitz heard from Greg Miller, who said he would represent
Stephanie Thomas and turn over her telephone and credit card
records to Zeitz in court tomorrow.

"Everybody . . . has a problem here," Zeitz told him. "I suggest you take a close look at what is going on, because it looks
like your client, Stephanie, has a financial interest in the outcome of this litigation."

On Tuesday, October 10th, Carl Poplar and Greg Miller
appeared before Judge Rosen on behalf of Eric and Stephanie
Thomas, both of whom were also in the courtroom. Stephanie,
tall and thin and somewhat reserved, was a contrast to Tracy,
who was short, with a roundish face, and who by all accounts
was lively and adventurous. Though Mellon and Kolodny were
present, it was Poplar and Miller who requested a postponement of the Thomases' depositions. Glenn Zeitz, Bill Conroy,
and Thomas Hinchey appeared for Ford. Also present was
Tamara Traynor, who told the judge that she, too, represented
Stephanie Thomas. Poplar, Miller, and Traynor said they would
not appear in the civil case against Ford but were only personal
counsel to the Thomases.

Carl Poplar, wearing his wire-frame glasses, told Rosen in his typically self-deprecating manner that the issues before the court couldn't be taken lightly, superficially, or cavalierly and that he needed more time.

"I have to point out to the court that I'm a new kid on the block as far as the knowledge of the dates of the deposition. I'm not requesting time because I failed to do this or I failed to do that. I'm requesting time because the issue of the deposition is new to me. The issues are huge. . . . Do I think the absence of granting my application for additional time, the failure to do that, would be inappropriate? Well, clearly nothing is inappropriate when it's within the discretion of the court, but I would ask Your Honor to exercise your discretion. . . .

"If Your Honor does not grant our extension," Poplar said, "it would be potentially disruptive tomorrow [at the deposition], because I will have to make decisions based on limited information."

Poplar asked for a thirty-to-sixty-day delay for himself and Miller, to give them time to review ten boxes of documents Tom Mellon had assembled for them. This did not include the fifty boxes of material from Ford, he added. But he did need to review the history, complexity, science, and tactics of the case.

Rosen noted that what was really being discussed was Dr. Thomas's potential exposure to criminal charges. And that, the judge said, had been around since March, when Ford's experts' reports were given to Tom Mellon.

"It's very hard for me to use the word *criminal,* Your Honor," Poplar replied, "so I was a little timid."

Zeitz opposed a delay. He told Rosen that when the issue of redeposing Dr. Thomas was being argued before the court, Carl Poplar was already involved in the case, "and if there was a failure to communicate . . . that was between Mr. Mellon and Mr. Poplar and their respective clients." Ford should not have to suffer because of opposing counsel's difficulties.

Zeitz then proceeded to run down the many positive statements that had been made about Eric and Tracy's marriage—by Mellon and by Dr. Thomas in his interrogatories. He noted the interview Dr. Thomas gave the *Philadelphia Inquirer*, in which he said he had not had an affair before Tracy's death. All of these statements had been made under "Mr. Poplar's watch," Zeitz said.

He then told the court that Ford had now obtained—independent of Dr. Thomas—records of 140 phone calls between Thomas and Stephanie that he had failed to disclose to Ford, all of which took place as Thomas was increasing the face amount of Tracy Thomas's life insurance. Zeitz had now introduced in court a connection between the phone calls and the amount of life insurance on Tracy, thus implying a possible motive for murder.

Dr. Thomas had several options if the depositions went forward, Zeitz said: to take the Fifth, the consequences of which were self-evident; not to show up and be in contempt of court; or to withdraw the lawsuit and figure out what to say to the media. There was another possibility: Dr. Thomas could come in and testify truthfully.

Zeitz then said it was Thomas who had chosen to bring the suit against Ford. If he had come into it with clean hands, he wouldn't have a problem. Dr. Thomas had created his own lies; Ford didn't create them. "He brought it upon himself."

Rosen then asked Mellon why Dr. Thomas had not disclosed all of his phone numbers and calls during discovery. The attorney ruefully admitted that Thomas hadn't disclosed them to him, either. Since Thomas had not been candid with his own attorney, the issue of sanctions against him had now arisen. Sanctions could obligate the court to inform the jury of Thomas's lies should the case go to trial.

"There are times when lawyers don't know everything," Rosen said, "or they're told things and not other things."

Eric Thomas, who'd been sitting next to his wife but looking straight ahead through the hearing, now turned to her for the first time. Mellon, expressionless, looked toward the Thomases, who did not return his glance.

"I've been lied to before," Zeitz said, seeing Mellon's predicament.

Then Conroy told the court that Ford wanted the depositions to take place the following day, as previously ordered. His client, he said, was now being sued for defamation. Meanwhile, Dr. Thomas had gone to the newspapers and on *Good Morning America* and stated, while not under oath, that he hadn't had an affair. This was harmful to his client. All Conroy wanted was the opportunity to ask some of the same questions that reporters had asked Dr. Thomas—but this time under oath.

"Dr. Thomas seems to want it both ways," Rosen said. "He had very aggressively pursued this claim, which is his right, but now that there are some serious questions, [he wants] to put the brakes on."

This was the same argument that Zeitz had tried to make earlier—that Thomas had called Ford's theory frivolous, but now Poplar was asking the court for additional time because of serious Fifth Amendment concerns against self-incrimination. If Ford's allegations were frivolous, how could Thomas be concerned about criminal exposure?

Poplar told Rosen that he hadn't been involved in the case as long as the court seemed to think. And just as important, he hadn't been consulted about the interviews that Thomas had given. "I was extraordinarily bothered by that," he said.

A delay in the depositions wouldn't prejudice anyone, he said. "The decision-making process will be made not by seat-of-the-pants lawyering but by careful lawyering, thoughtful lawyering, and it's still going to be, you know, a judgment call in this case. Everything is a judgment call that you do, except how to answer questions."

Conroy and Zeitz sat back and admired an able adversary.

"I don't care how bad the truth is," Poplar continued. "A bad truth is better than a good lie."

Having heard both sides, Rosen addressed the courtroom: "What Dr. Thomas is facing potentially is the possibility of a capital-murder charge. This is the worst-case scenario . . . but I'm looking at balancing prejudice—there's no question there's some prejudice to Ford in delaying this. . . . This case was initiated by Dr. Thomas. He walked into this. He knew what he was doing. He's a sophisticated fella. He's a bright gentleman. But he is facing . . . the possibility of capital murder. . . . He's facing a potential death sentence. . . . If you fellows [Ford] are right, this was—and I said if—this is a calculated homicide of a woman and her unborn child. It may be an accident, as plaintiffs have argued. But in weighing the balance, I've got to come down on the side of a potential capital case. I've got to. . . ."

Those in the gallery who had been watching the Thomases during the judge's comments found no discernible reaction on Eric Thomas's face. He remained impassive. Only once did he look down at his feet. That was when his wife, who was eight months pregnant with the couple's second child, took his hand.

"I'm going to give him a stay," Rosen said. "I'm going to give him a two-week stay, and then we're going to revisit this."

Rosen then canceled all the scheduled depositions and set a date of October 25th for the attorneys to report back to him.*

By now it was evident that Carl Poplar was in charge of the case, which was no longer about whether an air bag had killed Tracy Thomas but about whether Eric Thomas had lied under oath.

The local newspapers and some national outlets reported that Judge Rosen had postponed the Thomases' depositions. Some reports explained that Thomas could now be facing a charge of capital murder.

A few days later, on Saturday, October 14th, Eric and Stephanie Thomas attended funeral services, at the Mount Olive Baptist Church, for Dr. Callaway, seventy-seven, who had sold his practice to Dr. Thomas.

* * *

---

* At the October 25th conference, Rosen stayed it a second time and set another conference date for November 9th.

Meanwhile, Glenn Zeitz continued to dig into Eric Thomas's life. At the Cape May County surrogate's office he obtained documents Thomas had filed after Tracy's death in which he had said under oath that his wife was virtually destitute. Her jewelry had no value. Her clothing and her interest in their home and in the dental practice also had no value. This seemed odd when in photographs Tracy was always wearing pearl necklaces, earrings, and other jewelry. From Thomas's statement, one would have thought she belonged in a pauper's grave.

Continuing to comb through the Thomases' past, Zeitz obtained the pleadings in the Haleys' divorce, the American Express statements of Sean and Stephanie Haley before their divorce, and the insurance records of all the parties.

Zeitz also retained psychologist Elliott Atkins to examine Thomas at a future date. He believed the court would grant such a request because Thomas had added emotional distress to his original claim against Ford.

As a criminal-defense attorney, Zeitz never wanted his clients to have to face an inquiry by a psychiatrist. But now Zeitz was on the other side, and a court-ordered psychological evaluation could give him an invaluable window into Thomas's thinking.

TWELVE

Memory of Tracy

AUTHORITIES RE-OPENING
CAPE AIR BAG DEATH CASE

The Cape May County Prosecutor's Office plans to reopen its investigation into the 1997 death of a Middle Township woman.

On Tuesday, Acting Prosecutor David Blaker said he plans to request Dr. Thomas's telephone records from both the day of the accident and the months leading up to the accident. The phone records came to light during a U.S. District Court conference this month.

"We'll request the information we do not have which relates to the telephone calls," Blaker said. "We'll see where that leads us."

THE PRESS OF ATLANTIC CITY
October 18, 2000
By Michael Miller

Bill Conroy was pleased that the same D.A. he had met in February was now reopening the case. The next day, October 19th, the *New York Times,* the *Baltimore Sun,* the *Washington Post,* the *Detroit News,* and the *San Francisco Examiner* ran stories about the reinvestigation of the case. Meanwhile, the matter of the Thomases' depositions was still pending. At an October 25th conference, Judge Rosen stayed* the depositions once again until November 9th—to give Poplar and Miller more time to prepare. Then, on November 3rd, Poplar filed a motion to formally stay Dr. Thomas's redeposition once more and requested that the matter be heard on the November 9th court date, thus delaying the depositions again. He also informed the court that he was requesting a guardian ad litem to protect the interests of Alix Thomas. Another reason for requesting a stay, he said, was that no deposition was necessary until Alix's interests were ensured.

Attorneys for both sides wanted a guardian to recommend the proper course of action for the child. The guardian's report should include, Mellon wrote, "a full investigation of all aspects of the case" and a "clear and concise statement regarding the continued litigation of this case on behalf of the minor child, separate and apart from the considerations of Plaintiff, Dr. Eric Thomas."

Also on November 3rd, Greg Miller requested a delay in Stephanie Thomas's deposition because she was expecting a baby later that month and for some of the same reasons Poplar and Mellon had mentioned.

---

* The suspension or stopping of a case or some phase of it, such as a deposition.

Five days later, on November 8th, Bill Conroy filed a reply opposing Poplar's and Miller's motions for delaying the deposition. At the same time, he asked the court to disqualify Tom Mellon's and James Pickering's law firms as counsel in Dr. Thomas's lawsuit against Ford. The two attorneys had been wearing too many hats for too long, Conroy said. They'd been wrestling with the dual interests of Dr. Thomas and Alix Thomas, and this precluded proper representation of either party To emphasize his point, Conroy used the letter that Glenn Zeitz wrote to Tom Mellon on October 2, 2000, in which he said: "I also appreciate your statement to me that should we prove the 'affair' you will drop the lawsuit and sue your client for your costs, since he lied to you. I know that you will honor that *pledge* also."

The appointment of a guardian was the only issue the plaintiffs and the defense seemed to agree on. But the depositions should not be delayed, Conroy said, because the information obtained from Eric and Stephanie Thomas was exactly what the guardian would need in order to determine what was in the best interest of the minor child.

Conroy argued that Dr. Thomas himself had competing interests in the case. First, he had a financial interest in the lawsuit; second, it was in his interest to have the recently reopened criminal investigation dropped, so that he could avoid a possible criminal prosecution.

The minor child, Alix, had different interests, Conroy noted. Like her father, she had a financial interest in pursuing the suit against Ford. But *unlike* her father, she had a financial interest in pursuing a civil lawsuit against her father for the wrongful death of her mother and a further interest in the criminal prosecution of her father. Finally, she had a personal interest in the case against Ford, since her interests and her father's interests were in dramatic opposition to each other.

The guardian ad litem—not Thomas—had to decide what the child should do: one, drop the suit against Ford and achieve some normalcy in life; two, continue with the lawsuit; three, drop the suit but file a civil wrongful death action against her father for the murder of her mother; or four, proceed against Ford *and* her father. Under each of these four scenarios, Conroy pointed out, the depositions of Eric and Stephanie Thomas were crucial for the guardian to assess the situation.

Dr. Thomas, Conroy argued, was at a fork in the road. He could proceed with the lawsuit and hope that Ford's investigation wouldn't reveal incriminating evidence, or he could dismiss his suit and hope that the prosecutor's office would lose interest. This might have been Dr. Thomas's plan from the very beginning, Conroy said. Months before he filed the lawsuit against Ford, he had said to Donald Rose: "If things get out of hand and they ask too many questions, I'm going to drop it [the civil lawsuit]."

As to his own client's interests, Conroy pointed out that Ford had been sued for putting a defective product on the market and then for defaming Dr. Thomas. Both Ford and the public had an interest in knowing the truth; therefore, the depositions of Eric and Stephanie Thomas must go forward.

On November 9th, Judge Rosen heard oral arguments on the motions. He began by agreeing that the circumstances required the appointment of a guardian ad litem.

"How can you possibly represent the interests of a man and a child in this case when there is a serious allegation that her father killed her mother?" Rosen asked Tom Mellon.

Rosen ordered that Warren Faulk be appointed guardian ad litem for Alix Thomas "for the limited purpose of evaluating the case and giving the court a recommendation regarding how the case should proceed, if at all, vis-à-vis the minor child." Faulk was to submit a report to the court no later than January 4, 2001. Mellon was to pay the guardian's fees and costs, which might amount to as much as $10,000. All parties were instructed to supply Faulk with any information he requested as well as any additional information that might assist him in his task.

Rosen decided to postpone Stephanie and Eric Thomas's depositions to a date convenient to the parties between January 25, 2001, and February 2, 2001.

The judge then said he would withhold his decision on the disqualification of Mellon and Pickering on the issue of conflicts. He set a hearing on the matter for December 13th.

Bill Conroy then informed Rosen that his client intended to file a counterclaim or a motion against Dr. Thomas to recoup its legal costs. Dr. Thomas had lied to them, Conroy said, and he had cost Ford hundreds of thousands of dollars in fees.

Warren Faulk was a seasoned attorney who had argued before the United States Supreme Court. He often dealt with defamation and personal-injury matters. As guardian ad litem for Alix Thomas, Faulk would determine if she should remain a party to the suit filed against Ford, pull out of it, or file a claim against her father. His first task was to schedule interviews with Eric and Stephanie Thomas, Doris and Donald Rose, and Wendy. Faulk also arranged to visit the Thomases' home, to observe Alix's interaction with her parents.

Then he would meet with Tom Mellon, Elliott Kolodny, Carl Poplar, Greg Miller, Tamara Traynor, Bill Conroy, and Glenn Zeitz to get their opinions. After that he planned to review the background of the Thomas family; the expert, police, and autopsy reports; the NHTSA report; the results of the polygraph tests; and the claims of the parties. There was an enormous amount of work to be done before he could turn in his report to Judge Rosen on January 4th.

In mid-November, Mark Singer, a writer for the *New Yorker,* took an interest in the Thomas case after hearing about it from a friend. Singer drove down to the federal courthouse in Camden, New Jersey, where he reviewed the court documents that were available to the public. Afterward, he visited Cape May Court House and began contacting local people who knew Thomas. It was rough going. He met a "wall of silence."

Buzz Keough, Cape May County bureau chief of the *Atlantic City Press,* told Singer that his paper also had had a hard time finding anyone who was willing to talk. "It was like your classic small town thing. Everybody seems to run into him, and if you talk about the guy and he sees your name in the paper, well . . ."

Chuck Leusner, the mayor of Middle Township, told Singer that it was all ridiculous. "It's possible that he was having an affair, but that doesn't make him a murderer. [We never talk about it] at the Rotary Club. He's not the talk of the town." Thomas was still a respected citizen. "This community is such that no one is going to allow any wedge to be driven between them."

Some of Thomas's friends did speak to Singer, because they disapproved of Ford's actions. "They have deeper pockets than any law firm," Dennis Roberts told Singer. "The issue is that they don't want to pay on the lawsuit. . . . They're saying whatever they need to. The people that believe he's innocent far outweigh the people that think he's guilty."

Of course there were others who didn't want to be quoted by name. "Got out of the Army and bought a modest little practice. Within a year he's putting in a fancy pool, he's got a nice-size Mercedes, a big fancy SUV. Later I discovered there's $400,000 in life insurance. People don't have that much life insurance on a thirty-six-year-old who's helping out around the office."

That same week, November 29th, at Burdette Tomlin Memorial Hospital in Cape May Court House, Stephanie Thomas gave birth to a boy. She and Eric named him Logan.

Mark Singer would end his *New Yorker* article, which was published in December 2000, with the following paragraph:

"If there was something on my husband's* mind, he'd let you know what it was," she [Barbara Callaway] said. "But this, he

---

* Dr. Callaway, from whom Dr. Thomas had purchased the practice, had died on October 14, 2000, just a month earlier.

just didn't comment on it at all. We expressed our sympathy with Dr. Thomas after his wife died. We were just in sympathy with him. I had no reason to believe anything else was amiss. When I read about the murder allegation on the front page of the newspaper, I just went right over to his house and told him I didn't believe a word of it and I was angry at Ford and I thought it was cruel and they shouldn't do that. I said, 'It's not fair.' He said, 'It gives me sleepless nights, and this craziness has to be over sometime.' And that was the end of that conversation."

Though some of Thomas's friends had told the local newspaper that he was "prospering," it was likely that the newspaper and TV reports were hurting his practice.

Mark Singer had also contacted Tom Mellon, who took this opportunity to correct the omissions in Emilie Lounsberry's *Philadelphia Inquirer* article. On December 1st, he sent Singer a packet of documents supporting his client's position. Included among the papers was his and Pickering's response to Ford's brief to disqualify them, which he had filed the very same day.

In his brief, Mellon argued that disqualifications are "the most drastic remedy with often far reaching, sometimes devastating complications." Noting that Alix's interests must come first, he argued that any premature disqualification would affect those interests.

For example, if the guardian recommended that Alix pursue her claim against Ford and the court accepted that suggestion, who was better able to continue with the lawsuit than the attorneys who had been handling the case all along? After all, they were most familiar with the many complexities of the case. It should be obvious to the court, Mellon wrote, that "if the disqualification is granted before the determination is made, Alix Thomas may lose a valuable claim [against Ford]."

In addition, Mellon wrote, if the guardian recommended dropping the claim against Ford, there was no conflict of interest, since Thomas and his wife already had private counsel. A conflict would develop only if the guardian advised that Alix pursue a claim against Ford and against Thomas at the same time.

"It is clear that if this Court were to grant the pending motion [disqualification] it would be acting prematurely and precipitously," Mellon wrote.

The attorney attacked Conroy's and Zeitz's ethics.

In a footnote, Mellon stated that Zeitz had violated Judge Rosen's orders to have an "off-the-record" discussion,* during a chambers meeting on September 28, 2000, when Ford attached and thereby published Zeitz's September 29, 2000, letter to Mellon in their November 8th memorandum of law.

Ironically, the plaintiffs and the defense were accusing each other of violating a principle of law but could document this breach of ethics only by violating it. The good feeling Mellon had for Zeitz had clearly eroded. In his brief, Mellon wrote: "Zeitz utterly fails to be candid [with the court] regarding his own comment since he intentionally did not disclose his own statement: 'I only have to prove an affair and the defense will win, I don't have to even prove murder, the affair is enough.'"

---

* Which is published on pages 253 and 254 of this book.

AGGRESSIVE DEFENSE/LAWYERS:
FORD'S MURDER ACCUSATION
EXTREME TACTIC

The plaintiff was drunk. Another was a liar. One killed himself by intentionally setting his own car ablaze.

Ford Motor Company has defended itself in product-liability lawsuits by turning the tables on its aggressors. But never before has the auto giant accused anyone of murder.

Until now.

"You'd better know what you're getting into when you file a lawsuit against an automaker because you're in for a fight," Los Angeles attorney Robert W. Mansell said.

Mansell represented Sonny Velazco, a 61-year-old baker who lost an eye in 1995 when an airbag in a Ford Mustang Cobra deployed after a low-speed collision in California. Ford argued that Velazco's son, who was driving the car, was to blame for the accident.

The automaker filed a cross claim against the son for causing the accident.

"But the automaker can present an argument only if it has facts to support it," Rutgers Law School Professor Bernard W. Bell said. "Automakers have to establish why the plaintiff's medical condition, character flaws or criminal history are relevant to the case," he said.

"If there is no factual predicate to justify a lawyer believing that this person's husband killed the wife, then there's a serious question whether the lawyers lived up to their professional responsibility," Bell said.

"I've seen them [the automaker] concoct extreme theories that were just not believable and the jury has punished them," said product-liability specialist Robert M. Palmer of Springfield, Mo.

That happened last year when a jury demanded that General Motors pay $4.8 billion in punitive damages, the largest product-liability award in U.S. history.

Six people suffered severe burns in 1993 when a drunken driver struck their 1979 Chevrolet Malibu and the gas tank burst into flames.

Brian Panish, the family attorney, argued that GM chose to place the gas tank behind the rear axle of the car near the rear bumper to save money. GM defended itself by saying its gas tanks were safe and the drunken driver who struck them was to blame for the accident.

The jury sided with the family and awarded $107 million. An appeals judge reduced the punitive damages to $1.09 million.

Panish also represented the family of Ron Archer, a 42-year-old man who was burned to death while driving a Ford LTD in 1978. The family sued Ford, claiming the car caught fire after gas fumes from the fuel system leaked into the passenger compartment.

"Ford through innuendo and allegations tried to claim he was trying to commit suicide. The jury didn't buy it," Panish said.

The family received a $1.96 million award.

"We only take the cases we really believe in," Palmer said. "If you lose, you'll have advanced $200,000 of your own money."

"This puts plaintiffs who sue a large company at an immediate disadvantage," Rutgers' Bell said.

THE PRESS OF ATLANTIC CITY
December 11, 2000
By Michael Miller

By December 12th, as part of the discovery process, Thomas and Stephanie's attorneys provided numerous documents to Ford that Conroy and Zeitz had been awaiting eagerly. Included were telephone, credit card, and bank account records. Most important were Thomas's office appointment books for the period from September 1, 1996, through June 1, 1997. Many of the dates of Thomas's absences from his office coincided with trips Stephanie had taken before and after the accident. Thomas's claim that there had been no extramarital affair was beginning to look more and more like a flat-out lie.

On December 13th, Judge Rosen heard oral arguments on Ford's motion to have Tom Mellon and James Pickering dismissed as counsel for Thomas, the estate, and Alix Thomas. He decided to postpone his decision until after Warren Faulk had filed his guardian ad litem report.

Meanwhile, Mellon's experts were preparing supplemental reports for the guardian, to show that the air bag had killed Tracy Thomas. Mellon believed these new reports would counter Ford's defense, which was based primarily on Dr. Baden's opinion.

Halbert Fillinger, a forensic pathologist and former chief medical examiner for Philadelphia; Gerald Feigin, the current medical examiner for Gloucester County, New Jersey; and Dennis Shanahan, Wayne Ross, and Donald Jason all issued reports supporting Dr. Thomas's original claim and denying the findings of Dr. Baden, Conroy's world-class forensic pathologist.

Dr. Ross stated that "while we will agree that the air bag itself may not cause petechial hemorrhages to the eyes, it is the rapid deployment of the air bag that loads the neck, chest, abdominal complex and forces Mrs. Thomas [backward] into the driver's seat. This force pushes the clothing into the neck and, at the same time, propels her [back] into the seat. Her neck hyperextends and loads the head restraint region. This results in significant forces being generated through the neck—muscle—spinal cord. This leads to bleeding of the spinal cord. Any bleeding around the spinal cord is indicative of severe trauma. Clearly and unquestionably, this bleeding did not occur from strangulation. It did, however, cause a spinal cord injury."

Ross, who discounted Baden's opinion that there was no spinal cord injury, wrote that such an injury may "manifest significant damage in the following hours to days." Since Tracy Thomas's body had been immediately cremated, he added, there was no way Dr. Baden could prove that the spinal cord was not injured and that the air bag was not the instrument of death.

Dr. Jason also criticized Baden's findings. He wrote that the "bruises about the muscles of the back of the neck also mark the place of trauma most consistent with being caused by Tracy's head and neck being thrown backward to strike the headrest on deployment of the air bag so close to her face."

Gerald Feigin stated that "Dr. Baden mentions air bag deployment, which takes less than one tenth of a second from start to finish, cannot compress vessels for a long enough period of time to cause petechiae. I agree with that. However, because it [the air bag] is so rapid and so forceful it is enough to cause mechanical petechiae. It has to be importantly observed that petechiae are not just caused by strangulation and asphyxia, but can be caused by a variety of reasons and are not specific or diagnostic for any cause of death. As previously mentioned, these petechiae are not hypoxic related but are traumatic related."

Dr. Fillinger added that there was no external injury pattern on Tracy Thomas's neck. Only if one had been detected would Baden's conclusions be valid.

The new reports were sent to the guardian ad litem so he could consider them while making his decision.

On January 5, 2001, as expected, William Faulk issued his report to Judge Rosen and sent copies to the attorneys. In this fourteen-page document, Faulk described in detail the process he had undertaken, including whom he had interviewed and visited.

Faulk provided a complete background of the Thomas family, a history of the accident, and a review of the many official reports and contentions. He summarized the findings of plaintiffs' and Ford's experts, noting differences. He also noted the polygraph tests, which had concluded that there were "no deceptions indicated." Finally, Faulk noted that he had reviewed all the depositions, and quoted at length medical examiner Gross's letter that said he refused to adjust his original findings.

"I believe I now have a good understanding or an insight into the legal issues and personal interests implicated in this litigation, particularly as they relate to Alix Thomas, and thus feel confident in reaching the conclusions and in making the recommendations contained herein," Faulk wrote, and then gave his decisions: "After much consideration and weighing of these alternatives, I am certain that it is in Alix Thomas's best interests to recommend to the Court that the litigation proceed as it is presently joined, with Dr. Thomas pursuing the wrongful death and survival actions against Ford and TRW on behalf of the Estate and with Alix as a beneficiary of any recovery made by the Estate."

Faulk listed the reasons: First, "the evidence with regard to the cause/manner of Tracy Thomas's death, at least at this time, preponderates in favor of an accidental death rather than an intentional killing." He cited the medical examiner's findings and the plaintiffs' "four well-respected and experienced forensic pathologists and medical examiners" as the primary reason.

Second, he wrote, "If the evidence suggesting manual strangulation was more persuasive, it is my opinion that it is the role of the State of New Jersey, through the County Prosecutor, and not the role of this five-year-old child, to make such an accusation against Dr. Thomas."

Third, he said, Alix was better off financially if things stayed as they were: "From an economic standpoint Alix has the security of a professional father and a well-educated adoptive mother who seem able to provide the necessities and some luxuries of an upper middle class family."

Faulk added that if it was later proved that Dr. Thomas had killed Tracy Thomas, Alix was not waiving her right to sue her father. She would still be entitled to all the life insurance proceeds and all the property that her father and her natural mother had jointly owned at the time of Tracy's death.

But most important, Faulk emphasized, for "social, psychological and emotional considerations," Alix should not become her father's accuser.

When Bill Conroy read Faulk's report, he was furious. On Sunday, January 7th, he wrote a letter of protest to Judge Rosen, pointing out that the guardian's report referred to supplemental experts' reports provided by Mellon that had never been supplied to Ford. Because Ford hadn't had an opportunity to respond to those experts' reports, the guardian's objectivity was undermined. Conroy now accused Mellon of "conduct [which] has tainted the process which led up to Mr. Faulk's Report."

Kolodny had told Faulk on January 1st that the supplemental reports "had not been served upon Ford but that it was his [Kolodny's] 'intention to do so.'" As of January 7th, Conroy wrote, he still did not have those reports, although Faulk's report had been submitted on January 5th.

Conroy asked Judge Rosen for an opportunity to submit to Faulk Ford's expert reports in rebuttal.

When he received a copy of Conroy's letter, Tom Mellon replied to the court on January 8th. He had followed the court's explicit request, he said, to supply Faulk with any helpful information, and added that "your [Judge Rosen's] instructions did not require the parties to exchange expert reports." Ford could also have supplied Faulk with additional information, Mellon said, but "the fact that Ford has been unable to find any experts to bolster Dr. Baden's opinion is not surprising."

Mellon's letter convinced Conroy to bolster Dr. Baden's initial findings. Ford's attorney believed so strongly that Tracy had been strangled that he was now ready to contact the renowned pathologist Werner Spitz, who had often differed with Michael Baden. In the O. J. Simpson civil case, for example, Spitz told the jury that Ron Goldman, who was murdered with Nicole Brown Simpson, had died more quickly than Baden had asserted, thereby allowing Simpson more time to conceal the crime and return to his home.[*]

Nevertheless, Conroy now turned to Spitz, whom Zeitz had mentioned two years ago but Conroy had passed over, and would also get in touch with Jan Leestma, a world-class expert in the field of neuropathology.

On January 9th, Conroy called both men, and a few days later sent them the relevant materials.

JUDGE TURNS DOWN REPORT

A judge [Rosen] said yesterday that he would not accept a court-appointed lawyer's recommendation that the 5-year-old daughter of a Cape May County dentist who Ford Motor Co. says killed his wife, should remain a party to the father's lawsuit against the automaker.

In an emergency hearing in U.S. District Court yesterday [January 9], lawyers for Ford assailed the report on Alix Thomas.

Ford's lawyers said they never received expert reports that the plaintiffs submitted to the court-appointed attorney, Warren Faulk.

U.S. Magistrate Judge Joel B. Rosen sided with Ford lawyers and gave them 45 days to submit a rebuttal. Faulk will then have the opportunity to look over the rebuttal and write a new recommendation for Rosen.

---

[*] Simpson was held liable for the death of his ex-wife and Ron Goldman in a civil case.

"What happened here was a clear attempt to poison the well," [Glenn] Zeitz said.

"[Tom] Mellon said in court yesterday that he did not submit the reports to Ford because he believed them to be covered by attorney-client privilege."

THE PHILADELPHIA INQUIRER
Wednesday, January 10, 2001
By Aamer Madhani

Glenn Zeitz read and reread Faulk's report several times, hoping to tease out of it a line of attack for Ford. After much consideration, he concluded that on the evidence, Faulk was saying that the scales were almost equally balanced, but that since Thomas's interests were aligned with Alix's, the case should go forward.

Zeitz also realized that Stephanie, who, as Alix's adoptive mother, had a financial interest in the outcome of the case, might never drop the lawsuit. Zeitz believed that Stephanie had given up almost everything—including real estate property—in her divorce in order to marry Thomas and had entered the marriage in debt. Now Zeitz saw that she was not only benefiting from the insurance proceeds—a theory that he planned to advance at trial—but that as Alix's adoptive mother, Stephanie was also a beneficiary of the child's part of the lawsuit.

It now appeared to Zeitz that the Thomases were working hard to conceal their premarital affair. It made him wonder what else they might be hiding. He was eager to take Stephanie's deposition, which was now only weeks away.

★ ★ ★

On January 18th, the parties met with Judge Rosen to discuss various issues, which included the upcoming depositions.

First Rosen dealt with some lagging discovery matters. He decided that rather than appoint a monitor or micromanage the discovery himself, he would give everyone until August 31, 2001, to finish all fact discovery. The parties assured the court that these eight additional months would give them ample time to get the job done.

Zeitz wanted to know if the Thomases were going to assert marital and/or spousal privilege during their depositions, which were now scheduled for January 31, 2001. He added that Fifth Amendment issues could surely be raised.

"I don't know what he's talking about," Carl Poplar told Judge Rosen. "I don't know that there will be an assertion of privilege, so I don't know how we can deal with it. If Mr. Zeitz gives us every question in advance that he's going to ask, we'll say problem or no problem, but I don't know that there is going to be an assertion of any kind of privilege."

"I appreciate your suggestion," Rosen told Zeitz. "I just don't think it's practical. Let's wait and see what happens."

Then Rosen addressed Ford's motion to disqualify Mellon and Pickering's law firms because of an alleged conflict of interest. "I'm going to dismiss [this motion] without prejudice until after Mr. Faulk's [new] report comes in.* If we have to revisit it, I will. I just don't want it hanging around, it's not ripe, and Mr. Faulk's report may have some impact on it, one way or the other."

---

* Ford would have the right to refile the motion at a later date if they wished to.

Conroy agreed with the court.

Zeitz then informed the court that Ford had retained a psychologist: Thomas was alleging emotional distress due to defamation and in his original suit had claimed mental and psychological injuries. Ford had a right to conduct a defense medical-psychological exam, because the parties were going to trial.

Rosen said he wanted to wait until the guardian's supplemental report was issued before responding, to see if there would be any changes in Thomas's pleadings. Much hinged on Faulk's amended report, which was due by the end of March.

The next morning, January 19th, Bill Conroy was off to Chicago and Michigan to see Jan Leestma and Werner Spitz. He took with him a set of micro slides of Tracy Thomas's spinal cord that Dr. Gross, under court order, had prepared for the defense.

Conroy's gamble paid off. His new experts' opinion was that there had been no injury to Tracy's spinal cord and that Dr. Baden had been correct in his initial findings. Spitz and Leestma agreed to issue written reports by the first of March, which would then be submitted to the guardian ad litem.

When Conroy returned from his trip, he was confronted by a rumor that Thomas's attorneys had advised their client to drop everything and walk away from the lawsuit, but that Stephanie wanted to go ahead. According to the rumor, Thomas wanted a way out, but Stephanie wanted to clear their names first. This suggested to Conroy that if Thomas had killed his wife, Stephanie had no knowledge of it. She hardly would have insisted that he risk the exposure of the upcoming depositions.

In the absence of official word, Conroy proceeded to prepare for trial.

The following week, he and Glenn Zeitz began preparing for the Thomases' depositions.

Zeitz's strategy was to imply a conspiracy: Tie Eric and Stephanie's affair to the insurance that Thomas had bought and then increased just before the accident. Conroy's strategy was to show that Thomas's damage claims were baseless. How could he claim the loss of companionship with Tracy if he was sleeping with Stephanie prior to the accident?

Two days before the scheduled depositions, Eric and Stephanie were prepped by their attorneys. Thomas continued to insist that he had not had an affair with Stephanie before Tracy's death. Yes, they had talked many times, as the phone records indicated, but he had been sexually faithful to Tracy until several months after her death.

The Thomases' lawyers and their clients decided to meet for lunch. While he was driving with Thomas to meet Stephanie and her lawyer, Mellon's cell phone rang. It was Stephanie's attorney, who wanted to know if Mellon was with Thomas. Yes, Mellon responded. Then pull off the road and call me from the first pay phone, the lawyer said. Mellon explained to Thomas that he had a bad connection and had to stop and use a landline.

While Thomas sat in the car, Stephanie's attorney told Mellon that Stephanie had been forthcoming for the first time about the affair with Eric and that Thomas might have a problem with Ford's questions.

★   ★   ★

On January 31st, the videotaped redeposition of Dr. Eric
Thomas took place in a courtroom at the federal courthouse in
Camden, New Jersey.

As always, the attorneys climbed the short flight of steps and
passed through the metal detector and scanning machines on
their way to an empty courtroom that Judge Rosen had secured
for the deposition.

Inside the room, whose windows overlook apartments in
downtown Camden, the attorneys' tables had been pushed
together to form a single twenty-foot conference table.

Thomas walked into the room alone, so coolly that Conroy
thought for a moment he might be medicated.

Minutes before they were to start, with everyone gathered
around the table, Carl Poplar handed Bill Conroy a few sheets
of paper.

"Dr. Thomas has revised some of his original answers to
these interrogatories," Poplar told Conroy as he handed him
some papers. When Conroy took the documents, he suggested
to Zeitz that they step over to the other side of the room.

As Conroy read each page, he handed it to Zeitz:

ORIGINAL QUESTION:

1. During the six-month period of time following the accident in
question, please identify the dates and locations of each vacation
and/or trip that you went on outside of the State of New Jersey.

2. With respect to each trip and/or vacation identified in the
preceding Interrogatory response, please provide the following
information:

a. The purpose of the trip and/or vacation;

b. The individuals with whom you traveled on the trip and/or vacation;

c. The individuals with whom you visited during the trip and/or vacation;

d. The location where you stayed during the trip and/or vacation; and

e. Whether you played golf during the trip and/or vacation, and if so, the number of times you played and the location during each trip and/or vacation.

ORIGINAL ANSWER [MAY 3, 2000]:
During the period in question, Plaintiff made three trips outside of the State of New Jersey. Plaintiff does not recall the exact dates of these trips but believes they occurred during the period in question. On one occasion Erik and Alix Thomas traveled to South Carolina to visit Dr. Thomas's parents. Dr. Thomas and Alix stayed in the Thomas home. On one occasion, Dr. Thomas and Alix traveled to Massachusetts to visit the Roses, Tracy Thomas's parents. Dr. Thomas and Alix stayed in the Rose home. On one occasion, Dr. Thomas traveled to Colorado to attend a medical conference. Dr. Thomas does not recall the location where he stayed, but generally recalls that it was in a hotel. Dr. Thomas did not play golf on any of these trips.

Dr. Thomas now answered in the following manner.

REVISED ANSWER:
1–2. By way of further response, during the six-month period following the accident in question, Dr. Thomas traveled to Newark, New Jersey, Antigua, and Tampa, Florida.

Dr. Thomas does not recall the exact dates of these trips, but believes they occurred during the period in question. The purpose of these trips was to meet Stephanie Haley Thomas. Dr. Thomas does not recall the

*exact locations where he stayed, but generally recalls that he stayed at a
hotel. Dr. Thomas did not golf on any of these trips.*

ORIGINAL QUESTION:

6. With respect to your relationship with Stephanie Haley
Thomas, please provide the following information:

> a. Identify when you first met Stephanie before the
> accident in question;

> b. Describe the nature of the relationship with Stephanie
> from the time that you first met her up until the time
> that you married Tracy Thomas. This should include
> your statement of whether you were romantically
> involved with Stephanie and if so, the circumstances,
> before you met Tracy;

ORIGINAL ANSWER [SPRING 2000]:
*(a) Plaintiff does not recall the exact date but it was sometime in High
School, approximately 1978; (b) Plaintiff dated Stephanie in High
School. Their relationship was one of friends thereafter;*

REVISED ANSWER:
> *6(a)–(b). By way of further response, during the period Dr.
> Thomas dated Stephanie in high school and then for
> approximately the first year of college he had a romantic
> relationship with Stephanie. Their relationship was one of
> friends thereafter until the Winter of 1996.*

ORIGINAL QUESTION:

> c. State whether you had any contact with Stephanie
> from the date of your marriage to Tracy up until the

time of the accident in question. If the answer is yes,
please identify the dates of such contacts and the
purpose for them;

ORIGINAL ANSWER:

*(c) Yes. Plaintiff does not recall the specific dates but occasionally
spoke with Stephanie on the telephone and Eric and Tracy
Thomas would occasionally see Stephanie at Church when they
were visiting Dr. Thomas's parents in South Carolina;*

REVISED ANSWER:

*6(c). By way of further response, Dr. Thomas also met Stephanie
in Newark, New Jersey, and Boston, Massachusetts, in December
of 1996 and January 1997. Dr. Thomas had numerous telephone
conversations with Stephanie. By way of further response, during
the Newark, New Jersey, trip, Dr. Thomas and Stephanie hugged
and kissed. In Boston, they had sexual intercourse.*

ORIGINAL QUESTION:

d. Please state when you last spoke with Stephanie before the
accident in question, where the conversation took place, and the
purpose of the conversation.

ORIGINAL ANSWER:

*(d) Plaintiff does not recall the exact date, however, in the year
prior to Tracy Thomas's death, Eric and Tracy Thomas spoke
with Stephanie when they met in Church while Eric and Tracy
Thomas were visiting Dr. Thomas's parents in South Carolina;*

REVISED ANSWER:

*6(d). By way of further response, Dr. Thomas spoke with
Stephanie numerous times in the thirty days preceding the*

accident. Dr. Thomas does not recall the exact date, but believes
the last telephone call took place on or around January 30,
1997. Dr. Thomas does not recall his exact location, but he was
either at his home or office in Cape May Court House.

ORIGINAL QUESTION:

e. Please state when you first spoke with Stephanie following the accident in question, where the conversation took place, and the purpose of the conversation;

ORIGINAL ANSWER:

(e) Dr. Thomas was called by Stephanie and her mother shortly
after Tracy Thomas's death. Tracy Thomas's death was
announced during services at a Church in South Carolina. The
purpose of the conversation was to express their condolences to
Dr. Thomas;

REVISED ANSWER:

6(e). By way of further response, Dr. Thomas called Stephanie
on February 10, 1997, after he was released from the hospital,
and explained to her the terrible tragedy that happened.

ORIGINAL QUESTION:

(f) During the first six months following the accident in question, identify each date and location that you physically met with Stephanie and the purpose of the meetings;

ORIGINAL ANSWER:

(f) Plaintiff does not recall the exact date but during the period
in question Dr. Thomas saw Stephanie Haley Thomas in

*Church during the Easter holiday when he was visiting his
parents in South Carolina; and*

REVISED ANSWER:

*6(f). By way of further response, Dr. Thomas does not
remember the exact dates and locations, but generally
remembers physically meeting with Stephanie in Newark, New
Jersey, in March of 1997, in Orangeburg, South Carolina,
around Easter of 1997, in Tampa, Florida, in May of 1997,
at his home in Cape May Courthouse, New Jersey, in June of
1997 and in Antigua in August of 1997. Dr. Thomas also
recalls meeting with Stephanie in San Antonio, Texas, but is
uncertain whether or not this meeting took place during the
first six months following the accident in question. During
their meetings in Newark, New Jersey, and Orangeburg, South
Carolina, Dr. Thomas and Stephanie talked about what was
happening in their lives and their feelings that God may be
punishing them for their tryst in Boston. During their
meetings in Tampa, Florida, Cape May Courthouse, New
Jersey, and Antigua, Dr. Thomas did have sexual intercourse
with Stephanie.*

ORIGINAL QUESTION:

g. Please state when you first became romantically
involved with Stephanie following the accident in
question.

ORIGINAL ANSWER:

(g) Sometime in the summer of 1997.

REVISED ANSWER:

6 (g). By way of further response, Dr. Thomas first became

romantically involved with Stephanie in May of 1997 when
they met in Tampa, Florida.

Thomas E. Mellon, Jr., Esquire
Elliot Alan Kolodny, Esquire
Mellon, Webster & Mellon
87 North Broad Street
Doylestown, PA 18901

DATED January 30, 2001

After he had read the last answer, Conroy leaned over to Zeitz and whispered: "Dr. Thomas's current credibility problems with a jury just got a lot worse."

"Not to mention potential perjury problems," Zeitz replied, "because of the previously sworn answers that he now admits were knowingly false."

Conroy noted that though the document was dated the previous day, Dr. Thomas had dated and signed it only this morning and on several pages he had written corrections in his own hand, using the same pen he used for his signature. These admissions had clearly not come easily to Thomas.

Zeitz, who had no idea that Stephanie's lawyer had called Mellon two days before, wondered when Poplar and Mellon had learned that their client had lied to them. Even if it was only days ago, he couldn't understand why they had waited until the morning of the deposition to tell Ford that Thomas was going to change his story. It was an unusual procedure. Zeitz knew that because of attorney-client privilege, he might never find out.

Waiting for the videographer to adjust his camera, Zeitz

realized that he and Conroy still didn't know whether Thomas was going to let these new answers speak for themselves and take the Fifth Amendment, or use this renewed deposition to cleanse his soul.

Thomas looked typically calm as he sat between Mellon and Poplar. Conroy and Zeitz were joined at their side of the table by Thomas Hinchey, who had taken the doctor's first deposition a year and a half earlier, and Ann Walsh for TRW.

Conroy began by showing Thomas a credit card bill that listed the purchase of a Delta Airlines ticket. Who was the ticket for? Thomas replied that it was for Stephanie and that he had bought it two months after Tracy's death for use the following month. He met Stephanie in Tampa, Florida, he said. Conroy established that Stephanie was still married at the time and living with her husband, Sean Haley.

When was the last time you saw Stephanie prior to the death of Tracy?

In January, Thomas replied, after taking a sip of water.

"And that was where, sir?" Conroy asked.

"The location was Boston, Massachusetts."

"Why were you in Boston at that time?"

"I was attending a dental conference in Boston and speaking to a group of students," Thomas said.

Since Mellon had once told the court that Thomas was there with his family when they accidentally bumped into Stephanie, Conroy asked: "Did Tracy and Alix go with you on this trip?"

"No," Thomas said. "Tracy and Alix did not go with me on this trip."

"Where did you stay?"

"To the best of my recollection, I stayed at the Westin Hotel in Boston."

After discussing how the hotel bill was paid, Conroy asked: "And where did Ms. Arrington [Stephanie's maiden name] stay during this time, sir?"

"During this time, Ms. Arrington stayed with me at my room."

"So this is two or three weeks before your first wife's death when this was happening up in Boston?"

"Yes," Thomas replied.

"Did you have sexual intercourse, Dr. Thomas, with Stephanie Arrington during this period of time?"

"Yes, I did."

Thomas now seemed resigned. It was likely he understood that Conroy already knew the details and that there was no point in lying. Thomas then admitted that neither Tracy nor Stephanie's husband knew about the meeting in Boston.

After establishing that Stephanie had called him just after the accident, while he was still in the hospital, Conroy asked Thomas about his phone records for the month of January 1997, just before Tracy's death.

"Do you recall receiving over sixty telephone calls from Stephanie during the month of January?"

"To the best of my knowledge, I recall receiving numerous phone calls from Stephanie."

". . . Looking at item number forty-five, [a call on January 1, New Year's Day, 1997, 10:45 P.M.] to (609) 463-8196. That's your home phone number, sir?"

"Yes."

"And [you made the] call ... at 10:45 P.M. [and it lasted] 162 minutes?" Conroy asked.

"Yes."

Thomas then told Conroy that he couldn't recall what he had discussed or how many conversations he'd had with Stephanie in December 1996 or January 1997.

Thomas was noticeably less forthcoming when Conroy asked about his meeting with Stephanie in December 1996 in Secaucus, New Jersey.

"And did you slept [sleep] together that evening, sir?" Conroy wanted to know.

"Could you define the word *slept together*?"

It took Conroy a number of tries to get Thomas to admit that Stephanie had slept in the same room. But Thomas was vague about the details. Maybe it had two beds, maybe she didn't sleep in his bed, maybe she slept on the couch. Yes there was kissing, but there was no touching of the genitalia, and no sex.

Conroy then turned to Thomas's first replies to Ford's supplemental interrogatories, which he had submitted the previous year. Conroy wanted to show that the doctor supplied the answers and knew that he was lying under oath.

"To the best of my knowledge, these questions were answered [by me] telephonically to my attorneys."

"Did you then know that the answers, that some of the answers that you then [gave] under oath, were false?"

"What I knew then was that I was not forthcoming with this information because I was trying to hide the fact of my relationship with Stephanie," Thomas replied, adding that he didn't understand why his private life was relevant to the case.

When Conroy asked again whether he knew he was lying, he said, "What I'm telling you is that I did not understand the significance of my incomplete answers to the interrogatory questions."

Conroy took a hard look at Thomas before he tried again to make Thomas admit that he had intentionally failed to identify trips he'd taken with Stephanie.

"You forgot to put them in?" Conroy asked.

"Yes."

"And the trips to Antigua and Aruba were both vacations, correct, Doctor?"

"Correct."

"Are you telling us that you forgot about those vacations when you answered these interrogatories in the spring of 2000?"

"Yes."

Zeitz, watching the proceedings, glanced over at Tom Mellon, who looked as any lawyer would who had spent a lot of time and a great deal of his own money only to have his efforts come to nothing. Zeitz sympathized with him.

"Dr. Thomas, do you agree, sir, that you knowingly gave false answers originally to interrogatory number one when you failed to disclose the trip to Antigua and the trip also to Aruba? You knew about the trips, sir, but you intentionally decided not to disclose them; isn't that the truth?"

"No, that's not the truth," Thomas replied.

Conroy went through each of the interrogatories concerning the trips Thomas had taken, trying to get him to admit he had lied. But each time, Thomas gave the same answer: "At the time [it] was from the best of my recollection. . . ."

Conroy persisted. "And is it true, Dr. Thomas, that when you signed the verification, the original verification for these answers, that you knew the information that you were supplying was false, knowingly false, because you had seen Stephanie in Boston and you had seen her in North Jersey in December?"

"This is correct. I lied because I was trying to protect the memory of Tracy and the dignity of Stephanie and Alix, as well as myself, because of the humiliating circumstances," Thomas replied.

Finally, Conroy got the answer he wanted: an admission that would allow Ford to sue Thomas—or to ask the court for monetary damages—for its legal and investigative costs from the spring of 2000 to the present.

Zeitz was struck that each time Thomas admitted he lied, he added: "I did not disclose that information because I was trying to protect the memory of Tracy." But how, Zeitz wondered, could his denials of an affair protect the memory of Tracy, who was an innocent and injured spouse: a mother who made funny faces at Alix, never allowing her daughter to have a sad moment. Her memory didn't need Eric Thomas's protection.

Zeitz also noticed that Thomas, throughout Conroy's questioning, showed little emotion, hardly any anger, and certainly no tears, but remained low-key and poised.

Conroy then addressed the statements Thomas had made to the Roses, the medical investigators, the police, the polygraph examiners, and the media. He also asked about the events that took place before and after he and Tracy got into the car. Then he asked about Tracy's life insurance.

". . . You were already in contact with Stephanie Arrington before you [applied] for life insurance in 1996, correct?" Conroy asked.

"Yes."

"Why did you apply for life insurance in November of 1996?"

"We applied for life insurance in 1996 because we were in the process of buying a home and it was recommended . . . that we had life insurance. And . . . we [had no] life insurance since we were out of the military," Thomas replied.

"Am I correct that Tracy did not know that you and Stephanie were in contact at the time when this application was made for life insurance?"

"Yes."

"Yes, that she did not know?" Conroy asked.

"Yes."

"Am I correct, Doctor, that this is an amendment to the application for the life insurance policy . . . it's dated January 6, 1997."

"Yes."

"Now, if we go to paragraph two, it says—why don't you read to us what it says there," Conroy suggested.

"Number two. 'I am now applying to change the amount of life insurance shown on the application from $150,000 to $200,000,' " Thomas read.

"And [on] January 6th, when you prepared this application, this amendment on January 6, 1997, I'm assuming you had not told Tracy about the time you had spent with Stephanie in North Jersey in December, correct, a month before?"

"Yes."

"And the trip to Boston was a couple of weeks after this

January 6, 1997, application was prepared, correct, the trip to Boston where you met with Stephanie, correct?"

"Yes."

Thomas, who had been answering questions for almost six hours, took a break.

When Thomas and the lawyers returned to the table, Conroy returned to the subject of the insurance. He asked what Thomas had done with the proceeds.

Thomas said that he had spent about $125,000 of the $400,000 he received.

Conroy then asked him how much money he had put away for Alix. "Can you tell me how much is in that account now?"

"No, I can't. I don't know," Thomas replied.

"Is it less than $10,000, more than $10,000?"

"To the exact figure, I don't know."

"Well, can you give me a rough number?"

"No."

". . . Are you certain that you drew money against the life insurance and placed it into [a] trust account for Alix?"

"I don't remember."

Conroy then wanted to know when Thomas had disclosed his extramarital affair to his attorneys. This was relevant to the costs Ford had incurred in their effort to get to the bottom of his story.

Carl Poplar objected that the answer was covered by attorney-client privilege and told his client not to answer. Conroy rephrased the question. When had Thomas decided to disclose the information to his attorneys? Again Poplar objected. The question wasn't relevant, he said. Conroy believed it was, because if Thomas's attorneys had known about his lies for a long period of time, they themselves might be liable for sanctions.

Judge Rosen was called to the courtroom to rule on Poplar's objection. He permitted Conroy to ask when Thomas decided to tell his attorneys but not when he told them or what was said. The judge said that the timing of his decision went to Thomas's credibility but that everything else was privileged.

Rosen was still standing in the room when Conroy asked: "Dr. Thomas, when did you personally make the decision to disclose this, the extramarital affair that existed with you and Stephanie Arrington as of the time of your wife's death?"

"I don't know."

"Can you give me some rough idea?"

"I don't know when I decided."

"Was it after certain phone records began to surface concerning calls made by Stephanie Arrington to you before your wife's death?"

"I don't know when I decided."

Rosen stepped in. "Counsel, I think he's indicated that he just doesn't remember."

Conroy then asked "Why did you decide to disclose this affair, the extramarital affair with Stephanie Arrington?"

"The reason why I decided to admit to the private affair with Stephanie is because it seemed that a big deal was made of something that was irrelevant to the case," Thomas replied.

The deposition ended a few moments later. Eric Thomas

had spent eight hours answering Bill Conroy's questions, all of it videotaped so that jurors would eventually be able to see what had been asked and answered.

The following morning at 9:00 A.M. sharp, it would be Stephanie Thomas's turn.

THIRTEEN

Rules, Deadlines, and Orders

On the following day Zeitz walked into the same courtroom to take Stephanie Thomas's deposition. He didn't shake anyone's hand.

Already seated at the table with Stephanie were her lawyers Glenn Miller and Tamara Traynor. Stephanie was well dressed and a little more self-possessed than Zeitz had anticipated. Thomas sat in a spectator's seat, behind and a few feet away from his wife. Tom Mellon and Elliott Kolodny also appeared for the plaintiffs. Bill Conroy and Ann Walsh joined Zeitz.

Zeitz began abruptly: "Do you have any type of legal document or prenuptial agreement between yourself and Eric Thomas?"

"No, I do not," Stephanie replied.

"So then, is it correct . . . [that] you have never entered into any kind of agreement or contract or financial understanding with your current husband where you have . . . relinquished [your] right to share in the proceeds of a lawsuit, such as [this] case—is that correct?"

"That is correct."

That Stephanie Thomas had a financial interest in the outcome of the Ford lawsuit was a theme Zeitz would pursue throughout the day.

After determining that Stephanie worked and earned roughly $45,000 as a computer programmer while her ex-husband, Sean Haley, earned about $28,000, Zeitz asked her about their relationship.

"How long were you married?"

"The divorce was finalized in February of '98."

"So then you—" Zeitz began as he looked down at his notes.

"You can do the math," Stephanie replied curtly.

Zeitz then asked about her relationship with Eric Thomas. She confirmed that her father had been Eric's adviser while he was in college but that she and Eric had dated in high school, and that she wasn't in regular contact during their college years. This was different from what Thomas had said the day before, when he admitted that they where living together during his first year of dental school. Stephanie confirmed that she'd met Tracy before Eric married her and again after Eric returned from Germany with Tracy and Alix in October 1995. It was sometime later that her mother gave her Thomas's phone number.

"And then you dialed this number. What was your purpose in calling him after all those years he was in Germany?" Zeitz asked.

"I don't recall the exact purpose. To say hello to an old friend."

From Sean Haley's telephone bills, Zeitz established the number, frequency, and length of the calls Stephanie had made to Thomas, beginning on October 22, 1996. Some of the early calls lasted as long as twenty-seven minutes. Later calls lasted longer—for example, thirty-two and forty-six minutes on November 12, 1996. Zeitz asked Stephanie what she and Eric talked about. She said she couldn't recall exactly—just the things people talked about, like "how was Germany, how were mutual friends doing, family, about the practice, about my career, relationships, children— general conversations."

Stephanie then acknowledged that she told Thomas about her marital problems during the month of November 1996.

Then Zeitz asked about their face-to-face meetings.

"And did you have occasion . . . around the middle of December of '96, to meet him and stay with him at the Embassy Suites in Secaucus, New Jersey?"

"Yes."

"And . . . in Secaucus, New Jersey, [did] the two of you stay together?" Zeitz asked.

"In the same hotel room, yes," Stephanie responded.

"Well, your husband didn't know you were going in December '96 to go see Eric Thomas, did he?"

"He knew that I was taking a trip, yes. He did not know that I was going to see Eric. . . . I told him it was business-related."

Stephanie then admitted that she had lied to her husband about the nature of the trip. She said she trusted Thomas enough to believe he wouldn't reveal that they had been together.

Zeitz then implied that a conspiracy had begun.

"So each of you went into this voluntarily, knowingly, and realizing what the potential consequences could be in your own marriage if either of your spouses found out about what happened, correct?" Zeitz asked.

After some objections from Ms. Traynor about the wording of the question, Stephanie answered. "I knowingly, yes, went into this knowing what the potential consequences were."

Stephanie confirmed what Thomas had said about their meeting in Secaucus—they kissed and hugged but did not have sex. She said that she was still in love with her husband, Sean, at the time.

Zeitz again asked about her telephone conversations with Thomas, but this time trying to link their talks to other matters.

Zeitz asked if Thomas had ever told her on December 19, 1996, that he had scheduled a walk-through for him and Tracy to go through their new home because their escrow was closing the next day.

"I don't recall. Not that I remember," Stephanie answered.

"And on December 20th, which is the date that he went to settlement with his wife to buy his house, there's one, two, three, four, five, at least five calls from you to him on that day, correct?"

"I don't know when he was closing on his house. That date had no significance to me."

"I mean, we're talking, are we not, about a man who's buying a house with his current wife, who just spent the week before with you in a motel room in North Jersey, correct?"

"Yes."

Then Zeitz asked Stephanie about the call she placed to Thomas's home on New Year's Day.

"Now, what were you talking about on New Year's Day 1997 for 162 minutes?"

"I don't recall the details of that conversation. Generally, perhaps the Secaucus trip. Once again, it was nice to see him, how I enjoyed seeing him. I don't recall specific details about the call."

From the answers, Zeitz knew that Stephanie had gone over every entry in the phone bills with her lawyers.

Next, Zeitz asked whether she and Thomas had talked on the phone about the life insurance he was purchasing for himself and Tracy.

"I don't know the amount of the life insurance on Tracy. As best I can recall, my first knowledge of that came via media, a newspaper article discussing the matter," Stephanie replied.

Zeitz then changed course.

"Well, there was a Boston trip where you met at the Westin Hotel in January of 1997, isn't that correct?"

"This is correct."

"And during that time, did you have sexual intercourse?"

"Yes."

Apparently, this exchange struck a nerve, for Stephanie's reply was combative.

"So . . . in January of '97, by doing that, how had your

feelings towards him changed from when you were together in December?"

"I was caring for him more. I would not have taken that step if I was not feeling that way."

"Did you tell him that you were ready to leave your husband at that time for him?"

"No, I did not."

"Did he tell you he was ready to leave his wife?"

"No, he did not."

In fact, Stephanie told Zeitz, after that trip to Boston, it was clear to her that Eric was not going to leave Tracy. She did not tell him that she was planning to leave her husband, she said.

Zeitz now doubled back to the phone calls.

"Now, during [this] series of calls [in early January 1997], it's your testimony, I gather, that you were unaware . . . that this was about the same time that he [was told] that the life insurance had been placed [approved] on his wife."

"That's correct, I knew nothing."

Though Zeitz got nowhere with that line of questioning, he asked Stephanie about each and every phone conversation between her and Eric from January 1, 1997, through the date of Tracy's death. She told the attorney that it was her mother and her friend Adrian Keepler who informed her there had been an accident on February 9, 1997. And only the next day, February 10th, did Eric's sister tell Stephanie about Tracy's death. Shortly afterward, Stephanie said, she tried to get in touch with Eric at the hospital, but failed.

"So you're leaving messages on his pager. Is that what you're doing now?"

"Yes. Understand, Mr. Zeitz—I was desperate." It was clear from her tone that she was, for the first time, telling the truth about her feelings.

"This is someone I cared about. I was trying to find out what was going on. . . . I'm calling, leaving a message: 'Eric call me. I hear something's happened,'" Stephanie said, then added, "Excuse me," and started to cry. She tried to continue through her tears: "And so out of desperation, I'm talking to voice mail, yes."

Not wanting to badger her, Zeitz suggested that they break for a moment. When Stephanie had composed herself, he asked about the calls, after the accident, between her and Eric Thomas. The number and frequency of these calls had increased as the days progressed. Then, the following month, they met face-to-face again.

"Where did you see him [Thomas] in March?" Zeitz asked.

"In the Secaucus area."

"Did you stay at the same Embassy Suites that you stayed at in December of '96?"

"I believe it, yes, it was the same."

"Did you have sexual relations at the time in March of '97 at the Embassy Suites?"

"No, we did not."

"You stayed in the same room?"

"Yes."

"Can you tell me what discussions you had at that time with him?"

At that point, Stephanie said, they discussed their affair and became depressed about what had happened. The act of committing adultery as it related to their faith made them think of God's punishment for the sins that they had committed.

It was their meetings that now interested Zeitz, and the changing nature of their relations. Stephanie, sitting with her hands folded in her lap, revealed that there was another meeting in Orangeburg, South Carolina, where Thomas met her at her parents' home while he was visiting his family. On that occasion, too, they didn't have sex.

"Did you meet him [Thomas] down in Tampa, Florida?"

"Yes, I did."

"So then would it be fair [to say] that the trip that you took to Tampa, Florida, where you met Eric Thomas was at least three months before you started your divorce complaint against Sean Haley?"

"Correct."

"And I gather that while you were down there, you had sexual intercourse; is that true?"

"In Tampa, yes."

Zeitz asked Stephanie whether they had discussed concealing their relationship.

"Yes," Stephanie said, then added, "No one would want to . . . admit that they were having an affair. That's not a favorable thing to do."

During a second break, Ann Marie Walsh walked over to Zeitz and whispered to him, "Stephanie pursued him. She went after him." This intrigued Zeitz, but for now he continued with his planned series of questions.

When the break was over, he established that a year before Stephanie's marriage to Thomas, in June 1997, she had sex with

Thomas while visiting him in his home, while Alix was asleep. He also got her to admit to numerous meetings with Thomas thereafter.

Zeitz then renewed the topic of money. He established that when Stephanie divorced Sean Haley in 1998, $14,000 of debt became her sole responsibility, and she also gave up any right to alimony from Haley.

"And during the two years that you've been married to Eric Thomas," Zeitz asked, "has he at any time, to your knowledge, attempted to take any life insurance policy out on your life?"

"No," Stephanie replied. Her cool expression could not hide the significance of her answer. For the implied question was: Why had Thomas bought life insurance on Tracy, ostensibly to protect his family, but not on Stephanie?

Zeitz then referred to Emilie Lounsberry's piece in the *Philadelphia Inquirer*, which said that in February 1999, Thomas, who collected $400,000 in life insurance benefits, filed his lawsuit. "Is this the article that you were talking about earlier," Zeitz asked, "when you found out about the insurance?"

"I believe it is."

Stephanie admitted that she'd lied to Lounsberry about the nature of her relationship with Eric Thomas before Tracy's death.

"So sometime after September 24, 2000 [when the article was published] and before today, you [decided] that you would acknowledge the affair—correct?"

"Correct. Somewhere in between there."

She and Thomas told their respective parents about the affair the previous year, she told Zeitz, who then questioned her

about her interview, on December 27, 2000, with Warren
Faulk, the guardian ad litem.

"So it's your testimony that when you met . . . you admitted
to him that there was an affair?"

"I believe I did."

With that, Stephanie Thomas's deposition ended after six
hours.

For Conroy and Zeitz the depositions of Dr. Thomas and
Stephanie were a success. Both had admitted to deceiving the
court, the defendants, and their own attorneys.

Driving home along Interstate 9, Zeitz thought about Ann
Walsh's comment that Stephanie had pursued Thomas. He had
analyzed Thomas and Stephanie from a male perspective, thinking that Thomas had been the pursuer. Walsh's observation that
Stephanie had chased Thomas made him realize he might be
wrong. If she was the driving force in the relationship, maybe she
had also been the driving force in the lawsuit. Perhaps Thomas
chose to expose himself to perjury charges rather than drop the
case because it was less painful than facing Stephanie. Zeitz had
not succeeded in linking her financial need to Tracy's life insurance. That required further investigation.

That evening, Bill Conroy, sitting alone on his back porch,
also reflected on Stephanie's story. She had said that she was
with her friend Carlisha Brown-Robinson just after Thomas's
sister told her that Tracy was dead. But Sean Haley had told
Conroy that he and Stephanie were in bed when she heard of
the accident through a telephone call. Which version was correct? Did Stephanie—not knowing that Haley had offered a
different version—have something to hide? Maybe both were

true—maybe it was Eric's sister who called Carlisha and not Thomas himself. The question of who called had been missed.

After the deposition, Zeitz called Emilie Lounsberry at the *Inquirer*. He told her that Stephanie testified that only after she read the article did she find out about the insurance proceeds. Lounsberry was surprised, because she and Stephanie had discussed the insurance at the interview.

So the question now was: When did Stephanie find out about the insurance money? Had Stephanie known about the money early on, or had Eric Thomas concealed the information from her even after they were married? This was hard to believe, for how else to explain the money for their wedding, cars, and trips when Thomas himself had testified it had come from the insurance proceeds.

With the depositions of Eric and Stephanie Thomas over, Carl Poplar and Tom Mellon gave no indication of Thomas's next move while they awaited the guardian ad litem's further report, due in late March. Until then, Conroy and Zeitz believed Mellon would prepare for trial.

Mellon was a tenacious lawyer, with a large financial stake in the case. He had probably spent $300,000 of his own money so far and would soon have to spend another $150,000 if the case went to trial. Mellon now seemed to have taken the position that Eric's affair with Stephanie wasn't the central issue and that he would win the case on the science alone. This suggested that a trial was inevitable, since Ford wasn't going to settle.

Conroy knew that even if they destroyed Thomas's credibility, Alix was still a sympathetic plaintiff whom Faulk would now represent. The danger for Ford was how to counter a jury's feelings for a child who had lost her mother. Conroy had seen it happen before. He knew that Alix could generate emotion to outweigh the science and her father's damaged credibility.

If Mellon could go to trial representing only Alix, without Thomas as a plaintiff, Alix would be the sole plaintiff and Ford would be accusing her father of murder.

Alix's case was Tom Mellon's ace in the hole and maybe the only card he had left.

With these thoughts, Conroy and Zeitz prepared for a jury trial, which meant deciding who would cross-examine the Thomases. Since both of them represented Ford, the court would not allow each of them to examine both Thomases. The rule was one attorney per defendant, per witness.

Conroy's plan was that Zeitz would withdraw his appearance on behalf of Ford and appear on behalf of TRW. In that way, both he and Zeitz could cross-examine both witnesses.

Zeitz would now have the Thomases' original insurance documents reviewed to see if Tracy had actually signed the request that her insurance be increased from $150,000 to $200,000. If a handwriting expert said the signature wasn't authentic, this finding would support Zeitz's theory that the insurance was bought or increased for a criminal purpose—premeditated murder.*

The polygraphers were also Zeitz's responsibility, since Conroy had little experience with the subject. The court had

---

* This analysis was never requested by Ford or any of its attorneys.

granted Ford's request to depose the examiners, and on February 12th, William Fleisher, Mellon's "friendly" polygraph examiner, was deposed in Philadelphia. Zeitz and Mellon were the only attorneys present.

After Fleisher acknowledged that polygraph results are not admissible in federal court, the examiner agreed with Zeitz that in general, the more information an examiner had, the more reliable the test results would be. Fleisher told Zeitz that in his pretest interview of Thomas, he had asked, "Why would someone do something like this?"—meaning, hypothetically, why would a husband cause his wife's death? Thomas had answered that a husband might do something, "if things were not right in the marriage." Fleisher assumed therefore that the Thomases' marriage was fine.

Fleisher acknowledged that he didn't know, at the time of the polygraph, about the affair and that Thomas had lied about it to his attorney. Fleischer also said that he was unaware that Ford was defending its case on the basis that life insurance proceeds were a possible motive for Tracy's murder, if a murder had in fact occurred.

The next day, the deposition of the other polygrapher, James McGowan, was taken at the offices of the Cape May County prosecutor. Again, Zeitz and Mellon were the only attorneys present.

McGowan told Zeitz that he had asked Dr. Thomas if he'd ever told a lie. Thomas told McGowan yes, he'd lied to his mother, and once about a surprise birthday party. When McGowan asked, "Have you ever told even one other lie to protect someone?" he said, "No."

Zeitz knew, of course, that Thomas had said in his deposition, two weeks previously, that he lied about his affair with Stephanie to protect Tracy's memory.

Had McGowan asked Thomas if he was withholding information? McGowan said he hadn't asked that question. Had McGowan ever questioned Thomas about an affair? No, said McGowan.

Zeitz was now convinced that the two examiners had not been told everything for a proper test: if they had known more about the case, they would have conducted their tests differently. Zeitz was sure he could now request that references to the polygraph results—or even references to the tests themselves—be barred.

On February 17th, Elliott Kolodny, Bill Conroy, Glenn Zeitz, and Thomas Hinchey appeared before Judge Rosen for a status conference.

On the agenda was Ford's request that Elliott Atkins, the defense's chosen psychologist, conduct an evaluation of Thomas. Conroy had not obtained a firm date from Thomas and felt the plaintiffs were delaying.

Zeitz reminded Judge Rosen that besides the issue of defamation, for which Judge Orlofsky would soon rule, Thomas had alleged emotional injury to himself. He also claimed "psychological, mental distress, emotional damages" from the death of his wife. There was no way for Ford to confront the damage claim except through an expert's psychological interview.

Kolodny replied that the real purpose of the test was to show that Thomas was capable of committing "heinous acts," which, he assured the court, his client hadn't done. Which of the plaintiff's claims would the tests be used to counter, and to whom would they be provided? Kolodny said he believed that Ford wanted to submit the results to the guardian ad litem.

Rosen acknowledged the possibility, but Zeitz assured the court that his request had nothing to do with the guardian's report. He agreed to put Ford's intentions in writing for the judge.

Many other issues were addressed during the session, including Wendy's health, which had delayed the Roses' depositions, and Kolodny's claim that Ford still hadn't provided the plaintiffs with an index to some fifteen boxes of documents.

Conroy listened patiently as Kolodny berated Ford for pursuing a "scorched earth" approach to discovery in this case. Conroy had accused the plaintiffs of the same methods, of not giving up information, but he wasn't going to let Kolodny turn this into a sideshow about discovery and take the focus away from where the evidence was leading.

Judge Rosen told both parties that August 31st was the final day for fact discovery: "I'm just telling you fellas—that date is carved in stone."

On February 21st, Conroy and Mellon were in Austin, Texas, to depose Sean Haley and Carlisha Brown-Robinson.

Conroy was hoping these depositions would strengthen the case against Thomas for sanctions and fees. Thomas may also have misrepresented other facts.

At 9:00 A.M. Carlisha Brown-Robinson, a well-spoken, attractive African American in her early thirties, appeared at the offices of Brown McCarroll & Oaks Harline in Austin. Carlisha said that her friendship with Stephanie Haley had begun in 1993 and that in December 1996 or January 1997 Stephanie first revealed to Carlisha that she was seeing or talking to Eric.

In February 1997, Carlisha said, "[Stephanie] didn't sound like she was doing well, over the phone, and so I asked her if she needed me to come and pick her up and . . . have a talk or have a drink or, you know, whatever."

Carlisha believed they had then met on a Sunday afternoon. Stephanie told her "something terrible had happened and . . . she was crying." Stephanie had said that "there was an accident and Eric was in the hospital and his wife was killed in the accident and that his wife was pregnant . . . and the baby was lost as well."

This was the first time Carlisha realized that Eric Thomas was married, but all Stephanie could say was that she needed to be with Eric. Carlisha advised Stephanie against going to New Jersey. Their conversation, she said, soon moved to their shared belief in Christianity, and that adultery was a sin. Soon afterward, Carlisha said, Stephanie told her that she wanted to be left alone, to grieve for Eric's wife and unborn child.

In June of 1997, Stephanie moved in with Carlisha for two weeks. This was awkward, Carlisha said, for Stephanie had told her husband that she was staying with a friend, meaning Carlisha, but in fact Stephanie was often gone, and Carlisha assumed that she was off somewhere with Thomas. It was a difficult situation for Carlisha, because both Sean and Stephanie were her friends. Carlisha's relationship with Stephanie became strained over this, and she asked her friend to leave. Not long afterward, Stephanie got her own apartment, and then in December of 1997, she packed up and left Austin for good.

When Conroy was done, Tom Mellon tried to tie down the weekend in February 1997 when Carlisha first heard about the accident from Stephanie.

At issue was how Stephanie learned about the accident so early. Tracy had died early Sunday morning and few people knew about it by the following morning or early afternoon. When Carlisha and Stephanie had their talk, had the tragedy just happened, Mellon wanted to know, or was it possible that their conversation took place a week afterward? "Recently" was the way Carlisha remembered it. "I mean, a couple of days, you know, not a week, not two weeks. . . . It was short enough that the news . . . was still very [fresh]."

With this vague recollection, the deposition came to an end. Sean Haley was next.

Haley repeated to Conroy that it was around Valentine's Day of 1997 when very late one night Stephanie's pager went off. Who could be paging her that late Haley wondered? Stephanie got out of bed, left the room, and returned some ten minutes later. She told her husband that she'd been talking to an old boyfriend. From then on, little by little, Haley tracked the relationship between Stephanie and Eric Thomas by looking at their old telephone and credit card bills. He was shocked, he said, to find that the affair went back as far as October of the previous year.

Did his wife admit that any of her meetings with Thomas had occurred before February of 1997? Conroy asked.

"Yes," Haley replied, and then confirmed that when Stephanie moved out of their place, she stayed with Carlisha Brown-Robinson on the weekends and came home during the week for clothes and other personal items. Eventually, she stayed at Carlisha's full-time.

The couple began to go to a counselor, on and off, and about that time Haley discovered that Thomas was giving Stephanie expense money.

Haley didn't understand what had happened between them. Stephanie had said she was in love with both of them. Then, in the summer of 1997, he called Thomas and asked him to back off. Thomas told Haley it was up to Stephanie, not him. When she continued to be in touch with Thomas, he understood they were headed for a divorce. He was "quite frankly, amazed and shocked." He considered himself a good husband.

Tom Mellon had a few questions when Conroy had finished. Were the reasons for the divorce financial? Haley said that he didn't really know. He was going to school at the time; maybe he should have been earning more money. Did Stephanie admit that she met Dr. Thomas before Tracy's death? Yes, Haley said. She had confirmed to him a trip to Boston and one to North Jersey.

That was all the attorneys wanted from Sean Haley.

In the past, Bill Conroy had always handled the forensic and engineering parts of his cases—it was what he did best. In the Thomas case, those issues still had to be addressed. Meanwhile, however, Conroy had spent almost a year and a half, much effort, and a lot of money, because Eric Thomas had lied about matters relating to his damage claims. He had filed a loss-of-consortium emotional-distress claim against Ford knowing that it was at least partly false. Conroy was irked that Thomas hadn't thought twice about his actions. Nobody should be allowed to get away with that, he thought. So Conroy drafted a motion to have the court sanction Thomas for his perjury.

Conroy reasoned that Thomas had a very profitable dental practice and the proceeds from Tracy's life insurance, which would allow the court to consider Thomas's ability to pay such a sanction, even though Ford had far more resources. Conroy thought the doctor owed Ford a little more than $100,000 for his time, effort, and expenses. He also knew that if he asked for too much, Thomas might only get a slap on the wrist.

On March 1st, Ford filed a motion for sanctions. Conroy stated that just months before, on January 31, 2001, Thomas had admitted what Ford had been attempting to prove for over a year: that before Tracy's death, he had been having an adulterous relationship with Stephanie Haley Thomas.

But before this admission, Thomas had lied about that relationship to his then-wife, Tracy, and to the media, the police, and his own attorneys, "who represented to this Court on numerous occasions that Dr. Thomas's marriage was untroubled and that he had not engaged in any adulterous affairs." Thomas, he wrote, had "knowingly permitted his own lawyers to falsely represent his marital fidelity" to the court "while he sat silently in the courtroom."

The affair was relevant, Conroy wrote, because it went to the issue of Thomas's "damage claim for loss of consortium and mental anguish." Moreover, Thomas's credibility affected every issue in the case, "including the fundamental factual issues of what happened the night of the accident."

If Dr. Thomas had been honest with the police, Conroy noted, the entire direction of the investigation might have been different and Tracy Thomas's body might never have been released for cremation—which had been done at Thomas's request.

"Although Ford does not know when Plaintiff's counsel learned that Dr. Thomas had lied in his first deposition about his infidelity, if Plaintiff's counsel did know about his infidelity at this hearing," Conroy wrote, "their silence forced Ford to undertake [unnecessary] discovery efforts. In addition, their silence forced this Court to expend unnecessary time and effort in handling Ford's application for a Court Order."

In conclusion, Ford asked the court to sanction Thomas "for his blatant and knowing disregard of the fundamental obligation to tell the truth under oath. . . . Specifically, Ford requests that this Court order Plaintiffs to pay Ford reasonable costs and attorneys' fees for the substantial expenses that Ford incurred because Dr. Thomas lied under oath and continued to lie until Ford's 20-month investigation uncovered incontrovertible evidence of his lies."

Conroy also asked Rosen to further sanction Thomas for "his willful affront to the integrity of the judicial process, and to deter others who would play fast and loose with the truth before this Court."

On the same day, March 1st, Conroy, still preparing for a trial, escorted Dr. Baden to the scene of Thomas's accident and then to Gary's Automotive Service, to reexamine Thomas's

Explorer. Following them was a group of newspaper reporters and photographers, and waiting for them at the garage was Elliott Kolodny.

The vehicle was now stored under a car cover behind one of the large garage doors. The group of attorneys positioned themselves behind one door so they could have some privacy. Once the hours'-long examination was over, everyone quickly got into their waiting cars to evade the media.

Kolodny, who seemed upset that his side was losing the public-relations battle to Ford, turned back to one local reporter and said: "I know you went to breakfast with Conroy. You don't have to answer, I know."

On March 12th, Dr. Jan Leestma, a leading neuroforensic pathologist and an expert in neuropathology, issued his written report on the death of Tracy Thomas. The letter, addressed to Bill Conroy, was intended to be forwarded to the guardian ad litem and used in the upcoming trial. Leestma's six-page report was convincing in its detail and addressed issues that had not surfaced before.

"After analyzing the above information, I basically concur with the findings of Dr. Gross that Tracy Thomas died of asphyxia and suffered blunt force injuries, but did not suffer a spinal cord injury that caused the asphyxia," Leestma wrote. He could not, however, "find any evidence that the deployment of the airbag caused spinal cord injury or her death.

"Given the open laceration on the lower lip and the laceration/abrasion on the left cheek-earlobe of Tracy Thomas, it would be reasonable to expect some trace of blood . . . on the airbag if it [had been the cause of death], or upon the seat upholstery,* because of the propensity for the lip and earlobe to bleed vigorously and immediately when lacerated."

Leestma made a further finding based on the microscopic slides of the brain that Dr. Gross had cut for Ford's experts.

"The finding of eosinophilic and shrunken ("red") neurons in the cerebral cortex, and well-developed edema in the white matter, are both highly supportive of ischemic/sypoxic change that would have required an hour or more to have formed after some event that caused hypoxia, such as asphyxia-strangulation, and/or an interval compromise of cerebral circulation, attended by some degree of cardiac activity and respiration; and ultimately death. This indicates that death could not have been instantaneous, or nearly so (minutes), as had been postulated by the plaintiff's experts secondary to acute spinal injury caused by the deployment of the airbag."

Leestma was drawing a comparison to a Polaroid photograph. You take a picture with an instant camera and after ten seconds, there's nothing there. After fifteen seconds, something starts to show vaguely. After a minute, however, the image has been developed and the picture is clear as day.

What Bill Conroy understood from Leestma's report is that it is not uncommon in strangulation cases for the victim to lose consciousness and yet still have vital signs and a heartbeat, though the person is virtually brain-dead. After strangulation, the lack of oxygen initiates an irreversible chain of events from which the victim can't recover. The question then is only how

---

* None had been discovered or noted in any report or finding.

long before the entire body shuts down. It is during this period leading to death that the neurons build up. Conroy knew that Mellon's experts could not refute this finding, which was consistent with Ford's defense.

Leestma's opinion could support at best two theories. There might have been a staged accident in which Tracy was dead before the car veered off the road and collided with the utility pole. In a second theory, Tracy was alive when she got into the car but something—perhaps a violent argument—had caused her to veer off the road. Perhaps, Zeitz theorized, a struggle followed and caused the marks on Tracy's neck that the autopsy report revealed.

However, it was more likely that if there had been an assault, it had taken place at the house, because Thomas had told different versions of the story to different people. To support this theory, Ford had made an interesting discovery: it is possible to have one body in an Explorer's driver's seat and have another person, sitting in the front passenger's seat, drive by putting a foot on the gas pedal and rotating the wheel as the car is moving.

Conroy also asked Ford to determine how long the car's battery held a charge. Thomas's Explorer had a fuel ignition cutoff switch, which shuts the engine off automatically on impact, and therefore the battery is no longer being charged.

The question was: What was the life of the car's battery at twenty-three degrees? Assuming that the Thomases left the house a little after midnight, as Thomas had said, would the interior and fog lights of the Explorer still be on at three A.M., when the police photographed it with those lights on?

Ford's engineers determined that after the engine was turned off in cold weather, the Explorer's lights would begin to fade after the first hour and are completely extinguished in about two hours.

It seemed to Ford that if the lights were still on at 1:52 A.M., when Fitzpatrick first arrived, and also at 2:35 A.M., when Detective Webster arrived at the scene, and also at 3:00 A.M., when the photographs were taken, Thomas must have left his home at least an hour later than he said they'd left. If Ford's tests were correct, the accident probably happened much closer to 1:52 A.M. [when Fitzpatrick came on the scene] than originally assumed.

The interior temperature of the car was another matter that Ford investigated. Ford believed that if Thomas's car had, as he claimed, sat unheated in twenty-three-degree weather for an hour and a half, its interior would have been very cold.

Dr. Fitzpatrick, the first person to open the door, had said that the car felt warm inside. Of course, that was a subjective judgment; what was warm to him, Conroy reasoned, might be cold to someone else.*

* * *

---

* In an interview for this book, Dr. Fitzpatrick said the temperature inside the car was equal to the temperature outside the car.

In Utah, Ford attempted to re-create the exact environment present at the time of Thomas's auto accident, but because the weather wouldn't cooperate, the tests were run with an exterior temperature of thirty-two degrees and an interior temperature of seventy-four. Within an hour the interior temperature had dropped to fifty degrees, and continued to drop. These results were inconclusive, and the test was rescheduled for later in the year.

Just before the March 19th deadline for handing over additional expert reports to the guardian ad litem, Conroy received reports from the experts he had retained; James Benedict, Michael Baden, Robert Mendelsohn, and Werner Spitz. As expected, all of their opinions supported Ford's defense, and were forwarded to the guardian.

Werner Spitz, possibly for the first time in his career, became an advocate rather than a mere expert when he concluded his report by stating: "In consideration of Mrs. Thomas's injuries, a history of Dr. Thomas's extramarital affair, increase of life insurance for Mrs. Thomas shortly before her death, inconsistencies in Dr. Thomas's deposition testimonies, his unusually rapid recovery following claimed prolonged unconsciousness and the circumstances surrounding Mrs. Thomas's death, it is my opinion that the death of Mrs. Thomas was a homicide and that a thorough police investigation is warranted."

Tom Mellon provided the guardian ad litem with only one additional report, dated March 12, 2001. It was written by a doctor named Hydow Park, who had reviewed Baden's, Benedict's, and Mendelsohn's opinions. Dr. Park concluded that those experts' opinions were flawed and that "the cause of death in the case of Mrs. Thomas is blunt force impact by the air bag deployment due to motor vehicle accident and the manner of death is accident."

On March 15th, Glenn Zeitz asked for an emergency conference before Judge Rosen. The plaintiffs had still not provided Ford with a date for Dr. Atkins to examine Eric Thomas.

Kolodny told the court: "I have been unable to speak with

any of the co-counsel involved in this case." It might take as long as two weeks before he would be able to confer with them, he said.

For Conroy and Zeitz this was the first hint that there might be a division among the plaintiffs' attorneys.

"There's a claim of emotional distress in the original case as well as the counterclaim," Rosen reminded Kolodny. "They want to have him examined by a psychologist. What's the problem?"

Kolodny argued that Ford may have an ulterior motive. He should have received a letter stating what Ford intended to do with the results of the examination, but all he'd gotten was a letter from the psychologist stating what his intentions were.

Rosen told Thomas's lawyers that the examination had to go forward. Kolodny could be present but must not participate or make comments, Rosen said. And since there was no case law he knew of that limited the use of discovery, the judge said, he would look into any improprieties by Ford if or when they arose.

Deflated, Kolodny said he would consult with his co-counsel and attempt to set a date. The court gave him eight days; otherwise, Rosen said, he himself would set the date.

Then Rosen asked how many additional or new experts the plaintiffs had hired. "Quite a few," Kolodny said.

"Is this [case] going to come to an end?" Rosen demanded.

"Judge, I certainly hope so. . . ." Kolodny replied. "But given, of course, the grave implications of this defense, you know, we've got a war here on several fronts."

"It is a war," Rosen said, his voice rising, "but I'll tell you the difference between war and law. In law there are rules and there are deadlines, and there are orders. . . . And I'm telling you—and I'm directing this at both sides—I'm not directing this at plaintiffs' counsel. This case has got to come to an end."

Kolodny was fighting on so many fronts that it must have been difficult for him to keep track of them all. First, the plaintiffs were defending their client against an allegation of murder. Second, they had to pursue discovery on their client's additional claims of defamation and intentional infliction of emotional distress. On a third front, they had to keep pressing Ford to cooperate with air-bag discovery. On a fourth, they were fighting Ford's motion for sanctions against Thomas for perjury. Finally, they were trying to avoid a psychological examination. And all this was going on as they prepared for trial.

Standing in the courtroom as Rosen chastised all of the lawyers for discourtesy and lack of professionalism, Glenn Zeitz read a press release that Mellon just issued, which contained an attachment: his motion requesting the court to exclude Dr. Baden's expert opinion on the grounds that while he'd said that he had reviewed Dr. Gross's slides, in fact he had looked over only photographs of the slides or, possibly, a duplicate set of slides.

Zeitz was surprised that Mellon was making such an ill-advised grandstand play at this time. Glenn Zeitz believed the motion itself seemed trivial. He understood that Mellon needed to contradict Ford's experts, but to quibble with a simple error in Baden's wording from a report issued a year ago was a desperate move.

As the attorneys continued to argue about discovery, Judge Rosen made it clear that he'd had it with both sides: "I am tired of the way counsel is conducting this case. You all better get a grip and step back or you won't be practicing in this court. I'm not picking on one side or another. Part of the problem with this case is counsel's lack of courtesy and professionalism to one another. I will not tolerate it anymore. . . . If you want to try cases here, you comport with the rules. . . . I have a feeling in this case the press is getting documents before the lawyers and the court. . . . So everybody's playing that game, I suspect, and it's really unfortunate. All right. Have a good day."

FOURTEEN

The Minor Child

On March 20, 2001, Warren Faulk, guardian ad litem, issued his supplemental recommendation to the court. "The new and supplemental reports of defendants' forensic experts," he wrote, "along with the new report submitted by plaintiff, simply point up the fact that [the] cause and manner of death [are] vigorously contested in this case . . ." Noting that competent and responsible experts can often disagree and that the experts in this case were all convincing, he did not change his conclusion "that the best interests of Alix Thomas dictate that this civil action continue with the parties and issues as they are presently joined."

It seemed to Zeitz that Faulk was saying he wouldn't play jury any longer, that it was an even closer call now between the experts than before, and therefore it was imperative that the case go to trial.

In a statement at the end of his report, Faulk noted that Alix Thomas could file a wrongful death action against her father if it was proved that he had intentionally killed her mother. Clearly, the door was open for her to seek damages in that event. It was also evident that the guardian ad litem would be keeping a close eye on the case.

On March 27th, Judge Rosen once more heard that Thomas's attorneys felt the indexing of the discovery and the information the Ford designees provided in their depositions were insufficient. Elliott Kolodny wanted to redepose Ford's employees and have the automaker provide a proper index. Thomas Hinchey said he'd give the indexing one more shot and then he'd throw his hands up and surrender. In the end nothing, as usual, was resolved regarding discovery. There were only pledges to keep trying.

Tom Mellon had informed Zeitz that he wanted to videotape the psychological examination of Thomas and to be present at it. This meant that Zeitz or another Ford attorney would have to be present as well. "This is my big moment," Zeitz said as he addressed the court.

"I spoke to Dr. Atkins . . . and this is the first time in thirty years that I've ever had anybody want to videotape what was going on between the psychologist and the individual who is going to be examination [*sic*]. I, certainly, did not intend on being there, and I don't think anyone from Ford was going to be there. We anticipate this would be a routine psychological defense examination."

Rosen noted that nothing in this case was routine.

Mellon's reason for the request was that he didn't want his client subjected to questions that didn't address his state of mind as it related to his claims for mental distress, the accident, and defamation that were still before the court. How could the plaintiffs keep Dr. Atkins within the perimeters if they weren't there?

Again trying to strike a balance between giving Thomas some type of protection that Mellon felt was needed and protecting Ford's rights, Judge Rosen told Thomas to appear at Dr. Atkins's office on May 4th for a psychological evaluation. He could have his own psychologist and lawyer present, but only as silent observers. In addition, there would be no videotape, only an audiotape, should the court have to resolve a dispute.

On March 30th, Thomas filed his response to Ford's motion for sanctions. Tom Mellon wrote that Thomas's additional responses to the supplemental interrogatories, depositions, and other documents that Ford had attached as exhibits spoke for themselves. Eric Thomas, his attorney noted, had no way of knowing what Ford suspected or had been attempting to prove. Tracy Thomas, he wrote, had signed the original insurance application to increase her life insurance, and at the same time, Thomas had also increased his own insurance from $400,000 to $500,000. More to the point, Mellon said that Eric Thomas's relationship with Stephanie was "not relevant to any claim or defense in this action"; therefore, the alleged perjury on that issue was moot. In conclusion, Mellon said, regardless of what had taken place, "Ford would have undertaken all of the discovery that Ford did in fact conduct."

On that basis, Mellon asked Judge Rosen not to sanction Thomas. In addition, he requested that Ford's motion be stayed until at least the close of discovery on August 31, 2001, noting that the issue of sanctions didn't have to be resolved prior to trial. "On the contrary, the relief requested by Ford would in no way affect the trial on this matter."

Expanding on this theme, Mellon wrote that "Ford has continued its scorched-earth investigation into Dr. Thomas's personal life. . . . Ford continues to seek additional documentation of the relationship between Eric and Stephanie Thomas in the form of subpoenas directed to hotels, florists, and telephone companies. . . . It is clear that Ford has spared no expense in investigating every facet of Dr. Thomas' background and will continue to do so regardless of any information it obtained from Dr. Thomas in the course of discovery."

Conroy, for his part, felt that the plaintiffs' unrelenting pursuit of pointless discovery materials was also a scorched-earth tactic. It would be up to Judge Rosen to decide which argument—if either—had merit.

ADS FOR FORD'S NEW EXPLORER
SIDESTEP SAFETY ISSUE

When it comes to image polishing, the Ford Explorer sport utility vehicle would seem to need some real elbow grease, given all the negative publicity about Firestone tire problems and rollover deaths involving the Explorer. But when Ford Motor rolls out its extensive new advertising campaign this month for the completely redesigned 2002 Explorer, the company will be dealing with the safety issue in a nonintuitive way—by largely ignoring it.

But the spots [television commercials] will not mention the many changes that Ford has made to reduce the risks that the Explorer will roll over or kill other motorists in crashes. Two magazine ads will run lists of features that will include optional side-curtain airbags—but will not explain that the airbags are designed to protect occupants' heads and necks in the event of a rollover.

Ford's strategy has some similarities to the approach that Johnson and Johnson took after seven people died in Chicago in 1982 when they consumed cyanide-laced Tylenol capsules. That is not a coincidence, because Ford officials reviewed Johnson and Johnson's crisis-management tactics.

THE NEW YORK TIMES
April 2, 2001
By Keith Bradsher

AIR BAG SUCCESS STORIES

On January 13, 1997, Terri was driving her 1995 Ford Explorer to work on the freeway. The roads were slick from the morning mist and a semi truck jackknifed in front of her and slid across several lanes.

"Having only moments to react, I slammed on my brakes and tried to stay in my lane for fear of getting hit by other cars," says Terri. "In my mind, I truly thought I was going to die."

To make the story even more incredible, at the time of the crash, Terri was 8 months pregnant.

According to Terri, "The impact with the semi was very

severe. In addition, another vehicle slammed into my passenger side, thus pushing me further under the truck and trailer. The hood of the Explorer was actually under the semi, and I was trapped in my car for over an hour. The dash had compressed and was crushing my legs."

"The air bag in my Explorer saved my life and our baby's life, without question—the fireman at the scene said it, the doctors treating me said it, the insurance adjuster handling the claim said it, and quite frankly, in my heart, I know it."

According to Terri, "In this case the driver's side air bag saved two lives."

"My vehicle essentially rolled over her driver's side. At first, I didn't know what was going on because there was smoke in the car, I thought there was a fire, but I realized it was the air bags. I don't remember them going off. I just remember knowing nothing I could do to avoid the crash, then the thought that my car was on fire, then no, it's the air bag. I climbed out of the passenger side and went over to her car.

"I expected that she'd be dead. In all reality, she should have been dead. The air bag definitely saved her life. Her roof caved in; the air bag saved her. I think I was mostly saved from injury. If I hadn't had an air bag, I would have been badly injured by the jolt of the accident. But I escaped with just minor neck injuries."

Advocates for Highway & Auto Safety
www.safeboards.org
*Profiles of individuals saved by air bags**

---

* Advocates for Highway and Auto Safety is an alliance of consumer, health, and safety groups, and insurance companies and agents working together to make America's roads safer.

On April 11th, federal judge Stephen Orlofsky handed down his opinion about whether Thomas's claims for defamation and intentional infliction of emotional distress would be allowed.

Orlofsky said that Ford's actions were protected by litigation privilege. He wrote, "If Ford's statements to the local authorities meet each element articulated by the New Jersey Supreme Court in *Hawkins v. Harris* . . . Thomas's defamation and emotional distress claims would be futile because . [of] the protection afforded by the litigation privilege."* To illustrate his ruling, he applied the requirements set forth in the Hawkins case. Ford's statements were made in the course of judicial proceedings, which included pretrial actions; they were also made in accordance with the law and only to achieve the objects of the litigation; and they had some connection or logical relation to the action before the court.

Orlofsky let stand Rosen's opinion that the Civil Rights Act of 1985 did not apply to this issue, but he reversed Rosen's opinion that Thomas could later seek punitive damages for what he claimed as emotional distress from defamation.

Ford should have "an unqualified opportunity to explore the truth" of its theory "without fear of recrimination," he said, but noted that "Ford's statements regarding Thomas are still subject to the control of this court and the rules of professional conduct governing Ford's attorneys."

---

* Hawkins, 141 N.J. at 207, 216, that is used to determine when the litigation privilege applies.

$58,000 FOR AIR BAG INJURY

A Polish court yesterday ordered an importer of Ford cars to pay 232,500 zlotys ($58,000) in compensation to an eight-year-old girl paralyzed when an airbag accidentally deployed. The girl was paralyzed and suffered brain injuries when the airbag opened in a Ford Mondeo in December 1998.

IRISH INDEPENDENT
April 19, 2001

Though Eric Thomas's claim of intentional infliction of emotional distress was no longer before the court, Judge Rosen had ordered that, on May 4th, Thomas submit to the psychological examination Ford had requested because his initial claim had been for mental anguish, emotional distress, and psychological injuries due to Tracy's death.

On May 1st, however, Bill Conroy was told by Carl Poplar that Eric Thomas would not appear for Dr. Atkins's examination. Apparently, Thomas was out of town on a prepaid vacation; moreover, a scheduling mistake had been made in Kolodny's office and Thomas had never been notified of the date.

Zeitz suspected that Poplar wouldn't want his client to undergo such a test, for fear the results might reflect badly on Thomas.

Conroy and Zeitz requested an emergency conference call with Judge Rosen and the plaintiff. Zeitz insisted that the psychological evaluation proceed as scheduled. On the phone, Thomas's attorneys replied that Dr. Thomas was in Myrtle Beach, South Carolina, and that in light of Judge Orlofsky's ruling, he was considering dismissing his claims for mental anguish, emotional distress, and psychological injuries, so there was no need for him to be examined by Dr. Atkins.

Zeitz argued that Thomas's attorneys had confirmed the date on numerous occasions in writing but had done nothing to deliver their client. His position was that the court had ordered the examination and he wanted it to proceed.

Judge Rosen gave the plaintiffs until Friday, May 11th, to advise the court whether Thomas was in fact going to pursue claims for emotional distress or defamation in connection with his case and if not he would set a new date for the examination.

On May 11th, Elliott Kolodny confirmed in writing that Thomas would *not* pursue these claims.

That Eric Thomas would drop the claims, rather than submit to an examination by a psychologist, told Conroy and Zeitz that Mellon's office was no longer in charge. So did Kolodny's sudden silence about the discovery issues that had so bothered him for a year. He no longer asked, "Where are the videotapes? Where are the indexes?" Conroy suspected that Tom Mellon might be reevaluating how to proceed with the case.

The court's rulings on Ford's motion for sanctions against Thomas for lying under oath and their cross-motions against Mellon's motion barring Dr. Baden's expert opinion were imminent. Conroy hoped that Rosen would rule that Thomas had perjured himself and impose sanctions. In that case, a whole new series of events would follow. The perjury might even be referred to the U.S. Attorney's office. The pressure on Thomas and his lawyers was building.

Against this background, Carl Poplar called Conroy. He wanted to explore the possibility of resolving the case outside of court but made it clear that he represented only Thomas and not Alix.

Conroy didn't want Poplar to think that calling him, rather than Zeitz, with whom Poplar usually conferred, could bring about a resolution more easily. He asked Zeitz to tell Poplar that the three of them could meet but that settlement was not on the table.

When the three attorneys met in Zeitz's office, Poplar hinted that Mellon, who had advanced the costs of the litigation, still wanted to go to trial. At the same time, it was more than likely that Poplar feared that Ford's aggressive defense might lead to criminal exposure for his client. Eric Thomas was already living under the shadow of the perjury charges, and the last thing Poplar wanted was for him to have to deal with the Cape May County Prosecutor's Office as well. Conroy understood that Poplar, a criminal attorney, would see these risks more clearly than Mellon might.

"What can we do to resolve this?" Poplar asked. When Conroy didn't answer, Poplar continued. "Can we do anything financially, in terms of at least the child?"

"Carl, let's just stop right here," Conroy replied. "This case gets resolved one of two ways: Either Dr. Thomas dismisses the entire case with prejudice against Ford or a jury is going to fill out a verdict form and tell us who's right."*

It was now clear that Poplar's hope of taking an offer back to Mellon and the guardian ad litem was gone.

---

* This means that the same claims can never be filed against the same party relating to the same incident.

"Are you guys going to seek reimbursement for fees and costs from Dr. Thomas or are you prepared to walk away from that?" Poplar asked, deflated.

Conroy said he'd have to consult with Ford. It was their money, and they were very upset.

Though Elliott Kolodny had stated in writing to the court that Thomas was withdrawing his claims for mental anguish and distress, he was slow to deliver the formal documents. On May 16th, Conroy wrote to Thomas's attorneys reminding them of their written commitment. Conroy also insisted that they file a formal stipulation that the dismissal is with prejudice. Conroy thought that Ford might not seek reimbursement for costs and expenses from Thomas, who had a wife and three children. He was not a business or a corporation with resources. The automaker did not want to be seen as vindictive. Nevertheless, Conroy wanted to keep the pressure on Thomas, so Conroy said in his letter that Ford was still considering what costs and expenses to recover. Ford's motion for sanctions was still, formally, before the court.

Conroy also noted that Dr. Atkins had not been able to refill the allotted time for Thomas's May 4th appointment, so Ford wanted Mellon's office to pay the cancellation fee of $2,300.

Conroy's letter went unanswered.

On June 1st, his office wrote once again to the plaintiffs, stating that if the stipulation of dismissal wasn't filed by June 4th, Ford would request that the court compel the dismissal. This letter was also ignored.

To Conroy, the silence meant that Thomas's attorneys had

not yet decided upon their next move. Left with no choice, on June 5th he filed a motion to compel Thomas to dismiss, with prejudice, his claims for mental anguish and emotional distress.

FIRESTONE WANTS PROBE
OF EXPLORER SAFETY

Bridgestone/Firestone Inc., asked federal regulators yesterday to investigate the safety of the Ford Explorer, saying its studies showed that "a substantial segment" of the nation's most popular sport-utility vehicle is "defectively designed," putting driver and passengers at risk.

"When tires fail . . . drivers should be able to pull over, not roll over," Bridgestone/Firestone President John T. Lampe said in a prepared statement. "The Explorer does not appear to give the driver that margin of safety to make it to the side of the road and change the tire."

Ford Chief of Staff John M. Rintamaki said in a prepared statement that Ford's tests show that "the Explorer performs the same as competitive SUV's before, during and after a tread separation. This problem does not exist with Goodyear tires." He added that "real-world data . . . show the Explorer is among the safest vehicles on the road."

THE WASHINGTON POST
June 1, 2001
By Caroline Mayer and Cindy Skrzycki

On Thursday, June 7th, Judge Rosen was to hear Ford's motion to compel Thomas to dismiss the claims that Elliott

Kolodny had said Thomas would dismiss but had so far refused to do. Ford's motion forced Kolodny to circulate the stipulation before court convened. It was signed by all parties by the time Judge Rosen took the bench.

The court also heard Ford's motion for financial sanctions against Thomas. Conroy reviewed the history of Thomas's lies to the court, the defendants and his own attorneys. Poplar, speaking only for Thomas, said that sanctions should not be granted because when Thomas informed his attorneys of ambiguities, inconsistencies, and misstatements Ford was informed and the matter was "straightened out." He added, "There is no issue of perjury."

Conroy told Rosen that the "straightening out" of the matter took place only after Thomas had been caught in his lies and after Ford had gone to great expense to prove he was lying.

Judge Rosen referred to the precedent set in the case of *Paula Corbett Jones vs. William Jefferson Clinton,* in which substantial sanctions were imposed upon the president. Poplar stated that in Thomas's case, the ambiguities have been cleared up and in Clinton's case they were not acknowledged until after the court had ruled. Rosen said he would not rule on the issue of sanctions at this time.

Next was Mellon's motion to exclude Dr. Baden's testimony. He argued that Dr. Baden had stated he'd reviewed certain slides taken by Dr. Gross when in fact he'd reviewed Dr. Gross's own review of the slides. Since Dr. Baden had never seen any slides when writing his initial report, Kolodny wanted the report stricken from the record.

Kolodny also wanted to depose Dr. Baden so he could

impeach him in a Daubert hearing or at trial.* Conroy argued that Mellon's motion had used buzzwords like "fabrication," "deception," and "deceit" and that this was simply an attempt at a media counterpunch to Ford's prior motion for sanctions against Thomas. Zeitz read into the record Mellon's press release to support Conroy's point. Conroy added that Werner Spitz, with fifty years of experience as a forensic medical examiner, concurred with Baden and that Baden himself had amended his report to say that he'd only looked at the microscopic slide report. Rosen withheld his ruling.

Though Thomas had now dismissed his claims for mental anguish and emotional distress, the case was far from over. Still remaining were all the original claims filed by the estate of Tracy Thomas and—even more important—the claims of Alix Thomas, who had lost her mother in the accident. The course the guardian ad litem was charting was still unclear.

Meanwhile, Tom Mellon pushed ahead, which meant Ford had to press ahead too.

Conroy's next job was to depose Mellon's experts on the spinal cord injury. Was it or was it not damaged? Then Conroy and Zeitz planned to file a motion with the court for a Daubert hearing, asking the court to bar all the plaintiffs' experts on the

---

* Based on *Daubert v. Merrell Dow Pharmaceuticals, Inc.*, this is a hearing to exclude baseless and unreliable expert testimony. In its role of "gatekeeper," the trial court scrutinizes proposed expert testimony to eliminate what falls short of the standards of reliability.

spinal-cord issue because they claimed to have seen an injury on the slides that the medical examiner, Dr. Gross, had said was not present.

Zeitz pursued his portion of the case aggressively, as if preparing for a criminal trial. First on his agenda was a hand-writing expert to determine whether Tracy Thomas's signatures were actually there on the insurance applications. Then he would trace the money: What did Thomas do with the insurance proceeds? What happened to Tracy's jewelry and other assets? How much money had been put away for Alix? Before Zeitz was done, he would account for every penny, as if he were a prosecutor and Thomas had been charged with murder.

On June 25th, Tom Mellon, Elliott Kolodny, Bill Conroy, and Thomas Hinchey went to Plainfield, New Jersey, to take the long-awaited depositions of Doris Rose and her granddaughter—Wendy's twenty-nine-year-old daughter, Bre, who had been close to Tracy despite the twelve-year difference in their ages. Donald Rose was too emotional to sit for a deposition. To Conroy's astonishment, Eric Thomas had come along to watch the proceedings.

The previous year, Mellon had told the court that he wanted these depositions. It was the Roses who had first gone to the police and accused Thomas of murder. Mellon wanted to prove that their accusations were based not on facts but on their anger over Eric's marriage to Stephanie. It was likely that Thomas himself insisted on these depositions to expose what he viewed as the Roses' bias against him.

Bre's deposition would help Ford, however.

Mellon asked her to describe her family's relationship with Eric Thomas in the months after the accident. She mentioned the incidents that had led Doris and Donald to become suspicious of him. If he had really been unconscious after the accident, why would he say "With all my medical training, I couldn't save her"? Why was Tracy driving the SUV and not sitting in the backseat with Alix? That wasn't like her at all. Why were there inconsistencies in Eric's retelling the events of that fateful night? Yes, she'd heard some of these suspicions from her mother and her grandparents, but she had also observed some things herself.

Bre said she believed that Eric Thomas had killed Tracy. She had concluded this after reviewing the police report, reading his conflicting statements, comparing what she knew to things he had said, and learning about his affair with Stephanie. The timing of Eric and Stephanie's marriage was also suspicious, but she, like her grandparents, had come to suspect him of murdering Tracy even before his remarriage.

After hearing her out, Mellon pointed out to Bre the evidence supporting Thomas's innocence—what the experts had said and how he'd passed two polygraphs. Bre agreed to read all the relevant documents, but she didn't expect to change her mind, she said.

Then Mellon asked about visits she'd had with Tracy in Germany.

"The second trip, was that about two weeks [long]?" Mellon asked.

"I believe so."

"Now, during that second trip, did you witness anything

different [from] the first trip in terms of their relationship?" Mellon wanted to know.

". . . She was pregnant then."

Bre then said that she didn't think Tracy was as happy then as she'd been on her first visit, though there was nothing concrete to base her feelings on. Tracy had not confided that she was unhappy with her husband.

Had Bre ever seen Eric be violent with Alix? Mellon asked. No, she said, but added that on a shopping excursion in Germany, Eric had stormed out angrily because Tracy had bought something without letting him see it first.

"Those are the things I remember that I thought were, you know, strange, but maybe that's what married people do."

"Are you describing Eric Thomas as a person who has a violent temper?" Mellon asked.

"I've seen that. I've seen the way he approached my little cousin and grabbed him by the shirt," she replied, referring to an incident in which Thomas became angry with a young child who had broken a glass of water.

"You remember something from approximately eight years ago involving a child that he grabbed, correct?"

"Yes."

Sometime later, Bill Conroy, picking up the same line of questioning, asked: "Do you believe that Dr. Thomas had a temper?"

"Yes," Bre replied.

Conroy had only one more question: "Do you know what happened to the jewelry that Tracy owned, including her wedding rings?"

"No, I don't," Bre said.

Thomas, who had been present for the four hours of questioning, had not uttered a sound or shown any emotion.

Half an hour later, at five P.M., the deposition of Doris Rose began and Conroy led off. Again, Thomas sat off to one side, as he had during the questioning of Bre.

Doris told Conroy about various conversations she'd had with Tracy, leading to one in the spring of 1996, when she discovered that Tracy and Eric were having problems. Tracy had told her that Eric was no longer "touching her," and she said she was tired, trying to run the business and taking care of Alix at the same time. "It was just overwhelming to her," Doris said.

Just before the accident, Doris could sense that Tracy was very unhappy about something, but "she wouldn't tell us anything. She was just so unhappy there." With that, Doris began to cry.

When she composed herself, she talked about Eric and Tracy's trip to Texas and quoted what Tracy said before leaving: "Mommy, if anything happens to me, take Alix to Cape Cod." Then, in a very emotional retelling of the events following that trip and surrounding Tracy's death, Doris talked about what Eric had said in the hospital, at the funeral home, at the memorial service, and later, when they were alone together in Tracy and Eric's house. All these comments, taken together, led her to conclude that he had been involved in her daughter's death. Throughout the deposition, Thomas hadn't once taken his eyes off her.

Doris talked about the trips he took, about his insistence

that they not talk about Tracy in Alix's presence, about his demands that they take down from their own walls pictures of their daughter and about their pursuit of visitation rights. She mentioned things he said that seemed so unlike the Eric they knew. "I shouldn't let you take her [Alix] because you might kidnap her," he'd said to her once.

"I'd never seen this side of him," Doris told Conroy.

She described the shock of finding out about Stephanie and then the suspicions that led to their request for the police reports. Their meeting with Detective Webster was very upsetting, too, she said. The police had not reacted to their inquiries. But the more they thought about it, the more they remembered things like Tracy telling Doris about the calls to Eric's cell phone, which would prompt him to go outside, where he could talk in private.

Her suspicions had begun to surface soon after the accident. The only reason she said nothing for so long was for the sake of Alix, who was upset enough by her mother's death.

When Tom Mellon took over, he asked about the relationships with the family—Wendy's and Tracy's, Eric's and Tracy's, Donald's and hers—before the accident. Doris became emotional as she talked in detail about all their many visits to Cape May Court House and how she shielded her husband from what she believed was Tracy's unhappiness.

Doris said that Eric began saying strange things, like, "You can't please everybody all the time." He'd made that comment three or four times, she said.

Mellon also took her through Eric's demand that the Roses take the pictures of Tracy down from their walls and how they finally did it just so they could see their granddaughter. As she spoke, Mellon tried to show that the Roses' suspicions of Thomas were based not in reality but on their personal antipathy to him as he presented obstacles in their relationship with Alix.

"Could you tell us in your own words, however you want to say it, what you believe happened the night of the accident?" Mellon finally asked.

"That [would be] speculation," Doris said. "I'm not here to say [what I think]. I want to hear what happened to my daughter."

Then Mellon turned to the time Tracy left Alix with the Roses when they traveled to Texas.

"Is this the time when Tracy said to you, words to the effect, Mamma, if anything happens to me—"

"Take Alix home to Cape Cod," Doris continued.

"When she said 'Mommy, take Alix to Cape Cod if anything happens to me,' did you think at the time that she was really talking about, God forbid, an airplane crash or something?" Mellon asked.

"No, no. That never entered my mind."

"On that date, February 1st, and the year would be 1997, is there anything that Eric said or did or anything that Tracy said or did to give you a clue that there was a problem?"

"No."

"Up to October of '98, is there anything that Eric said or did that said to you, this man may have murdered my daughter? Is there anything that Eric said or did?"

"No. I don't think so."

Then he turned to Bre.

"Are you aware of the fact that Bre, your . . . granddaughter, does believe that Eric murdered Tracy? Did you know that?"

"Bre is having . . . a very hard time. . . . She doesn't really want to talk about it. I don't really—she's a young girl. I just can't—she's hurting. We're all hurting in different ways. I'm not going to put what Bre—no. I'm not going to go there."

"Do you know whether or not Wendy believes in her heart—"

"Yes," Doris interrupted.

"—that Eric murdered Tracy?" Mellon finished his question.

"I believe she does."

And then Doris added: "I don't believe that an air bag killed my daughter. I don't know what happened, but I don't believe an air bag killed my daughter." Thomas stared at Doris expressionlessly and said nothing.

"Mrs. Rose, I think cynicism is a good thing," Mellon said, "and I think being a doubting Thomas makes a good lawyer. I think that's a very good thing. I think questioning authority is a good thing and I think having an open mind is a good thing. So I salute you to the extent that you're waiting for the truth to come out. But I'd like you to comment upon or explain to me why, if the federal government spent two years and Lord knows how much money, if the medical examiner after two grueling days with counsels questioning . . . if Dr. Gross gave hours [of] answers, if the polygraph experts did their job, if these other medical examiners . . . who worked for the state but looked at it at my direction, if all these people are saying the truth has come out and that Tracy was a victim of a horrible accident, that doesn't make Ford bad or anything, it was just a horrible accident, I don't understand . . ."

"Why I still have questions?" Doris replied. "I have no comment on that. I just don't know why. I just don't believe it. . . . Because of the circumstances. I don't believe it."

"What do you mean, the circumstances?" Mellon asked.

"What she [Tracy] told me . . . [and] the accident report."

Doris stated that the inconsistencies in Eric's statements and describing Tracy as clumsy was enough for her to question what had happened. Thomas still sat expressionless, as he had done all day.

"You find it hard to accuse Ford's air bag?"

"I just don't believe it."

"But you don't find it hard to accuse Dr. Thomas?"

"I saw that car. I just don't believe. When you look at that car, I just don't believe. I just don't believe it. That's all."

Doris wept as she talked about her ex-son-in-law.

". . . It was like a true betrayal [referring to his affair with Stephanie]. It was like a double—it was like something killed me because I thought so much of Eric."

"Mrs. Rose, I'm sorry. I'm tired," Mellon said.

Bill Conroy had a few more questions. "Do you know what happened to Tracy's jewelry?" he asked.

"No," Doris replied. "I don't know what happened to any of her possessions."

Thomas was still motionless.

The deposition concluded at 10:45 P.M. Doris Rose had been answering questions for almost six hours and the only word her ex-son-in-law had said to her was "Hello" when she first entered the room.

★   ★   ★

The next morning, June 26th, Conroy and Zeitz sent Mellon a letter asking him to stipulate that the polygraph results, which he had referred to several times during Bre's and Doris's depositions, were not admissible in Thomas's lawsuit against Ford.

The following day, Mellon replied: "Consider this letter as official notice that we intend to use the polygraph records," he wrote, adding that he believed that the law permitted this at trial.

Zeitz and Conroy were pleased to have smoked out Mellon's intention to use the polygraph tests. This meant he had no other way to restore his client's credibility.

The next day, June 28th, Zeitz responded to Mellon's letter and copied the guardian ad litem and Carl Poplar, citing a 1998 Supreme Court case in which polygraph evidence was ruled inadmissible in the federal system. Zeitz enclosed summaries of the polygraph examiners' depositions and other items to support his and Conroy's position. He also quoted from a *Philadelphia Inquirer* article on polygraphs: "Critics say that while polygraphs can catch a secretary who stole a stapler, they fail miserably on sociopaths who are trained to lie without a conscience."

Zeitz then added:

... you have practiced criminal and civil law for approximately thirty years. Mr. Poplar has practiced criminal and civil litigation since 1967. Eric Thomas successfully lied to both of you experienced trial lawyers with a combined total of over sixty years of experience. He only confessed at the very last moment before his videotaped deposition on January 31, 2001, when he knew he was caught in his deceptions and lies under oath.

The position you have taken on the polygraph has no basis

in law or fact. Once again, I am afraid that you have your legal feet planted firmly in the air. In the words of Kenny Rogers and The Gambler, you have to know when to hold 'em, and know when to fold 'em.

Three days later, on July 2nd, Carl Poplar called Zeitz. "We will agree to your terms," he said. Thomas, the estate of Tracy Thomas, and Alix Thomas would drop all their remaining claims against Ford. All of them.

"I'll pass that on to Conroy," Zeitz told Poplar calmly.

He dialed Conroy immediately. "Mission accomplished," he said. "They've folded."

At first, Bill Conroy thought maybe Zeitz was kidding. But after a moment's silence, Zeitz heard hooting and hollering from Conroy's end of the phone.

As always, it was an emotional moment for Conroy. Win or lose, he felt the outcome of every case very strongly. In this case, he had followed a path and stayed with it. He had taken a chance hiring Zeitz and his instinct had served him well.

Zeitz would put it a little differently: Conroy had picked up the scent in the woods and followed it. Either way, Conroy won.

A few minutes later, after composing himself, Conroy called Ford with the news.

Throughout the rest of the day, Glenn Zeitz had a hard time keeping his composure. He'd win a case and be up; he'd lose a case and be down. He understood what manic-depressives went through.

★ ★ ★

When Doris heard the news, she wept. Donald could not stop thinking about Tracy's death. He wondered whether it was murder, and if it was, was it premeditated or an act of passion.

These were the questions he asked himself as he drove to and from work each day. He might never learn how Tracy had died, but he could not stop wondering.

Judge Rosen called a court meeting for July 6th. Kolodny and Poplar appeared with Thomas. Mellon didn't show up—he'd left for an early vacation on Cape Cod. Warren Faulk represented Alix, Conroy and Zeitz appeared for Ford.

Faulk addressed the court first and informed Judge Rosen that Thomas had decided to dismiss his claims against Ford and that, on behalf of Alix, Faulk endorsed the voluntary dismissal.

Then Eric Thomas took the witness stand and was examined by Carl Poplar.

"Do you agree with the application that we're making to dismiss this case with prejudice with the understanding that it brings to a conclusion and it is not subject to be reinstated?"

"Yes," Thomas answered.

"Has Stephanie, your present wife, agreed to this application, that is the application to dismiss this case on your behalf and on behalf of the estate with prejudice?"

Again Thomas answered yes.

Bill Conroy then questioned Thomas.

"I would like to ask [whether] you understand that any claim that you or your minor daughter have are forever barred at this point, that no [party to this lawsuit] can bring any claim against Ford Motor Company as a result of the death of your wife in the future? Do you understand that?"

"Yes."

"And does your present wife understand that?"

And again Thomas answered yes.

The court noted that Ford would withdraw all of its motions and neither side would seek repayment of costs and expenses from the other.

Then an argument broke out. Kolodny stated the reason for the dismissal was that the plaintiffs could no longer finance the case. Poplar disagreed with that statement. Zeitz told the court that Ford did not agree that the case was being dismissed for economic reasons.

"Let's stick to the issues," Rosen told everyone. "Everyone has their views. As he left the bench, Rosen said, "And why people [do] what they [do] is their own decision."

It was unclear why Faulk had given up Alix's right to proceed against Ford. If, as Zeitz felt, the science in the case was a tossup, there was still a chance that a jury would award something to Alix, a sympathetic plaintiff. Faulk's action even prevented the child from suing Ford when she obtained majority at the age of eighteen.

DENTIST DROPS SUIT AGAINST FORD

Eric V. Thomas agreed yesterday not to bring any future claims against the automaker and Ford agreed not to seek any damage costs.

Thomas's lawyer, Carl Poplar, said he urged his client to drop the case because it would cost him more to pursue it than a jury might award.

"Let people who review the facts draw their own conclusions as to why this happened," said William J. Conroy, adding that U.S. Magistrate Joel Rosen was about to rule on whether Thomas should be sanctioned for lying under oath in denying that he and his current wife were having an affair at the time of his first wife's death.

Ford's lawyers yesterday shied away from saying Thomas killed his wife.

"That's for the prosecutor to make a determination, not us," said Glenn Zeitz, another Ford lawyer.

Thomas declined to comment after the brief court hearing.

ASSOCIATED PRESS
July 7, 2001

On July 18th, Bill Conroy filed the stipulation of dismissal, with prejudice, of Eric Thomas's, the estate's, and Alix Thomas's lawsuit against the Ford Motor Company and TRW, Inc. Both parties agreed to waive all costs, fees, and expenses The order was signed by Tom Mellon, James Pickering, and Carl Poplar for the plaintiffs; Bill Conroy and Ann Walsh for the defendants; and Warren Faulk as guardian ad litem for Alix Thomas. Judge Rosen also signed the order.

On July 31st, Tom Mellon faxed the following memo to everyone he had worked with on the Thomas case and to selected members of the media.

As you may know by now, the law firm of Mellon, Webster & Mellon has declined further participation in the *Estate of Tracy Thomas v. Ford* case.

Essentially, the case had several recent turning points. They are as follows:

- the reversal by the Court of our ability to litigate the defamation action; the elimination of our ability to focus the jury on the defamatory conduct by Ford greatly changed the trial strategy and, perhaps, the likely outcome of the case;

- receipt of the two expert reports supporting the conclusion of Dr. Michael Baden that Tracy Thomas died by homicide; the reports are authored by two distinguished members of the forensic pathology community, *viz.*, both Dr. Jan E. Leestma and Dr. Werner U. Spitz. These two physicians are, in fact, the authors of two of the leading volumes of forensic pathology;

- the continuing advanced costs necessary to litigate the case to completion were quite substantial, that is, estimates suggest that another $150,000 to $225,000 would be needed to finalize the trial on this matter; currently, we have expended $426,000.00;

- although we have spent conservatively 7,500 hours to date over the last three and one half years (Elliott Kolodny— 4,000 hours, Thomas E. Mellon, Jr.—3,500 hours), we estimate another 2,500 hours would be required to bring the case to a jury verdict;

- with the admission by Eric and Stephanie Thomas of their affair prior to the death of Tracy Thomas, a diminution in the value of the damages would occur; in fact, a strong argument could be made that Eric's claim of consortium was rendered valueless. Similarly, the claim by the minor child, Alix, regarding the loss of her mother, Tracy, was substantially diminished by the emergence of her loving stepmother, Stephanie;

- under New Jersey law, all costs are subtracted from the final award before an award of a fee is considered by the court; stated otherwise, assuming the jury were to return an award of $1 million, the advanced costs of $500,000 is subtracted first, *viz.*, the attorney's fee is based not on the $1 million settlement/verdict but only the figure left after subtraction of all the advanced costs or, $500,000. Ironically, the greater the financial commitment by Plaintiff's counsel, the lower the reward;

- the courts of New Jersey regulate the amount of attorney's fees in all cases. Instead of the usual forty percent (40%) fee for complex and costly plaintiff's cases, the court supervises the fee award with a descending scale, that is, the awards range from thirty-three percent (33%) to twenty percent (20%). Our experience and research suggested the Court would authorize an overall fee of twenty-five percent. By reducing the fee even further by a fair and appropriate referral fee, the remaining compensation to Mellon, Webster & Mellon would be totally inadequate. Even a "victory" would become a financial disaster. Jonathan Herr's volume *Civil Action* comes to mind;

- the continuing publication in the mass media of Eric's affair remained the focal point of the news stories, not the issue of safety involving the Ford product;
- Eric's criminal lawyer was decidedly unenthusiastic about our continued efforts to litigate the case; similarly, Stephanie's personal lawyer was equally unenthusiastic about the likely success of this case; finally, the Guardian for the minor child, Alix, offered little encouragement to proceed. Despite my best efforts to enlist their litigation support by forming a team to pool resources to bring this case to a conclusion, all declined. Finally, our local counsel had no interest in pursuing the case. Their collective opinions were unequivocal and unanimous, they all agreed that it was in everyone's best interest to discontinue the case.

Please understand I remain convinced of the truth of our allegations, that is, Tracy Thomas died as a result of the mechanical failure of the air bag which did not comport with known safety advances. Simply stated, Tracy Thomas died because the Ford Explorer air bag was far too aggressive. Since Tracy's death, Ford has reduced the aggressivity of this air bag by 100 percent. Our legal and engineering theories remain sound and, therefore, a products liability case was eminently viable.

However, I believe that Eric Thomas (and my law firm) were a victim of his deception regarding the affair with Stephanie Thomas. Also, I believe that Eric Thomas (and my law firm) have been victimized by the corporate bullying by Ford. Without question, the judicial process failed to protect an ordinary citizen in their dispute with a billion dollar corporate

monolith with unlimited resources. Ford has been known for
many years to engage in crash and burn litigation tactics. As
I've learned from my experience in tobacco litigation, this phi-
losophy can oftentimes be successful albeit without ethical or
moral decency. Hence, Goliath beat David into the ground.

On a personal note, the case represents a tremendous financial loss to Mellon, Webster & Mellon. As noted above, we have
not only lost a tremendous amount of actual dollars but, addi-
tionally, we have also lost many thousands of hours of uncom-
pensated time. I am not bitter but I am terribly disappointed.

Hopefully, we will be able to work with each other again in
the near future without the concomitant calamity.

The following week the Cape May County Prosecutor's Office
called Bill Conroy to say they would subpoena his entire file on
the Thomas matter.

MOTHER'S DEATH UNDER SCRUTINY

No one knew about the accident until around 2 A.M., more
than an hour after it happened.

Tracy Thomas was behind the wheel, ash-colored, her jaw
locked with her tongue protruding, her head resting on her
left shoulder. She had no vital signs. Six months pregnant, she
was pronounced dead at 2:21 A.M., at the age of 37.

If you believe Eric Thomas, his wife died from the over-
aggressive deployment of an airbag.

If you believe lawyers for Ford Motor Co., Tracy Thomas
was murdered.

Now, with Ford's files in their hands, Cape May County

prosecutors must decide if Eric is the victim of an unfortunate set of coincidences, his own duplicity and a powerful adversary, or if a car accident hid murder.

COURIER POST
[Cherry Hill, New Jersy]
August 5, 2001
By Kathy Matheson

OFFICE OF THE PROSECUTOR
COUNTY OF CAPE MAY

J. DAVID MEYER
County Prosecutor, Acting

FOR IMMEDIATE RELEASE
February 21, 2002

FOR FURTHER INFORMATION CONTACT:
J. David Meyer, Acting County Prosecutor
Cape May County Prosecutor's Office
(609) 465-1135

TRACY THOMAS DEATH INVESTIGATION

Cape May Court House, New Jersey—After consideration of the presently existing evidence concerning the death of Tracy Thomas on February 9, 1997, I have concluded that there is insufficient evidence to warrant criminal prosecution and am declining prosecution of this matter at this time.

The existence of two groups of qualified forensic medical experts firmly holding opposing views of the cause and manner of death based upon the same scientific evidence suggests both a substantial subjective component to their respective conclusions and that a definitive objective scientific solution is not available utilizing present knowledge and technology. As a consequence of the differing conclusions and opinions of these numerous experts, no reasonable jury could conclude, beyond a reasonable doubt, that this occurrence was an act of criminal homicide by manual strangulation, as opposed to a tragic motor vehicle accident fatality.

Although the self-evident influences upon the respective parties and their experts in the related civil action render the divergent positions and conclusions of each somewhat suspect, neither theory can be conclusively proved to the exclusion of the other warranting either formal criminal prosecution or formal closure of our investigation. Consequently, despite the fact that our active investigation of the presently available evidence is concluded, our investigation will remain open and we will continue to accept and consider any newly discovered evidence.

We may never find out how Tracy Thomas really died on the night of February 9, 1997. A jury may someday be asked to render a verdict in a new case, civil or criminal, one in which Eric Thomas is the defendant facing the charge of murder. But even that may not be enough for Alix Thomas. There will come a day—when she is old enough to understand more about her mother's death—when she will want her own answers.

In the meantime, all we know is that Eric Thomas engineered his own fate. If he had not sued Ford—a giant corporation and a mighty foe—it is unlikely that anyone would have questioned how his wife Tracy died. Nor would Thomas's affair with Stephanie have come to light.

Many professionals brought their expertise to bear in this case—forensic pathologists, jurists, automotive engineers, polygraphers, air-bag specialists, psychologists, and civil and criminal lawyers. But no high-priced specialist can save a human being from his own errors. If Eric Thomas, propelled by greed, is now caught in a web from which he cannot extricate himself, he has only himself to blame.

Epilogue

CAPE DENTIST'S IN-LAWS SUE
FOR DAUGHTER'S DEATH

The parents of a Middle Township woman who was found dead at the wheel of her Ford Explorer in 1997 said their son-in-law murdered her.

Donald and Doris Rose of Hyannis, Mass., filed a wrongful-death lawsuit in U.S. District Court on Monday, nearly two years after a forensic pathologist said Tracy Thomas was strangled, not killed by a faulty air bag as police and Cape May County prosecutors concluded.

In the lawsuit, the Roses say Tracy's husband, Middle Township dentist Eric Thomas, murdered her. "We believe the life of Tracy and our unborn grandchild was brutally snatched away," the Roses said in a statement. "We will not rest until her murderer(s) are brought to justice."

The Roses' attorney, Robert Pickett of Maplewood, N.J., said the family hopes the federal lawsuit will answer lingering questions about what happened to Tracy that snowy, winter night in Cape May Court House.

Eric Thomas, reached at his Middle Township home, declined to comment Monday.

Pickett said he plans to call on many of Ford's expert witnesses to prove his case. A civil case has a lower standard of proof than a criminal one, Pickett said.

In a criminal matter, the prosecution must prove the case beyond a reasonable doubt. In civil cases, the plaintiff must show a preponderance of the evidence. "We have the burden of proof. We'll prove he unfortunately killed his wife," Pickett said.

THE PRESS OF ATLANTIC CITY
March 26, 2002
By Michael Miller

Afterword

Dr. Eric Thomas and his wife, Stephanie, did not grant any interviews for this book. Two of their attorneys, Thomas Mellon and Elliott Kolodny, gave no formal interviews but did meet with me to discuss some aspects of the case and their points of view. Some of their subsequent conversations were off-the-record and several were on-the-record.

My reporting of the Eric Thomas case began when I read Mark Singer's article in the *New Yorker*. Shortly thereafter I purchased the rights to his material to develop a motion picture for CBS Television. The effect of that article, published in December 2001, has been noted and some of his research has been used with his permission in this work.

I wish to thank the following for their contributions: William J. Conroy, Wyn Evoy, Dr. Robert Fitzpatrick, Elliot Gross, Emilie Lounsberry, Wendy Rose Mahdi, Mike Miller, Jeannie Morrisson, Vincent Orlando, Bre Rose, Donald Rose, Doris Rose, Mike Voll, and Glenn A. Zeitz.

With much admiration for the unique talents of Jason

Epstein, I offer my grateful appreciation for his vital understanding and help with this book.

The legal and editorial assistance of Carlos Lozano cannot be underestimated in the preparation of this work, nor can the invaluable contribution made by Veronica Windholz, whose advice and suggestions helped shape this work.

Mimi Tyler of Spector, Gadon & Rosen, P.C., in Philadelphia aided me in obtaining material from the federal court docket, and I thank her for her help.

Thanks to my son Howard Schiller, who designed the book's jacket, and to my other son, Anthony Schiller, who worked on the final editorial phases of this book; to Rebecca Whittington, my vice president of Motion Picture projects; and to my personal assistant, Serra Haworth, who kept our work in order.

My thanks to Marjorie Braman, Cathy Hemming, Jane Friedman, James Fox, and Laurie Rippon at HarperCollins, who were all of fine help.

Last, and not least, a much-earned thanks to John Taylor Williams of Hill & Barlow, who has assisted me on five book projects.

Grateful acknowledgment is made to the following for permission to reprint previously published material.

Associated Press: Excerpts from various articles from January 19, 1998, through July 7, 2001, pertaining to the Thomas case and related matters. Copyright © 1998 and 2001 by the Associated Press. Reprinted with permission of the Associated Press.

Courier Post: Excerpts from two articles, July 19, 2000 and August 5, 2001. Copyright © 2000 and 2001 by Courier Post. Reprinted with permission of the Courier Post.

New Jersey Law Journal: Excerpt from the article "Ford Airbag-Death Case Places Old Nemeses in Opposition" is from the July 31, 2000, issue of the New Jersey Law Journal. Copyright © 2000 NLP IP Company. Further duplication without permission is prohibited. All rights reserved.

The New York Times: Excerpts from two articles, August 20, 2000, and April 2, 2001. Copyright © 2000 and 2001 by The New York Times Co. Reprinted by permission.

The Press of Atlantic City: Excerpts from various articles from April 12, 1997, through March 26, 2001, pertaining to the Thomas case and related matters. Copyright © 1997, 1998, 1999, 2000, 2001 by the Press of Atlantic City. Reprinted by permission.

The Washington Post: Excerpt from June 1, 2001, article. Copyright © 2001 by the Washington Post. Reprinted by permission of The Washington Post.